JUSTICE LEAGUE OF AMERICA

Hereby Elects...

JUSTICE LEAGUE OF AMERICA HEREBY ELECTS...

JUSTICE LEAGUE OF AMERICA

Hereby Elects...

GARDNER FOX
DENNY O'NEIL
STEVE ENGLEHART
GERRY CONWAY
WRITERS

MIKE SEKOWSKY
DICK DILLIN
PENCILLERS

BERNARD SACHS
JOE GIELLA
DICK GIORDANO
FRANK MCLAUGHLIN
INKERS

JUSTICE LEAGUE of AMERICA

HEREBY ELECTS

GREEN ARROW

TO MEMBERSHIP FOR LIFE ~~ WITH ALL PRIVILEGES AND GRATUITIES INCLUDING THE WEARING OF THE SIGNAL DEVICE AND POSSESSION OF THE GOLDEN KEY WHICH PERMITS ENTRY INTO THE SECRET SANCTUARY, ITS LIBRARY AND SOUVENIR ROOMS. IT IS HEREBY FURTHER RESOLVED AND ACTED UPON, THAT +++

GREEN ARROW

SHALL RECEIVE A SPECIAL COMMENDATION FOR HIS EXPERT ASSISTANCE IN THE CASE WE HAVE ENTITLED ON OUR SCROLLS +++

Doom of the Star Diamond!

WELCOME TO THE *JUSTICE LEAGUE, GREEN ARROW!*

SNAP!

The Roll Call

1. WONDER WOMAN
2. GREEN LANTERN
3. FLASH
4. J'ONN J'ONZZ
5. BATMAN
6. AQUAMAN
7. SNAPPER CARR
8. SUPERMAN

AND INCLUDING FOR THE FIRST TIME... GREEN ARROW

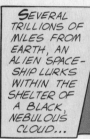

SEVERAL TRILLIONS OF MILES FROM EARTH, AN ALIEN SPACE-SHIP LURKS WITHIN THE SHELTER OF A BLACK, NEBULOUS CLOUD...

CARTHAN IS APPROACHING! READY STARBOARD DISINTOR-BEAMERS!

IN THE NEXT MOMENT, THE ONCOMING SPACESHIP HURTLES WITHIN FIRING RANGE...

INSIDE THE ATTACKING VESSEL CRIES OF UTTER AMAZEMENT RING OUT...

INCREDIBLE! CARTHAN'S SHIP'S BEEN DISINTEGRATED-- BUT CARTHAN HIMSELF IS UNHARMED! FIRE PORT BEAMERS AT HIM!

DISSOLUTION RAYS OF AWE-SOME POWER BATHE THE HELPLESSLY DRIFTING SPACE-MAN...

CARTHAN HAS BECOME INDE-STRUCTIBLE! THOSE RAYS WOULD TURN SOLID STEEL TO POWDER! BUT THEY DON'T HARM HIM! GET HIM INSIDE HERE WITH A SNATCH-BEAM!

SHORTLY, CARTHAN--WARLORD OF THE SPACE-FLEETS OF THE PLANET DRYANNA-- STANDS A PRISONER OF HIS PLANETARY RULER ...

XANDOR! I--I DON'T UNDER-STAND! WHY TRY TO DESTROY ME? I'VE JUST CONQUERED OUR ANCIENT ENEMIES THE SLYSSA FOR OUR PEOPLE!

EXACTLY! YOU'VE BE-COME A -- GREAT HERO!

MOST PEOPLE ON DRYANNA SECRETLY CALL ME A DICTATO YOUR FRIENDS--CERTAIN SCIENTISTS--HOPE TO OVERTHROW ME AND ESTABLISH A GOVERNMENT OF THE PEOPLE -- AND WANT YOU TO LEAD THE REVOLT!

...VIOUSLY I CANNOT LET U GO HOME TO *DRYANNA!* ST AS OBVIOUSLY I NNOT DESTROY YOU! L I CAN DO IS IM-ISON YOU! BUT BE-RE I DECIDE WHERE-- L ME! WHAT HAPPENED MAKE YOU INDESTRUCTIBLE?

IT OCCURRED WHILE I WAS ON A LONE SCOUTING MISSION AGAINST THE *SLYSSA...*

"*WHILE I WAS INVESTIGATING A BARREN PLANET TO USE AS A POSSIBLE SUPPLY BASE AGAINST THE ALIENS, I WAS CAUGHT IN AN ELECTRO-MAGNETIC DISTURBANCE..*"

I'VE NEVER ENCOUNTERED ANYTHING LIKE *THIS* BEFORE!

"*UPWARD ROM THE HIGHLY AGNETIC PLANET ETTED PIRALS OF RAW ENERGY, RAPPING ME ETWEEN HEM AND ATHING ME FOR N HOUR UNIMAG- ABLE ADIATIONS...*"

WH-WHAT'S HAPPENING TO ME...?

S *CARTHAN* ONCLUDES IS TALE...

AS A RESULT OF THAT FREAK ACCIDENT, AN *AURA*--INVISIBLE IN NORMAL LIGHT--HAS SURROUNDED MY BODY... ROTECTING ME FROM DESTRUCTION! OW TELL ME, WHAT DO YOU INTEND DOING WITH ME?

AFTER CONFERRING WITH HIS ADVISORS, *XANDOR* REACHES A DECISION...

I CAN'T IMPRISON YOU IN A JAIL OR ON A PLANET NEAR OUR HOME PLANET, FOR YOU COULD TELEPATH TO YOUR SCIENTIST FRIENDS FOR HELP! I HAVE ANOTHER PRISON UNDER CONSIDERATION, HOWEVER--A PLANET CALLED *EARTH!*

YOU'RE A VERY IMPORTANT MAN, SO WE'LL TREAT YOU WELL! I'M GOING TO GIVE YOU A FINE SPACESHIP--WHICH WILL BRING YOU ON AUTO-MATIC CONTROLS TO EARTH! HOWEVER--

WE ARE *TELEPORTING* THREE GOLDEN BOX-MACHINES AHEAD OF YOU, DESIGNED TO KEEP YOU ON EARTH PERMANENTLY! SHOULD YOU DECIDE TO LEAVE EARTH, THESE MACHINES WILL CAUSE YOUR AURA TO BE COATED WITH *OPAQALUX*--BLINDING YOU FOREVER!

BLIND, YOU COULD NEVER FI... YOUR WAY BACK TO *DRYANN...* OR LEAD A REVOLT AGAINST MY DICTATORSHIP! EARTH I... A DAWN ATOMIC ERA PLANET WITHOUT SPACE-TRAVEL! SO YOU'LL GET NO HELP THERE...

IF YOU *REMOVE* THE METALLIC COVERINGS OF THE BOX--MACHINES, YOU WILL BE ABLE TO ESCAPE FROM EARTH WITH YOUR EYESIGHT INTACT! *HOW-EVER*--THE INSTANT YOU RE-MOVE THE COVERINGS, YOU ACTIVATE THE MACHINES! ONCE TURNED ON...YOU'LL BE UNABLE TO TURN THE MACHINES OFF...AND THEY'LL DESTROY ALL HUMAN LIFE ON EARTH!

YOU'RE A HUMANITARIAN, *CARTHAN!* YOU WOULDN'T DELIBERATELY HARM THE BILLIONS OF PEOPLE ON EARTH-- EVEN TO SAVE YOURSELF! THAT'S WHY I'M SO CONFIDENT EARTH WILL BE YOUR HOME THE REMAINDER OF YOUR LIFE...

ON A WORLD TOO FAR AWAY FROM *DRYANNA* FOR *CARTHA...* TO TELEPATH FOR HELP, A SPACESHIP IS OUTFITTED FOR HIS JOURNEY TO EARTH...

THERE'S YOUR SPACESHIP, *CARTHAN!* IT WILL TAKE YOU AT SUPER-LIGHT SPEED TO EARTH WHETHER YOU WANT IT TO OR NOT! AFTER THAT-- YOU WILL BE YOUR OWN JAILOR! YOU WON'T DARE DOOM ANYONE ON EARTH-- SO YOU'LL LIVE OUT YOUR DAYS IN EXILE!

THROUGH HYPER-DIMENSIONAL GULFS, **CARTHAN** TRAVELS TOWARD EARTH AT MULTI-LIGHT SPEED...

AT LEAST I'LL BE ABLE TO STUDY THE CULTURE AND SOCIAL HABITS OF EARTH'S INHABITANTS WITH THE SUPER-INSTRUMENTS **XANDOR** GAVE ME!

AS HIS HIGHLY SENSITIVE COMPUTERS PICK UP REAMS OF INFORMATION...

WHY, THIS ISN'T AS BAD AS I FEARED! EARTH HAS A GROUP OF AMAZINGLY-ENDOWED HUMANS-- BANDED TOGETHER AND CALLING THEMSELVES THE **JUSTICE LEAGUE OF AMERICA**! ALL I NEED DO IS ASK THEIR HELP!

BUT AS HIS SPACESHIP, PROTECTED FROM DISCOVERY BY AN INVISIBILITY AND ANTI-RADAR BEAM, ENTERS EARTH'S ATMOSPHERE...

I **CAN'T** ASK FOR THE **JUSTICE LEAGUE'S** HELP! SOMETHING ABOUT MY **AURA** IS--**PREVENTING IT!** I WANT TO PLEAD FOR ASSISTANCE-- BUT I'M UNABLE TO DO SO!

WAIT! PERHAPS ALL ISN'T LOST! SUPPOSE I WERE TO PRETEND TO BE--**EVIL?** SUPPOSE I **DO** ACTIVATE THE MACHINES OF DESTRUCTION! SURELY THE **JUSTICE LEAGUE** WOULD FIND A WAY TO AVERT THE DOOMS! ONCE THAT WAS DONE, I COULD LEAVE EARTH WITH A CLEAR CONSCIENCE!

AT THIS MOMENT, IN THE HEADQUARTERS OF THE **JUSTICE LEAGUE OF AMERICA**, ITS MEMBERS ARE CONDUCTING A REGULARLY SCHEDULED MEETING--WITH **WONDER WOMAN** AS ROTATING CHAIRMAN...

WE'RE HERE TO DISCUSS THE ADMISSION OF NEW MEMBERS! DO YOU HAVE ANY SUGGESTIONS?

REMEMBER--ACCORDING TO OUR CONSTITUTION AND BY-LAWS--WE CAN ADMIT ONLY **ONE** NEW MEMBER AT A TIME!

HOW ABOUT **ADAM STRANGE?** HE'S ACHIEVED AN EXCELLENT RECORD!

YES, BUT **GREEN ARROW** HAS BEEN DOING FINE WORK FOR A LONG TIME!

HOW ABOUT THAT NEWCOMER IN **MIDWAY CITY?** HE'S KNOWN AS **HAWKMAN**...

AFTER AN HOUR OF FRIENDLY ARGUMENT...

MADAME CHAIRLADY, I MOVE THAT **GREEN ARROW** BE ELECTED UNANIMOUSLY!

I SECOND THE MOTION!

BUT BEFORE THE **AMAZON PRINCESS** CAN CALL FOR A VOTE...

ALL IN FAVOR OF **GREEN ARROW**... OHHH!

LIKE CRAZY, MAN! SPEAKING OF ARROWS.. WHERE'D *THAT* COME FROM?

IT APPEARED OUT OF THIN AIR!

IMPULSIVELY **BATMAN** LEANS FORWARD AND GRASPS THE SLENDER METAL SHAFT, AND AS HE DOES SO IT STARTS TO VIBRATE SOUND WAVES...

GREETINGS, **JUSTICE LEAGUE** MEMBERS! I HAVE NEWS FOR YOU! YOUR PROSPECTIVE NEW MEMBER--**GREEN ARROW**--IS MY PRISONER!

WHO IN THE WORLD--?

HOW DID HE LEARN ABOUT US AND OUR SECRET MEETING PLACE?

MY NAME IS **CARTHAN**! I COME FROM A PLANET MANY LIGHT YEARS FROM EARTH, TO ADD YOUR PLANET TO THE OTHERS I HAVE CONQUERED!

EVEN AS I TELEPATH MY THOUGHTS TO YOU THROUGH THE COMMUNICATOR-ARROW I FASHIONED--THREE ENGINES OF DOOM ARE GOING INTO OPERATION AT THREE DISTANTLY SEPARATED LOCALITIES ON EARTH! YOUR OBVIOUS ASSIGNMENT IS TO SMASH THEM--IF YOU CAN!

EVEN AT THIS INSTANT, MY ULTRA—WEAPONS ARE REMOVING THE METALLIC COVERINGS WHICH WILL SET THE DESTRUCTIVE ENGINES IN OPERATION.."

WHHIRRRRRRRRR!

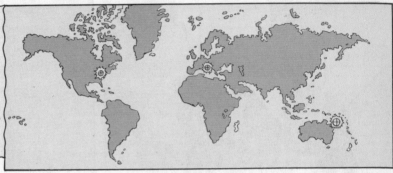

THESE ENGINES BEGIN ...CTIONING, THEIR *ALPHA*—...CRON-- AND *XI* RAYS ...L SEND A TRIO OF ...ASTERS ACROSS THE ...RTH! ...E MACHINE IS OUTSIDE ...YSTONE CITY--ANOTHER ...THE *PACIFIC OCEAN*, ...RTHEAST OF AUSTRALIA-- ...E THIRD AND LAST NEAR ...ME, *ITALY!*"

...EN THE VIBRATORY VOICE FADES AWAY...

BATMAN, THE TWO OF US MUST FIND THIS SPACE-VISITOR *CARTHAN*--AND FREE *GREEN ARROW!*

RIGHT! *J'ONN J'ONZZ*--I HAVEN'T BEEN TEAMED WITH YOU SINCE WE BATTLED *STARRO THE CONQUEROR!* LET'S HEAD FOR *KEYSTONE CITY!*

...'LL HANDLE ...E AUSTRALIAN ...CTOR, ...QUAMAN!

OKAY, *FLASH!*

THAT LEAVES ME TO TAKE CARE OF THE "ROMAN—MENACE"!

THE MEETING ROOM IS EMPTY, SAVE FOR THE WORRIED *SNAPPER CARR!* AS TIME SPEEDS BY, THE HONORARY JLA MEMBER GROWS MORE AND MORE RESTLESS, UNTIL...

I'M BLASTING OFF! I'M COMING UNGLUED FROM SUSPENSE! MAYBE BEATING FEET WILL CALM ME DOWN!

7

11

As the *AMAZON PRINCESS* and the *MARTIAN MAN-HUNTER* hurtle toward the first of the three deadly instruments of destruction placed on Earth, they discover their way to *KEYSTONE CITY* barred by monstrous insects..

HAS YOUR *MARTIAN-VISION* SPOTTED THE *DOOM WEAPON* CARTHAN SPOKE OF, *J'ONN J'ONZZ*?

YES, *WONDER WOMAN!* IT'S HIDDEN NOT FAR FROM HERE-- BUT TO REACH IT, WE HAVE TO FIGHT A PATH THROUGH THOSE GIANT INSECTS!

EVEN AS HE SPEAKS, THE *MARTIAN SUPER-SLEUTH* REELS UNDER THE SAVAGE ATTACK OF A TITANIC WASP AND A BUMBLE BEE..

THEIR TREMENDOUS STINGERS CANNOT PENETRATE MY MARTIAN SKIN-- BUT THE REPEATED BLOWS ARE DAZING ME!

FIGHTING FURIOU[S] HE BARRELS HIS WAY THROUGH THE SWARMING INSECT[S]

CARTHAN'S WEAPON MUST BE SOME SO[RT] OF GROWTH--CAUS[ING] MACHINE! THE NEA[RER] WE COME TO IT, TH[E] LARGER ARE THE INSECTS--AND ANIMALS--AROUND IT! EVIDENTLY HUMANS ARE NOT AFFECTED!

...EN, AS ...EAP-...OPPERS ...PRING ...ORWARD...

I COULD BREAK FREE IF ONLY THE GLUEY SAP THESE LEAFHOPPERS ARE EXUDING WEREN'T COVERING MY EYES--AND STICKING MY LEGS TOGETHER ...

...ABLE TO USE HIS JET-FLYING ...OWER, THE JLA MEMBER ...RASHES TO THE GROUND ...UST AS A HUGE FIREFLY ...ANDS BESIDE HIM ...

...FIREFLY GIVES OFF COLD ...IGHT--BUT WHEN IT'S THIS ...IZE THE USUALLY NEGLIGIBLE ...MOUNT OF HEAT IS ENOUGH ...O SET FIRE TO DRY LEAVES!

THE FLAMES ARE SPREADING-- WEAKENING ME! IF THEY AREN'T STOPPED SOON, I'M DONE FOR!

FAR ABOVE THE HELPLESS MARTIAN, WONDER WOMAN FINDS THAT, SHE TOO, IS IN DIRE TROUBLE!

MERCIFUL MINERVA! THAT HUGE CAT THINKS MY ROBOT-PLANE IS A BIRD ... AND IS TRYING TO CATCH IT!

NOW OTHER CATS ARE JOINING IT! I'VE GOT TO GET OUT--SEND MY ROBOT PLANE INTO THE SKY--OUT OF DANGER--AND CONTINUE WITHOUT IT!

9

THEN--AS THE *AMAZING AMAZON* RIDES THE WIND CURRENTS...

A *COOPER'S HAWK*--SWOOPING DOWN ON ME!

GRIPPED IN THE CRUEL PINCERS OF THE POWERFUL TALONS, *WONDER WOMAN* STRUGGLES TO FREE HERSELF FROM THE CRUSHING PRESSURE...

THIS BIRD IS A PREDATOR-- PREYING ON OTHER LIVING THINGS! IT'S HOLDING ME TOO TIGHTLY FOR ME TO BREAK LOOSE!

THEN, AS THEY PASS OVER THE FALLEN *MARTIAN MANHUNTER*, THE *AMAZON PRINCESS* YANKS LOOSE HER MAGIC LASSO...

MINERVA GUIDE MY AIM! THERE'S JUST ONE CHANCE FOR *J'ONN J'ONZZ* AND MYSELF! I MUST MAKE A PERFECT TOSS!

STRAIGHT AND TRUE FLIES THE GOLDEN ROPE! IT COILS AROUND THE ALMOST UNCONSCIOUS *J'ONN J'ONZZ* AND LIFTS HIM UPWARD...

WONDER WOMAN SAVED ME! I'M GETTING MY SUPER-STRENGTH BACK! NOW IT'S *MY* TURN TO GIVE *HER* A HELPING HAND!

THE *SUPER SLEUTH* INHALES WITH ALL HIS MIGHT! IN THE TERRIFIC DOWNDRAFT THUS CREATED THE *COOPER'S HAWK* FLUTTERS WEAKLY...

I DIDN'T INHALE HARD ENOUGH! I'LL HAVE TO TRY AGAIN

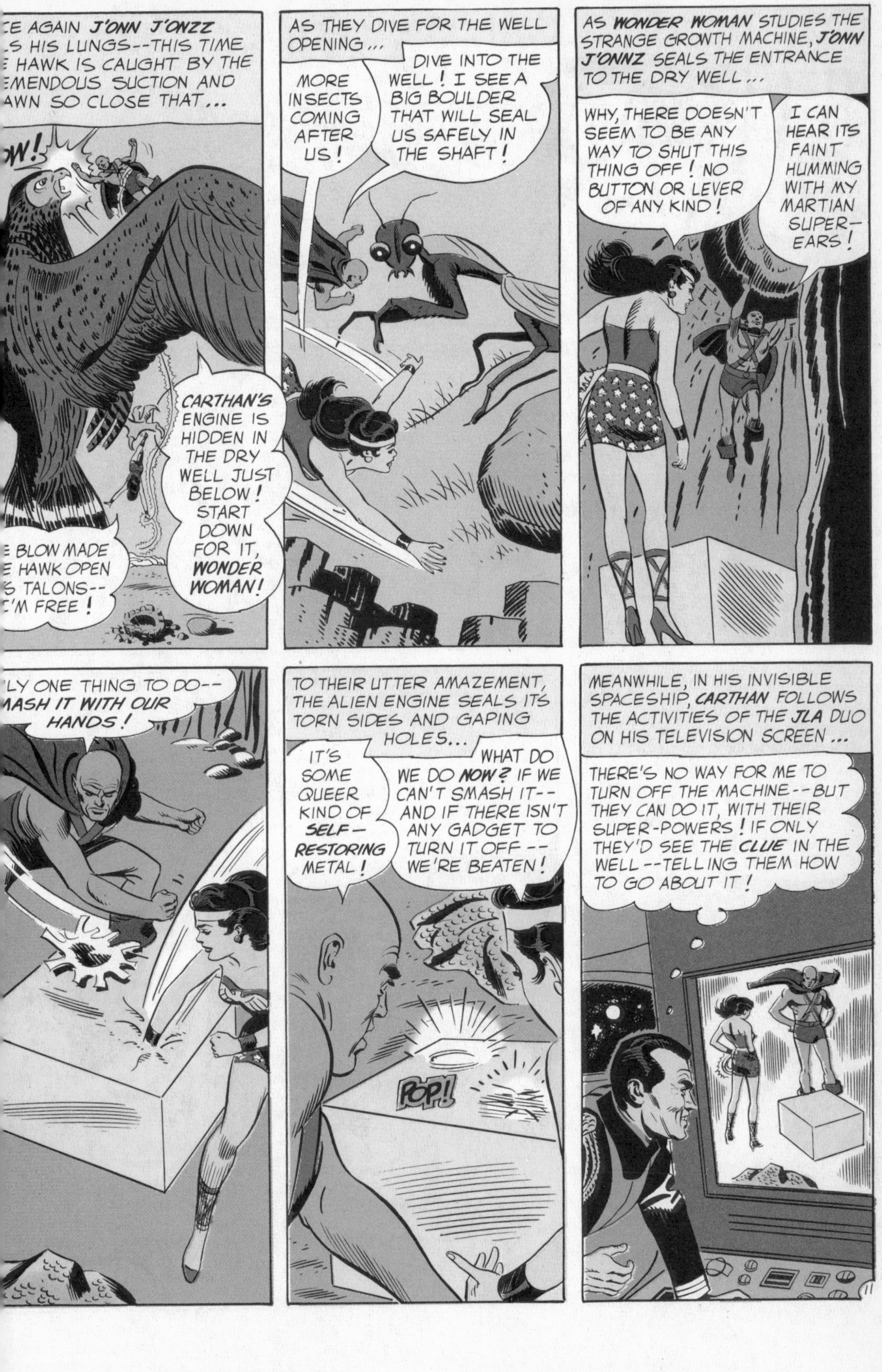
CE AGAIN J'ONN J'ONZZ
S HIS LUNGS--THIS TIME
HAWK IS CAUGHT BY THE
EMENDOUS SUCTION AND
AWN SO CLOSE THAT...
CARTHAN'S ENGINE IS HIDDEN IN THE DRY WELL JUST BELOW! START DOWN FOR IT, WONDER WOMAN!
E BLOW MADE E HAWK OPEN S TALONS-- I'M FREE!
AS THEY DIVE FOR THE WELL OPENING...
MORE INSECTS COMING AFTER US!
DIVE INTO THE WELL! I SEE A BIG BOULDER THAT WILL SEAL US SAFELY IN THE SHAFT!
AS WONDER WOMAN STUDIES THE STRANGE GROWTH MACHINE, J'ONN J'ONZZ SEALS THE ENTRANCE TO THE DRY WELL...
WHY, THERE DOESN'T SEEM TO BE ANY WAY TO SHUT THIS THING OFF! NO BUTTON OR LEVER OF ANY KIND!
I CAN HEAR ITS FAINT HUMMING WITH MY MARTIAN SUPER-EARS!
LY ONE THING TO DO-- MASH IT WITH OUR HANDS!
TO THEIR UTTER AMAZEMENT, THE ALIEN ENGINE SEALS ITS TORN SIDES AND GAPING HOLES...
IT'S SOME QUEER KIND OF SELF-RESTORING METAL!
WHAT DO WE DO NOW? IF WE CAN'T SMASH IT-- AND IF THERE ISN'T ANY GADGET TO TURN IT OFF-- WE'RE BEATEN!
POP!
MEANWHILE, IN HIS INVISIBLE SPACESHIP, CARTHAN FOLLOWS THE ACTIVITIES OF THE JLA DUO ON HIS TELEVISION SCREEN...
THERE'S NO WAY FOR ME TO TURN OFF THE MACHINE--BUT THEY CAN DO IT, WITH THEIR SUPER-POWERS! IF ONLY THEY'D SEE THE CLUE IN THE WELL--TELLING THEM HOW TO GO ABOUT IT!
11

FRANTICALLY, *WONDER WOMAN* AND *J'ONN J'ONZZ* EXAMINE THE MYSTERY MACHINE UNTIL ...

J'ONN J'ONZZ--LOOK! THIS IS THE METALLIC CLOTH COVER *CARTHAN* SPOKE ABOUT REMOVING! MAYBE IF WE REPLACE IT ON THE ENGINE IT WILL HELP US SOMEHOW!

AS THE COVER IS REPLACED...

SEE HERE! THE TOP OF THE COVER INDICATES IT SHOULD FIT SOME PART OF THE MACHINE--A MISSING PART--! IT MUST BE THE *OFF-ON HANDLE* WE'RE HUNTING! WHEN THE COVER WAS REMOVED, IT MIGHT HAVE CAUSED THE HANDLE TO DISAPPEAR INTO *ANOTHER* DIMENSION!

SECONDS LATER THE MAGIC LASSO IS TWIRLING SO FAST THAT IT SLIPS THROUGH THE DIMENSIONAL BARRIERS AND IS GUIDED BY *WONDER WOMAN'S* THOUGHTS INTO THE FOURTH-DIMENSION...

GOOD GIRL! YOU'VE CAUGHT IT! NOW GIVE IT A TUG TO THE LEFT--

NOTHING'S HAPPENING! I'LL TRY IT TO THE *RIGHT!*

AGAIN AND AGAIN THE *AMAZON* YANKS AT THE INVISIBLE LEVER UNTIL ...

YOU DID IT! I CAN'T HEAR THE MACHINE HUMMING ANYMORE!

I PULLED THE HANDLE *DOWN* INTO THE MACHINE! THAT MUST HAVE TURNED IT OFF!

AND WHEN THE *JLA* DUO EMERGES FROM THE WELL...

IT WORKED ALL RIGHT! THE INSECTS ARE GROWING SMALLER AS THE EFFECTS WEAR OFF!

NOW THAT W DISPOSED THIS MENA LET'S START AFTER *CARTHAN* I ONLY HOPE THE REST OF THE GROUP IS DOING AS WELL

DOOM OF THE STAR DIAMOND CHAPTER 3

...RACING SO SWIFTLY THAT HIS FEET DO NOT BREAK THE SURFACE TENSION OF THE WATER -- THUS ENABLING HIM TO STAY ABOVE THE SURFACE IN THE SAME MANNER THAT A FLAT STONE SKIRS ACROSS THE WATER-- **FLASH** *HURTLES TOWARD THE "DOWN UNDER" CONTINENT, PUSHING* **AQUAMAN** *BEFORE HIM...*

IT WON'T BE LONG NOW, *AQUAMAN!* WE JUST WENT PAST THE *SOLOMON ISLANDS!* NOW WE'RE ENTERING THE *CORAL SEA!*

NEXT STOP-- AUSTRALIA!

...AS THEY NEAR AUSTRALIA...

THE LAND IS SINKING INTO THE SEA!

THE MACHINE *CARTHAN* TOLD US ABOUT *MUST* BE CAUSING IT! DIVE DEEP, *AQUAMAN* -- SEE IF YOU CAN LOCATE THE MACHINE UNDER THE SURFACE!

THE ENTIRE CONTINENT WILL SOON BE UNDER THE SEA-- UNLESS I CAN DO SOME- THING ABOUT IT!

13

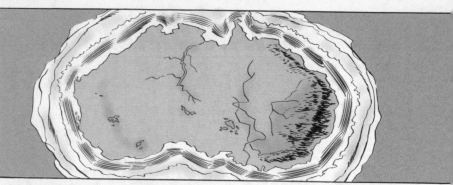

THE WATER FORMS A SOLID WALL--HELD UPRIGHT BY THE COMPRESSED AIR CREATED BY THE **FLASH'S** SPEED...

I DON'T KNOW HOW LONG I CAN MAINTAIN TH FANTASTIC PACE! IT'S UP TO **AQUAMAN** TO LOCATE THAT MACHINE IN A HURRY!

BELOW THE COOL WATERS OF THE PACIFIC OCEAN, THE **RULER OF THE SEA** QUESTIONS THE DENIZENS OF THE DEEP...

YES, WE HAVE SEEN AN ODD ENGINE DOWN ON THE SEA BOTTOM!

BUT BE WARNED-- NOTHING ALIVE CAN GET NEAR IT!

WHEN **AQUAMAN** APPROACHES THE SUBMERGED METAL BOX, HE IS REPELLED VIOLENTLY BY THE STRANGE FORCES SURROUND- ING IT...

OOF! WHATEVER REPELLING RAY THAT THING IS GIVING OFF HAS THE KICK OF A MISSOURI MULE! Hmmm-- IF I CAN'T GET NEAR IT-- MAYBE **FLASH** CAN!

SENDING OUT HIS MENTAL CA FOR HELP, THE **SEA SULTAN** IS SOON SURROUNDED WITH FIN FRIENDS...

BUT FOR **FLASH** TO EXAMINE THE ENGINE, I'VE GOT TO GET IT UP TO THE SU FACE! MY FISH FRIENDS WIL HELP ME DO THAT!

SOON A GROUP OF OCTOPI IS BUSILY WEAVING A HUGE SEAWEED BASKET...

KEEP WORKING! YOUR BASKET MUST BE BIG ENOUG AND STRONG ENOUGH BEFORE I CAN PUT MY PLAN IN ACTION!

...THE **GREAT BARRIER REEF**, SHORTLY AFTER, [SW]ORDFISH ARE CUTTING AWAY AT CORAL...

I WANT A LONG, STRONG PIECE OF CORAL!

[SIN]CE CORAL IS COMPOSED OF THE SKELETONS OF [MA]RINE CREATURES, IT CAN BE SAFELY THRUST THROUGH [TH]E REPELLING RAY OF THE DOOM MACHINE...

NOW--RAM THE CORAL INTO THE MACHINE--TILT IT ON EDGE-- AND **INTO THE SEAWEED BASKET!**

[TH]EN, AS THE SHARKS SWIM UPWARD WITH THEIR [BA]SKET-CATCH...

FLASH WILL BE RACING [AR]OUND THE CONTINENT SO FAST--HE'LL OUT-[RU]N THE SOUND OF MY VOICE! HOW CAN I TELL [HI]M WE NEED HIS HELP? THAT I CAN'T GET [NE]AR THE MACHINE?

WHEN THE MACHINE IS SET UP ON SHORE...

MY ONLY HOPE IS TO HOLD UP SIGNS-- JUST AS THEY DO AT AUTO-SPEED RACES--TO GIVE THE DRIVERS A MESSAGE!

I CAN'T GET [NE]AR THE [MA]CHI...!

[ARO]UND AND AROUND THE CONTINENT RACES THE **SCARLET** [SP]EEDSTER, KEEPING THE WATER FROM INUNDATING THE LAND, [UN]TIL...

[I] CAN'T GET [NE]AR THE [MA]CHINE!

NEED YOUR HELP TO TURN IT OFF!

AT THAT MOMENT IN **CARTHAN'S** SPACE-SHIP...

I HOPE **FLASH** REALIZES THAT HE HAS TO CAUSE COUNTER-VIBRATIONS TO NEUTRALIZE THE REPELLING VIBRATIONS OF THE BOX! IF HE CAN'T, THE BEAMS WILL EVENTUALLY PULL DOWN **ALL** THE LAND AREAS OF EARTH--TO THE BOTTOM OF THE SEA!

15

AS HE HURTLES AROUND THE *"DOWN UNDER"* CONTINENT, THE *FLASH'S* THOUGHTS KEEP LIGHTNING SPEED WITH HIS FLYING FEET AND-- THEN--

I'LL TAKE OUT A SPLIT-SECOND FROM MY CONTINENTAL *"RUNAROUND"* TO WORK UP VIBRATIONS TO COUNTER THE REPELLING VIBRATIONS!

BACK HE SUPER-SPEEDS AROUND AUSTRALIA, HOLDING AT BAY THE TONS OF SEA WATER...

DIDN'T WORK THE FIRST TIME! ON THE NEXT CHANCE I'LL TRY WHIRLING MY ARMS!

EACH SUCCEEDING EFFORT BY THE *SCARLET SPEEDSTER* MEETS WITH FAILURE UNTIL...

YOU'VE HIT IT, *FLASH!* I CAN GET THROUGH! JUST KEEP ON SPINNING-- UNTIL I REACH THAT TURN-OFF HANDLE!

SECONDS LATER...

IT'S OFF!

GOOD! BUT UNTIL THE NORMAL BALANCE BETWEEN LAND AND SEA IS RESTORED-- I'D BETTER STAY ON THE JOB!

SHORTLY THEREAFTER...

MISSION ACCOMPLISHED, *FLASH!* EVERYTHING HAS BEEN RESTORED TO NORMAL!

NOW WE CA GET AFTE *CARTHAN* - TRUSTING THA THE OTHERS H. DONE AS WELL AND WILL MEET US THE

DOOM OF THE STAR DIAMOND CHAPTER 4

AS THE *EMERALD WARRIOR* SWOOPS DOWN OUT OF THE SOFT ITALIAN SKY...

THIS IS A MOVIE SET, MADE FOR THE SCIENCE-FICTION PICTURE, *"GIANTS FROM GANYMEDE!"* THOSE GOLDEN GIANTS WERE PROPS USED IN THE MOVIE!

THOSE GIGANTIC GILDED STATUES HAVE *COME ALIVE!* SINCE THEY'RE *YELLOW* -- MY *POWER RING* CAN'T STOP THEM!

HURTLING ACROSS THE WAVES OF THE ATLANTIC--OVER THE MIGHTY ALPS TO ITALY--COMES *GREEN LANTERN!* AHEAD OF HIM LIES THE THIRD OF *KARTHAN'S* MYSTERIOUS DOOM MACHINES! BEFORE HIM ARE ALSO THE STRANGE AND DEADLY LIFE-FORMS THE MACHINE HAS CREATED!

THE MOVIE STUNT MEN MANIPULATED THEM BY WIRES FROM HELICOPTERS DURING THE FILMING OF THE PICTURE--BUT THERE'S NO NEED FOR WIRES NOW! THEY'VE *COME ALIVE!*

17

MY *POWER RING* IS JUST AS USELESS AGAINST THOSE "INVADERS" AS CANNON AND TANKS! SOME STRANGE FORCE FROM THE DOOM MACHINE HAS ENDOWED THEM WITH *LIFE*!

DODGING THE OUTSTRETCHED HANDS WHICH SEEK TO DESTROY HIM, THE *GREEN GLADIATOR* BEAMS HIS *POWER RING* AT A NEARBY FOREST...

ORDINARY METHODS WON'T OVERCOME THEM--SO I'LL TRY SOMETHING *EXTRA*ORDINARY!

FLAT GREEN BUZZSAWS FORM IN THE DEPTHS OF THE FOREST AND INSTANTLY BEGIN WORKING, SENDING HUGE SHOWERS OF SAWDUST INTO THE AIR...

BEHIND THEM, TREMENDOUS FANS ROTATE FASTER AND FASTER, SENDING THE SAWDUST TOWARD THE GILDED GIANTS WITH THE VELOCITY OF A HURRICANE...

I'VE GOT TO FORM A FINE LAYER OF SAWDUST OVER THE SURFACE OF THE GIANTS--THEN COAT MORE AND MORE LAYERS OVER THE FIRST ONE!

SOON THE "GIANTS FROM GANYMEDE" ARE THICKLY COATED WITH THE FINE PARTICLES OF WOOD SHAVINGS...

SINCE THE FIRST LAYER IS IN CONTACT WITH THE *YELLOW SURFACE* OF THE CREATURES, MY RING HAS NO EFFECT ON IT--BUT IT WILL WORK ON THE OTHER LAYERS COATING THEM!

...DER THE RAYS OF THE **POWER RING** THE SAWDUST ...DENS INTO **PETRIFIED WOOD!*** ENCASED IN THICK ...LLS OF SOLID STONE, THE ALIEN TITANS CANNOT ...VE!

WELL, THAT TAKES CARE OF **THAT** TROUBLE!

...ditor's Note: PETRIFIED WOOD IS CAUSED BY ...NERALS REPLACING THE WOODY STRUCTURE ... TREES OR SAWDUST WITH QUARTZ!

TO HIS CHAGRIN, **GREEN LANTERN** LEARNS HIS TROUBLES ARE ONLY BEGINNING...

THE LIFE-FORCE THAT ANIMATED THE GIANTS IS WORKING ON OTHER SUB- STANCES NOW! THOSE BUILDINGS-- STARTING TO MOVE...

...PROBE BEAM FROM THE **POWER** ...NG STABS THIS WAY AND THAT ... LOCATE THE LIFE SOURCE...

...MUST FIND THE MACHINE ...REATING THOSE LIFE RAYS ...D DESTROY IT! ODD-- MY ...NG CAN'T SEEM TO MAKE ...CONTACT WITH IT!

AND THEN...

THERE'S THE ANSWER! THE LIFE RAY IS HIDDEN IN A **GOLDEN BOX**! THE RING EMANATIONS CANNOT TOUCH IT-- BUT THEY'RE **GLOWING** TO ATTRACT MY ATTENTION!

GREEN LANTERN SURROUNDS THE GOLDEN BOX WITH A FORCE-FIELD BUT THE YELLOW LIFE RAYS EASILY PENETRATE IT...

IT'S NO USE! THE RAYS THEMSELVES ARE GOLDEN! BUT IT SHOULD BE SIMPLE ENOUGH FOR ME TO TURN THE MACHINE OFF WITH MY HANDS!

19

LUNGING FORWARD, HE REACHES FOR THE YELLOW HANDLE BUT AS HIS FINGERS WRAP AROUND IT...

OOOHH! THE LEVER IS **ELECTRIFIED**! I--I CAN'T MOVE!

FROM HIS **POWER RING** SHOOTS A GREEN BEAM ...

MY FEET ARE GROUNDING ME! IF I COULD FREE THEM FROM CONTACT WITH THE EARTH, THE FLOW OF ELECTRICITY WON'T AFFECT ME TOO MUCH!

THE **POWER RING** SHOVEL DIGS THE GROUND UNDER **GREEN LANTERN'S** FEET UNTIL HE HAN[G] SUSPENDED IN THE AIR BESIDE THE BOX--

I'M FREE!...

WITH A WRENCH OF MIGHTY MUSCLES, HE YANKS DOWN ON THE LEVER ...

I'VE SHUT IT OFF!

HIS MISSION ACCOMPLISHED, THE **JLA** MEMBER HEADS HOMEWARD ...

I WONDER IF THE OTHERS MADE OUT AS WELL AS I DID? NO TIME TO FIND OUT, THOUGH! I'VE GOT TO LOCATE **CARTHAN** AND HIS SPACE-SHIP AND GIVE A HELPING HAND TO **SUPERMAN** AND **BATMAN**!

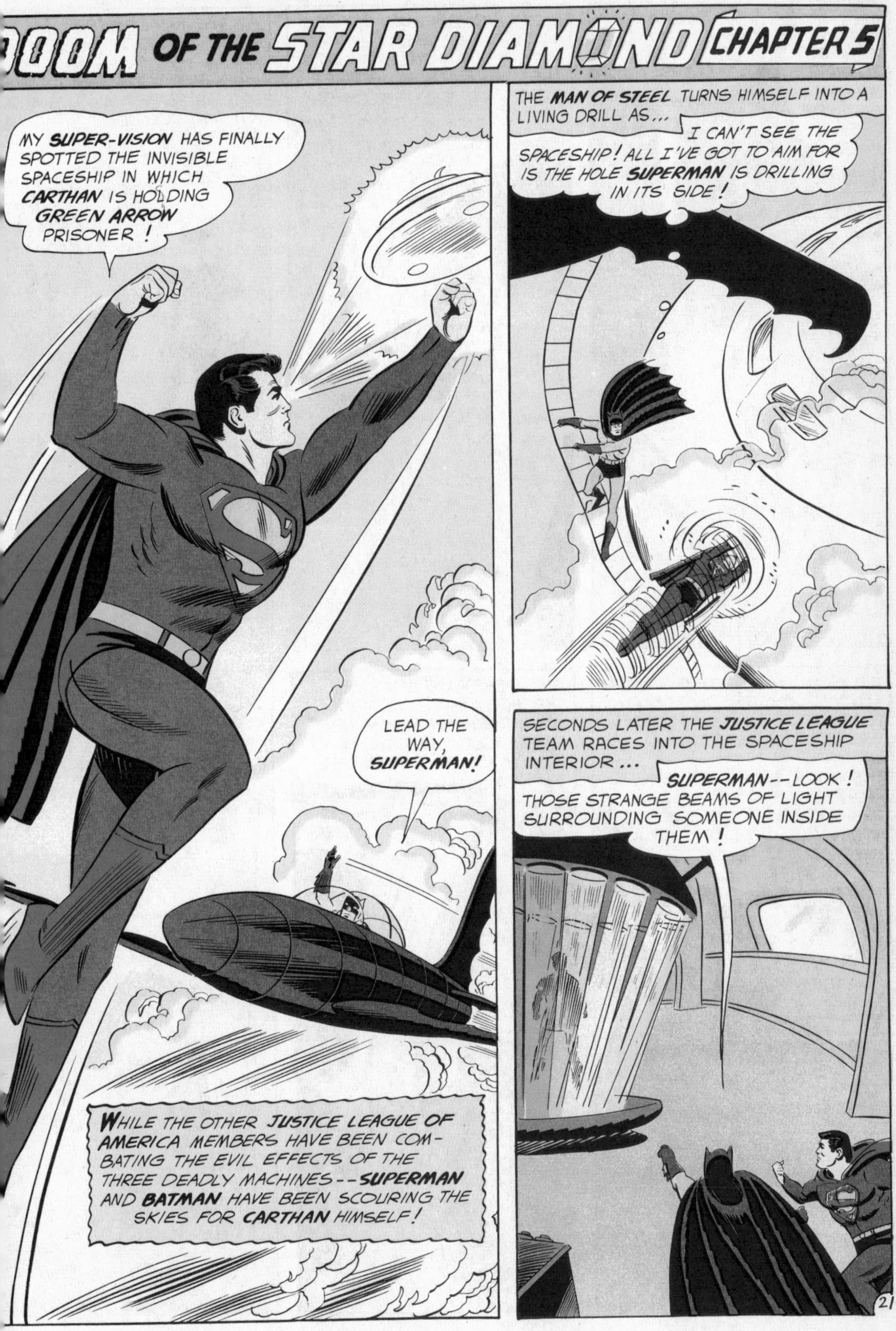
DOOM OF THE STAR DIAMOND CHAPTER 5
MY SUPER-VISION HAS FINALLY SPOTTED THE INVISIBLE SPACESHIP IN WHICH CARTHAN IS HOLDING GREEN ARROW PRISONER!
LEAD THE WAY, SUPERMAN!
WHILE THE OTHER JUSTICE LEAGUE OF AMERICA MEMBERS HAVE BEEN COMBATING THE EVIL EFFECTS OF THE THREE DEADLY MACHINES--SUPERMAN AND BATMAN HAVE BEEN SCOURING THE SKIES FOR CARTHAN HIMSELF!
THE MAN OF STEEL TURNS HIMSELF INTO A LIVING DRILL AS...
I CAN'T SEE THE SPACESHIP! ALL I'VE GOT TO AIM FOR IS THE HOLE SUPERMAN IS DRILLING IN ITS SIDE!
SECONDS LATER THE JUSTICE LEAGUE TEAM RACES INTO THE SPACESHIP INTERIOR...
SUPERMAN--LOOK! THOSE STRANGE BEAMS OF LIGHT SURROUNDING SOMEONE INSIDE THEM!
21

WHY--IT'S *GREEN ARROW*! I'LL HAVE YOU OUT OF THERE IN A JIFFY!

NO, *BATMAN--WAIT*! DON'T TOUCH THOSE LIGHTS!

THOSE LIGHT BEAMS ARE ACTUALLY DEADLY RAYS! IF ONE OF THEM WERE TO TOUCH YOU, YOU WOULD DIE!

THESE RAYS WON'T BOTHER *ME*, *GREEN ARROW*! I'LL GET YOU OUT!

As THE MAN OF STEEL EASILY PASSES THROUGH THE DEATH RAYS....

GOOD ENOUGH, *SUPERMAN--* BUT THAT DOESN'T SOLVE THE PROBLEM OF GETTING ME *OUT*!

I'VE ALREAD[Y] THOUGH[T] OF THA[T] WATCH

THE MIGHTY HANDS OF *SUPERMAN* RUN THROUGH THE SOLID LEAD FLOOR AS IF IT WERE MADE OF MELTING BUTTER...

THIS FLOOR IS OF SOLID LEAD TO PROTECT YOU FROM THE RAYS WHILE YOU'RE IN THE PRISON! HOWEVER, I CAN USE THAT SAME LEAD TO PROTECT YOU ANOTHER WAY!

SINCE THE RAYS CAN'T GET THROUGH LEAD I'LL MAKE A HUGE EGG IN WHICH TO CARRY YOU! THE RAYS WON'T TOUCH YOU AS I BRING YOU OUT!

MOMENTS LATER...

GREAT WOR[K] *SUPERMAN*! I'VE BEEN MIGHT[Y] CURIOUS AS TO HOW *CARTHAN* CAPTURED *GREEN ARROW*!

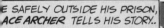

Panel 1 (partial left): SAFELY OUTSIDE HIS PRISON, ...ACE ARCHER TELLS HIS STORY..

WAS RETURNING FROM A CASE ...HE ARROW CAR WHEN ALL ...A SUDDEN A QUEER LIGHT ...FORMED AROUND ME...

Panel 2: "I WAS LIFTED UPWARD AT AN INCREDIBLE SPEED BY WHAT CARTHAN LATER TOLD ME WAS A SNATCH BEAM..."

I'M PARALYZED... UNABLE TO MOVE!

"THEN I FOUND MYSELF IN THE DEATH-RAY PRISON WITH CARTHAN JUST BEYOND IT..."

I HATE TO DO THIS TO YOU, GREEN ARROW... BUT IT'S PART OF MY PLOT TO STIR THE JUSTICE LEAGUE OF AMERICA INTO ACTION!

WHILE GREEN ARROW IS CON- CLUDING HIS STORY, THE OTHER JUSTICE LEAGUE MEMBERS ARE RETURNING FROM KEYSTONE CITY, AUSTRALIA, AND ITALY...

MY MARTIAN X-RAY VISION HAS SPOTTED CARTHAN'S SPACESHIP! I'LL LEAD THE WAY!

...AS THE QUINTET OF WONDER-BEINGS HURTLE INTO THE SPACESHIP THROUGH THE HOLE DRILLED BY SUPERMAN...

A GLOWING BUBBLE FORMING AROUND US!

WE'RE CAUGHT INSIDE IT!

HOLDING US LIKE QUICK- SAND --

23

AS THE BUBBLE COALESCES, HARDENS-- THE FIVE JUSTICE LEAGUE MEMBERS FIND THEMSELVES IMPRISONED INSIDE A GIGANTIC HOLLOW DIAMOND...!

THE *JUSTICE LEAGUE* CONSIDERS ME THEIR ENEMY! FOR MY OWN SAFETY I HAD TO IMPRISON THEM-- UNTIL I CAN EXPLAIN!

THERE ARE TINY FLAMES ENCASED IN THE DIAMOND-- WEAKENING ME!

AND GOLDEN FLAKES-- WHICH MAKE MY *POWER RING* USELESS!

IF ONLY I KNEW WHERE TO STRIKE THE JEWEL AND SPLIT IT IN TWO--

THE STRE[SS] POINT C[AN] ONLY B[E] DETERMIN[ED] FROM OUTSI[DE] THE GEM

AT THIS MOMENT, *SUPERMAN, BATMAN,* AND *GREEN ARROW* DASH INTO THE ROOM...

OHH! THERE'S *KRYPTONITE* IN THAT DIAMOND-- IT'S SAPPING ALL MY STRENGTH!

THERE'S THE ONE RESPONSIBLE FOR IT ALL-- *CARTHAN* I'LL HANDLE HIM!

SWIFTER EVEN THAN THE LUNGING *BATMAN* IS THE FLIGHT OF *GREEN ARROW'S* SLENDER SHAFT-- WHICH BOUNCES HARMLESSLY OFF *CARTHAN'S* PROTECTIVE AURA AS...

NOTHING CAN HARM ME-- CAN'T YOU UNDERSTAND?

I'VE GOT TO CONVINCE MYSELF!

KNOCKED OFF HIS FEET, *CARTHAN* FALLS BACKWARD AGAINST THE SPACESHIP MACHINERY...

WHY DIDN'T MY AURA PROTECT ME?

ZZZZZZTT!

AS HE COLLAPSES TO THE FLOOR, THE SPACEMAN TOUCH[ES] HIS HEAD...

OWW! MY HEAD[--] IT *HURTS!* THEN-- THAT MEANS[--] MY PROTECTIVE AURA HAS SUD[--]DENLY FADED AWAY!

SOON CARTHAN IS POURING OUT HIS STORY TO AN ASTOUNDED BATMAN AND GREEN ARROW...

NOW AT LAST I CAN GO BACK TO MY OWN WORLD--BUT FIRST I HAVE TO RELEASE YOUR FRIENDS FROM THE DIAMOND! OH, *NO!* WHEN YOU THREW ME INTO THE MACHINERY, *BATMAN*--I WRECKED IT! I CAN'T RELEASE THEM!

WAIT! THERE'S A SLIM CHANCE! EVERY DIAMOND HAS A *STRESS POINT*...IF I KNEW WHERE THIS ONE IS, I COULD SPLIT THE DIAMOND WITH ONE OF MY DIAMOND-TIP ARROWS!

BEFORE CLEAVING A DIAMOND, DIAMOND-CUTTERS SOMETIMES SPEND MONTHS STUDYING IT TO DISCOVER THE *STRESS POINT!* WE DON'T HAVE THAT MUCH TIME! LUCKILY, I'VE MADE SUCH A STUDY ON MY HOME PLANET! AIM HERE, *GREEN ARROW!*

WITH SWEAT BEADING HIS FORE-HEAD, THE *AMAZING ARCHER* DRAWS FAR BACK ON HIS GREAT BOW...

I MUST HIT THE DIAMOND *EXACTLY* AT THE POINT INDICATED-- WITH *EXACTLY* THE RIGHT FORCE-- OR I'LL DOOM THE *JUSTICE LEAGUE* TO A TERRIBLE FATE!

N THE NEXT NSTANT THE BOWSTRING TWANGS AND...

GREAT SHOT, GREEN ARROW! YOU SAVED THEM!

25

FOR A FEW MOMENTS THERE IS WILD CONFUSION UNTIL *BATMAN* AND *SUPERMAN*, TOGETHER WITH *GREEN ARROW*, CONVINCE THE OTHER MEMBERS THAT THE MAN THEY THOUGHT WAS AN ENEMY IS REALLY A FRIEND...

MAYBE WE OUGHT TO GIVE YOU A HELPING HAND AGAINST *XANDOR*!

YOU'VE HELPED ME PLENTY! OVERCOMING *XANDOR* IS-- MY FIGHT!

LATER, AFTER *CARTHAN'S* SHIP HAS BEEN REPAIRED AND HAS DEPARTED FOR THE STARS, THE *JUSTICE LEAGUE* MEMBERS RETURN TO THEIR SECRET HIDE-OUT TO COMPLETE SOME UNFINISHED BUSINESS...

ALL IN FAVOR OF *GREEN ARROW* BEING ACCEPTED AS A NEW MEMBER SAY *AYE*!

AYE!

HEY, WAIT FOR ME-- I VOTE AYE TOO!

MAN, I'M COMING UNGLUED! CLUE ME IN ON WHAT HAPPENED AGAINST *CARTHAN*!

IF YOU'RE SAYING WHAT I *THINK* YOU'RE SAYING, *SNAPPER*, I WANT TO HEAR THEIR ADVENTURES, TOO! I WAS IN PRISON WHILE THEY WERE STOPPING THOSE DOOM MACHINES!

SNAP!

SNAP!

AND SO WHILE A POP-EYED *SNAPPER* "KEEPS THE MINUTES OF THE MEETING", EACH OF THE *JUSTICE LEAGUE* MEMBERS TELLS HIS STORY...

WHEN WE FOUND THE BOX HAD NO HANDLE...

SNAPPER, YOU HAVEN'T TAKEN DOWN A THING WE'VE SAID! GET WITH IT, MAN-- GET WITH IT!

SNAP!

SNAP!

*T*HE *JUSTICE LEAGUE OF AMERICA*, AUGMENTED BY *GREEN ARROW*, TAKES OFF ON ANOTHER SUPER-ADVENTURE IN THE NEXT ISSUE!

The End

I'VE BEEN ASKED TO TELL YOU THIS STORY! *SUPERMAN, BATMAN, HAWKMAN* AND THE REST OF THE *JUSTICE LEAGUE* SAY IT'S *MY* STORY... MINE AND *BLACK CANARY'S!*

AS MOST OF YOU KNOW, MY NAME IS *GREEN ARROW!* IN MY SPARE TIME I FIGHT CRIME IN *STAR CITY!* BUT MOST DAYS I OPERATE AN INVESTMENT COMPANY AS *OLIVER QUEEN--*

"*I* DON'T THINK I NEED ADD THAT I'M RICH! OR, *WAS* RICH, UNTIL ABOUT A MONTH AGO! I WAS IN MY BOARD ROOM..."

THE QUEEN FUND

...STENING TO THE LIES OF JOHN ...LEON!"

...ESE DOCUMENTS ...OVE YOU DELIB- ...RATELY MISHANDLED ...E CITY'S MUNICIPAL ...ONDS FOR YOUR ...WN PROFIT!

THOSE SO-CALLED DOCUMENTS ARE *FORGERIES,* DELEON-- AND YOU *KNOW* IT!

PERHAPS! BUT THERE'S NO WAY IN THE WORLD YOU CAN *PROVE* IT!

YOU'RE *THROUGH,* QUEEN--*FINISHED!* ONCE NEWS OF THIS GETS OUT, NO BUSINESSMAN WILL COME NEAR THE *QUEEN FUND!*

"I KNEW DELEON HAD FRAMED ME-- TO FORCE *MY* ACCOUNTS TO DO BUSINESS WITH A COMPANY *HE* CONTROLLED! BUT, AS HE SAID, I COULDN'T PROVE IT! AND I KNEW HE WAS ALSO RIGHT IN SAYING THAT MY OUTFIT WAS DEAD..."

-223

"*I NEEDED TO BE ALONE...TO THINK! I WANDERED AIMLESSLY, MY STEPS UNCONSCIOUSLY CARRYING ME TO A CRUMBLING SLUM AREA OF THE CITY...*"

"*SUDDENLY, I HEARD A CALL FOR HELP, AND SAW--*"

A MUGGING! IT'S A FINE OPPORTUNITY TO TRY OUT MY NEW *GREEN ARROW* GEAR!

"*QUICKLY, I PULLED MY COLLAPSIBLE BOW FROM MY QUIVER AND, WITH A TWIST OF THE WRIST, SNAPPED INTO READINESS! THEN, I FITTED A SLIM, PLEXALUMINUM SHAFT TO THE SPUN-GLASS STRING--*"

"*--AND LET FLY!*"

TWAAAA

AANG

"*A MOMENT LATER, THE PLASTIC ARROWHEAD EXPLODED, AND--*"

F-F-Z-Z-Z-LT

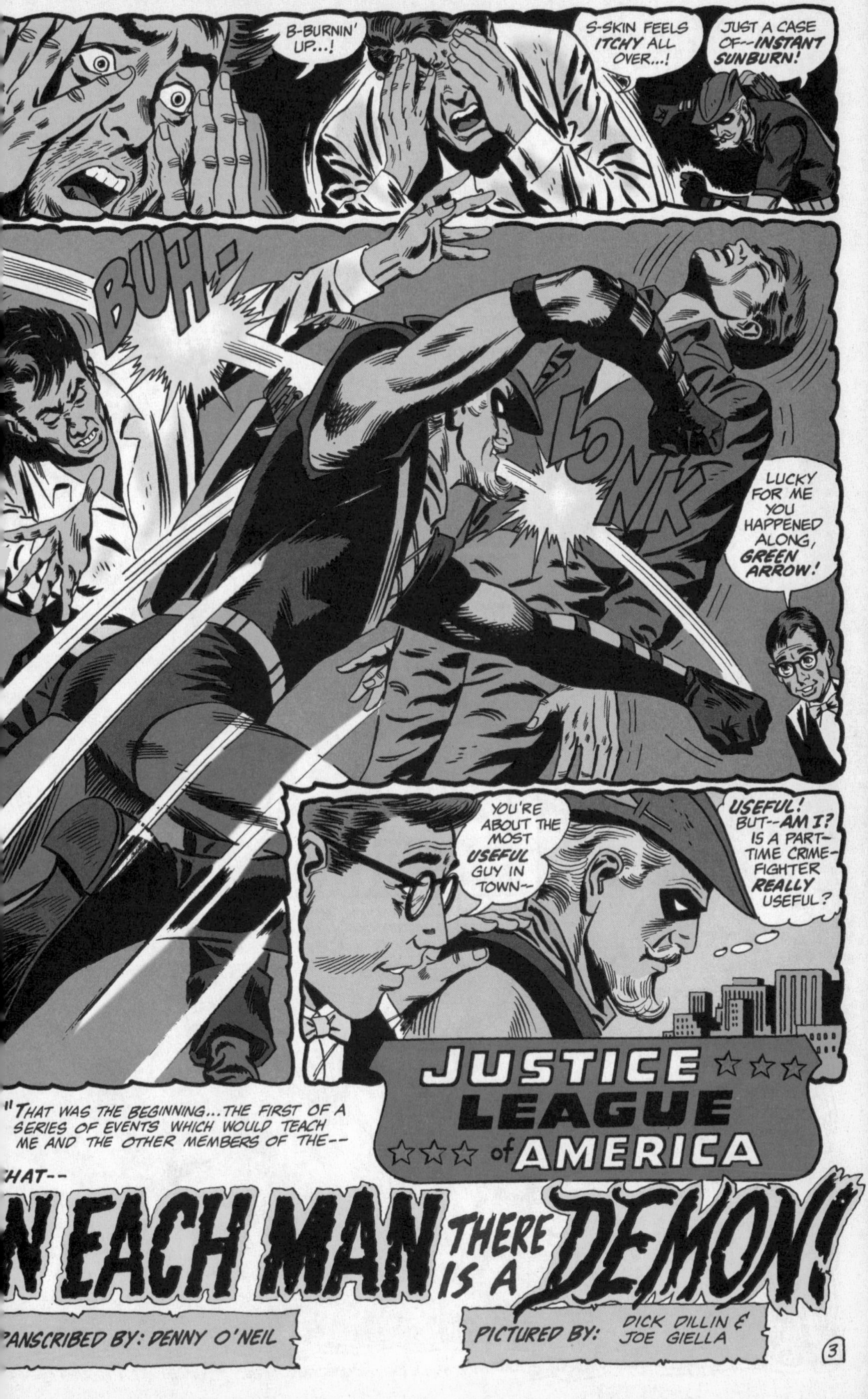

B-BURNIN' UP...!
S-SKIN FEELS ITCHY ALL OVER...!
JUST A CASE OF--INSTANT SUNBURN!
BUH-
LONK
LUCKY FOR ME YOU HAPPENED ALONG, GREEN ARROW!
YOU'RE ABOUT THE MOST USEFUL GUY IN TOWN--
USEFUL! BUT--AM I? IS A PART-TIME CRIME-FIGHTER REALLY USEFUL?
"THAT WAS THE BEGINNING...THE FIRST OF A SERIES OF EVENTS WHICH WOULD TEACH ME AND THE OTHER MEMBERS OF THE--
JUSTICE LEAGUE of AMERICA
HAT--
N EACH MAN THERE IS A DEMON!
ANSCRIBED BY: DENNY O'NEIL
PICTURED BY: DICK DILLIN & JOE GIELLA
3

PERHAPS YOU'D BETTER LET *ME* TELL THE NEXT PART, *GREEN ARROW!*

SURE, *BLACK CANARY!* AFTER ALL, *YOU* WERE THERE--AND I *WASN'T!*

"I WAS AT *JUSTICE LEAGUE* HEADQUARTERS--T~ SUBJECT OF A MILD *ARGUMENT...*"

I MOTION THAT WE WAIVE ALL REQUIREMENTS AND VOTE *BLACK CANARY* A JLA MEMBER *IMMEDIATELY!*

HOLD *ON, SUPERMAN!* I YIELD TO *NO ONE* IN MY ADMIRATION FOR *BLACK CANARY'S COURAGE* AND *VIRTUE...*

...AND I KN~ HER *EAR~ TWO* RECO ADMIRABL BUT I WON~ WHETHER S~ ACCUSTOM~ *OUR* KIND C MISSION--O~ KIND OF *DANGERS*

MANY OF OUR TASKS INVOLVE *MORE* THAN ORDINARY *CRIMINALS!*

AS *HAWKMAN* DRONED ON, MY MIND WANDERED TO MY HOME--*EARTH-T* AND THE TERRIBLE EVENTS OF A WEEK PAST...WHEN THE *JUSTICE LEAGUE* TEAMED WITH THE *JUSTICE SOCIETY* AGAINST THE STAR-CREATURE *AQUAR*

*A TALE FULL OF *SOUND AND FURY* TOLD IN *JLA* ISSUES *73* AND~

A SHUDDER OF HORROR, I RECALLED HOW *AQUARIUS* [CAUS]ED THE DEATH OF MY HUSBAND, *LARRY*--"

"--AND HOW *SUPERMAN* INVITED ME TO *EARTH-ONE*... WHERE PERHAPS I COULD...FORGET--"

[I] SNAPPED OUT OF MY REVERIE WHEN *HAWKMAN'S* VOICE ROSE IN ANGER..."

[I] KNOW SHE'S A [JU]DO-EXPERT-- [BU]T *JUDO* SIMPLY [IS]N'T *ENOUGH* AGAINST THE SORT OF FOES *WE* TACKLE!

HOW DO YOU *KNOW?* IT SEEMS TO ME SHE SHOULD HAVE A *CHANCE!*

STILL, WE HAVE NO RIGHT TO ENDANGER HER *NEED- LESSLY!*

PLEASE STOP TALKING ABOUT ME AS IF I WEREN'T *HERE!* ALL OF YOU--STOP *BICKERING--*

"SUDDENLY I FELT AN ODD *SINGING* INSIDE MY HEAD-- LIKE NOTHING I'D EVER FELT BEFORE--*EVER!* IT SEEMED TO MOVE *OUTSIDE*--"

5

35

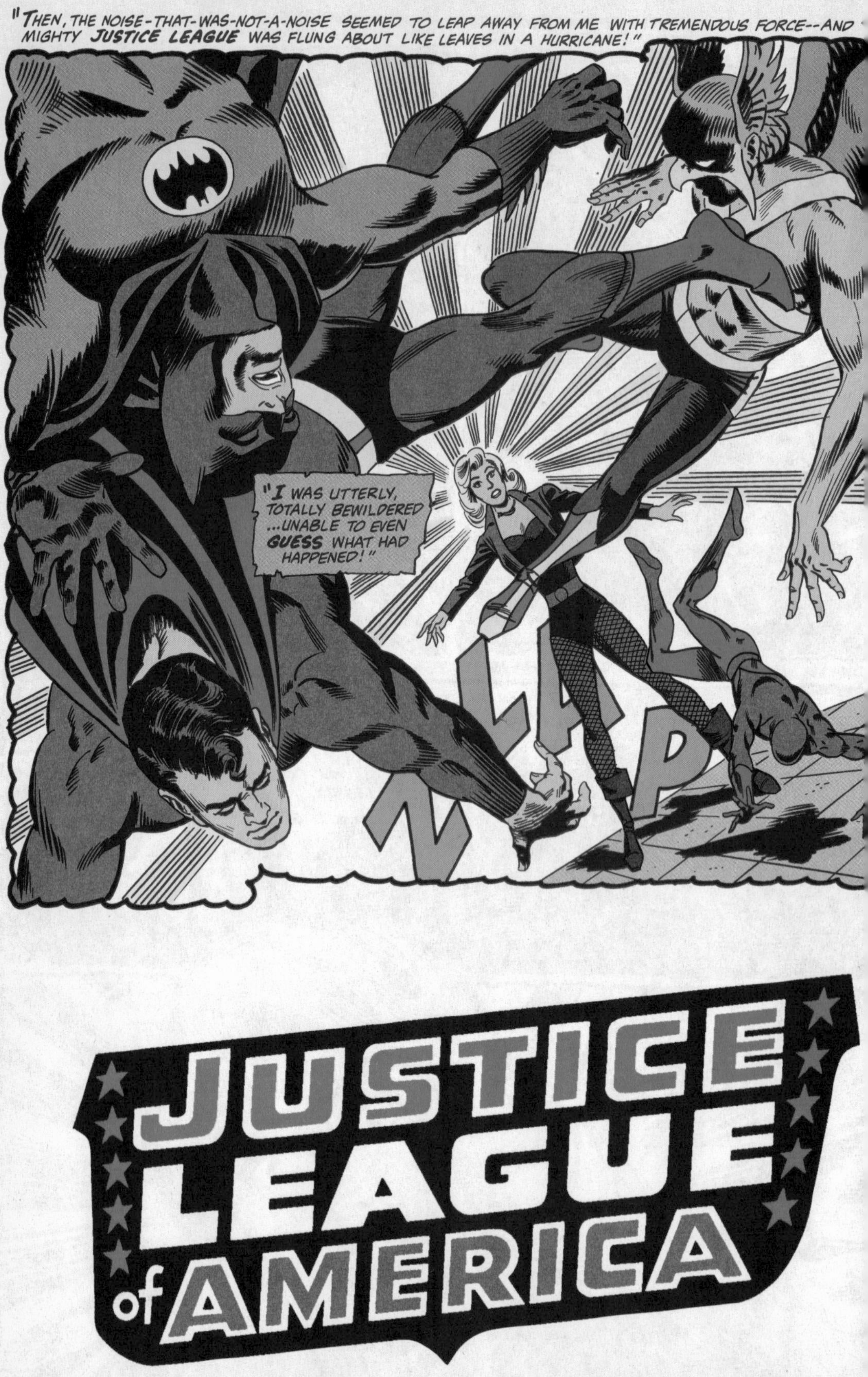
"THEN, THE NOISE-THAT-WAS-NOT-A-NOISE SEEMED TO LEAP AWAY FROM ME WITH TREMENDOUS FORCE--AND MIGHTY JUSTICE LEAGUE WAS FLUNG ABOUT LIKE LEAVES IN A HURRICANE!"
"I WAS UTTERLY, TOTALLY BEWILDERED ...UNABLE TO EVEN GUESS WHAT HAD HAPPENED!"
ZLAP

JUSTICE LEAGUE of AMERICA

WHILE **BLACK CANARY** WAS AT JLA HEADQUARTERS, I WAS ON MY WAY TO SEE CERTAIN DR. OYAL...

I NEEDED HELP--AND I KNEW IT! THE FIRST PSYCHIATRIST I CONSULTED HADN'T CLEARED UP MY PROBLEM*...

*SEE BRAVE AND BOLD #85!

"I'D HEARD OYAL HAD DEVELOPED A REVOLUTIONARY NEW THERAPY! I POURED OUT MY SOUL TO HIM--"

SO YOU SEE, DOCTOR, I DON'T KNOW WHICH IS REALLY **ME**--OLIVER QUEEN, FINANCIER ...OR **GREEN ARROW**, CRIME-CRUSADER...

A HIGHLY COMPLEX CRISIS, YOU HAVE!-- AN **IDENTITY** CRISIS, I BELIEVE!

FORTUNATELY, I AM IN A POSITION TO ASSIST YOU! I HAVE RECENTLY PERFECTED A DEVICE THAT WILL REVOLUTIONIZE PSYCHIATRY--

MY **ID-ACTUALIZER!** IT WILL DIG DEEPLY INTO YOUR SUBCONSCIOUS AND ENABLE YOU TO **SEE** WHAT YOU REALLY WISH TO BE!

RELAX! THE TREATMENT IS QUITE PAINLESS--

"I SLIPPED INTO A TRANCE FOR A MOMENT--"

WHA--WHAT IS **THIS**? IT SHOULD NOT BE **OCCURRING!**

WHO ARE **YOU**? WHERE DO YOU **COME** FROM?

7

I AM THE **REAL** GREEN ARROW-- THE WARRIOR WHO LIVES WITHIN OLIVER QUEEN'S BODY-- --HIS **FIGHTING** SPIRIT!-- HIS **SELF!**

THIS IS MOST **UNEXPECTED**-- UTTERLY UNSCIENTIFIC!

I DON'T KNOW WHAT THAT THING **IS**... OR WHAT IT WAS **BABBLING** ABOUT... BUT SOMETHING TELLS ME IT BETTER BE **STOPPED!**

TAKE IT FROM HERE, **BLACK CANARY!**

AFTER I'D **ACCIDENTALLY** KNOCKED THE **JUSTICE LEAGUERS** DOWN...

"**SUPERMAN** AND **ATOM** DECIDED TO FIND OUT **HOW** I'D DONE IT! THEY USED THE JLA'S **BIONIC COMPUTER** TO TEST MY PHYSICAL RESPONSES..."

IF YOU READ THOSE DIALS LIKE **I** READ THOSE DIALS--WE'VE GOT AN **INSTANT-MUTANT** SITTING HERE!

THAT'S THE WAY I READ THEM ALL RIGHT!

WILL **ONE** OF YOU PLEASE **EXPLAIN?**

GAL, WHEN YOU SENT US FLYING, YOU DID IT WITH **ULTRA-SONIC WAVES!**

BUT--**HOW?** I DIDN'T **SAY** ANYTHING!

YEAH...AND **THAT** IS WHAT'S FREAKY! APPARENTLY, YOUR BRAIN **GENERATED** THEM WITHOUT YOUR **WILLING** IT!

SWOP

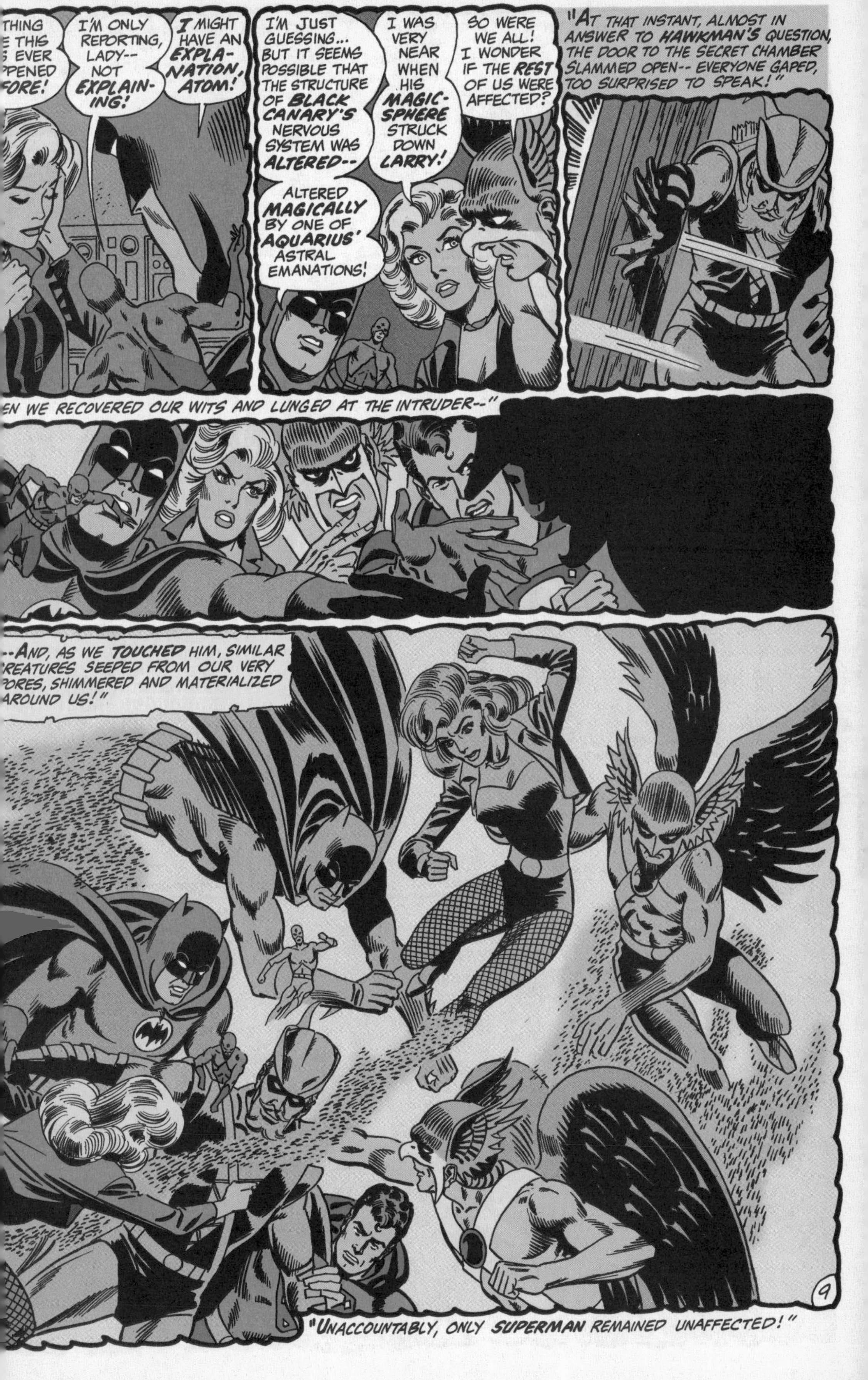

THING E THIS S EVER PPENED FORE!
I'M ONLY REPORTING, LADY-- NOT EXPLAINING!
I MIGHT HAVE AN EXPLANATION, ATOM!
I'M JUST GUESSING... BUT IT SEEMS POSSIBLE THAT THE STRUCTURE OF BLACK CANARY'S NERVOUS SYSTEM WAS ALTERED--
ALTERED MAGICALLY BY ONE OF AQUARIUS' ASTRAL EMANATIONS!
I WAS VERY NEAR WHEN HIS MAGIC-SPHERE STRUCK DOWN LARRY!
SO WERE WE ALL! I WONDER IF THE REST OF US WERE AFFECTED?
"AT THAT INSTANT, ALMOST IN ANSWER TO HAWKMAN'S QUESTION, THE DOOR TO THE SECRET CHAMBER SLAMMED OPEN-- EVERYONE GAPED, TOO SURPRISED TO SPEAK!"
EN WE RECOVERED OUR WITS AND LUNGED AT THE INTRUDER--"
--AND, AS WE TOUCHED HIM, SIMILAR REATURES SEEPED FROM OUR VERY PORES, SHIMMERED AND MATERIALIZED AROUND US!"
9
"UNACCOUNTABLY, ONLY SUPERMAN REMAINED UNAFFECTED!"

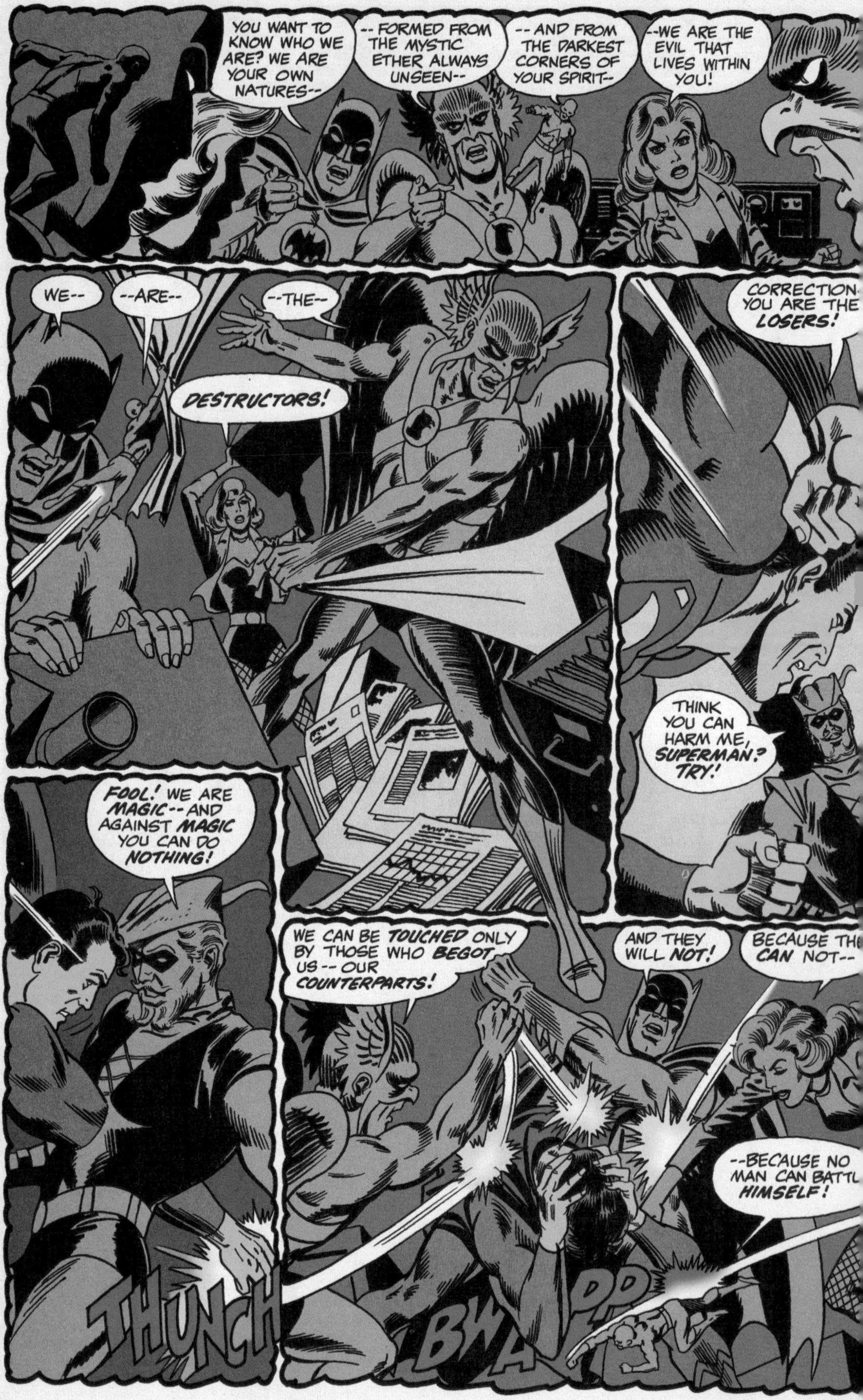

YOU WANT TO KNOW WHO WE ARE? WE ARE YOUR OWN NATURES--
-- FORMED FROM THE MYSTIC ETHER ALWAYS UNSEEN--
-- AND FROM THE DARKEST CORNERS OF YOUR SPIRIT--
--WE ARE THE EVIL THAT LIVES WITHIN YOU!
WE--
--ARE--
--THE--
DESTRUCTORS!
CORRECTION YOU ARE THE LOSERS!
THINK YOU CAN HARM ME, SUPERMAN? TRY!
FOOL! WE ARE MAGIC--AND AGAINST MAGIC YOU CAN DO NOTHING!
THUNCH
WE CAN BE TOUCHED ONLY BY THOSE WHO BEGOT US -- OUR COUNTERPARTS!
AND THEY WILL NOT!
BECAUSE TH CAN NOT--
--BECAUSE NO MAN CAN BATTL HIMSELF!

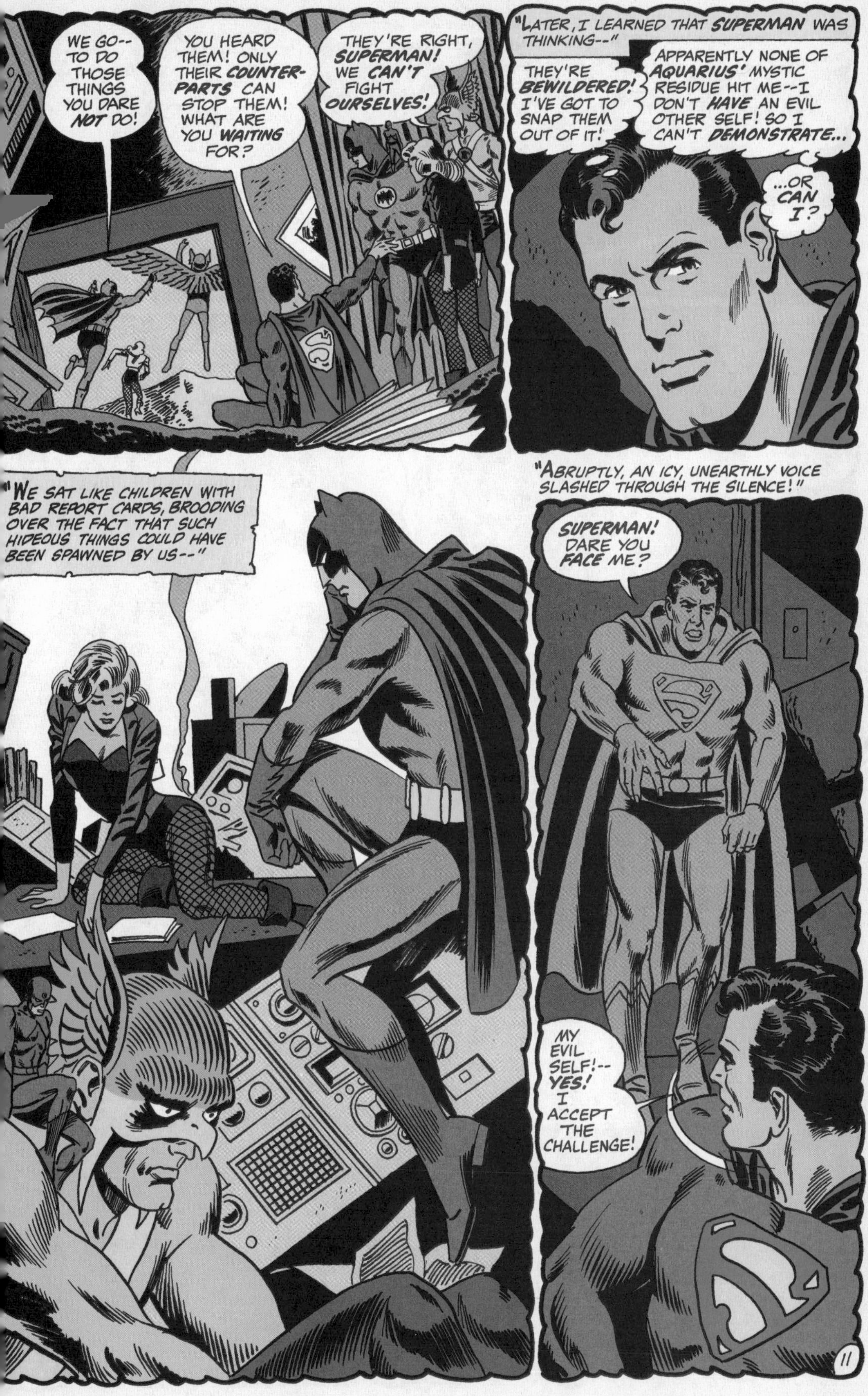
WE GO-- TO DO THOSE THINGS YOU DARE NOT DO!
YOU HEARD THEM! ONLY THEIR COUNTER-PARTS CAN STOP THEM! WHAT ARE YOU WAITING FOR?
THEY'RE RIGHT, SUPERMAN! WE CAN'T FIGHT OURSELVES!
"LATER, I LEARNED THAT SUPERMAN WAS THINKING--"
THEY'RE BEWILDERED! I'VE GOT TO SNAP THEM OUT OF IT!
APPARENTLY NONE OF AQUARIUS' MYSTIC RESIDUE HIT ME--I DON'T HAVE AN EVIL OTHER SELF! SO I CAN'T DEMONSTRATE...
...OR CAN I?
"WE SAT LIKE CHILDREN WITH BAD REPORT CARDS, BROODING OVER THE FACT THAT SUCH HIDEOUS THINGS COULD HAVE BEEN SPAWNED BY US--"
"ABRUPTLY, AN ICY, UNEARTHLY VOICE SLASHED THROUGH THE SILENCE!"
SUPERMAN! DARE YOU FACE ME?
MY EVIL SELF!--YES! I ACCEPT THE CHALLENGE!
11

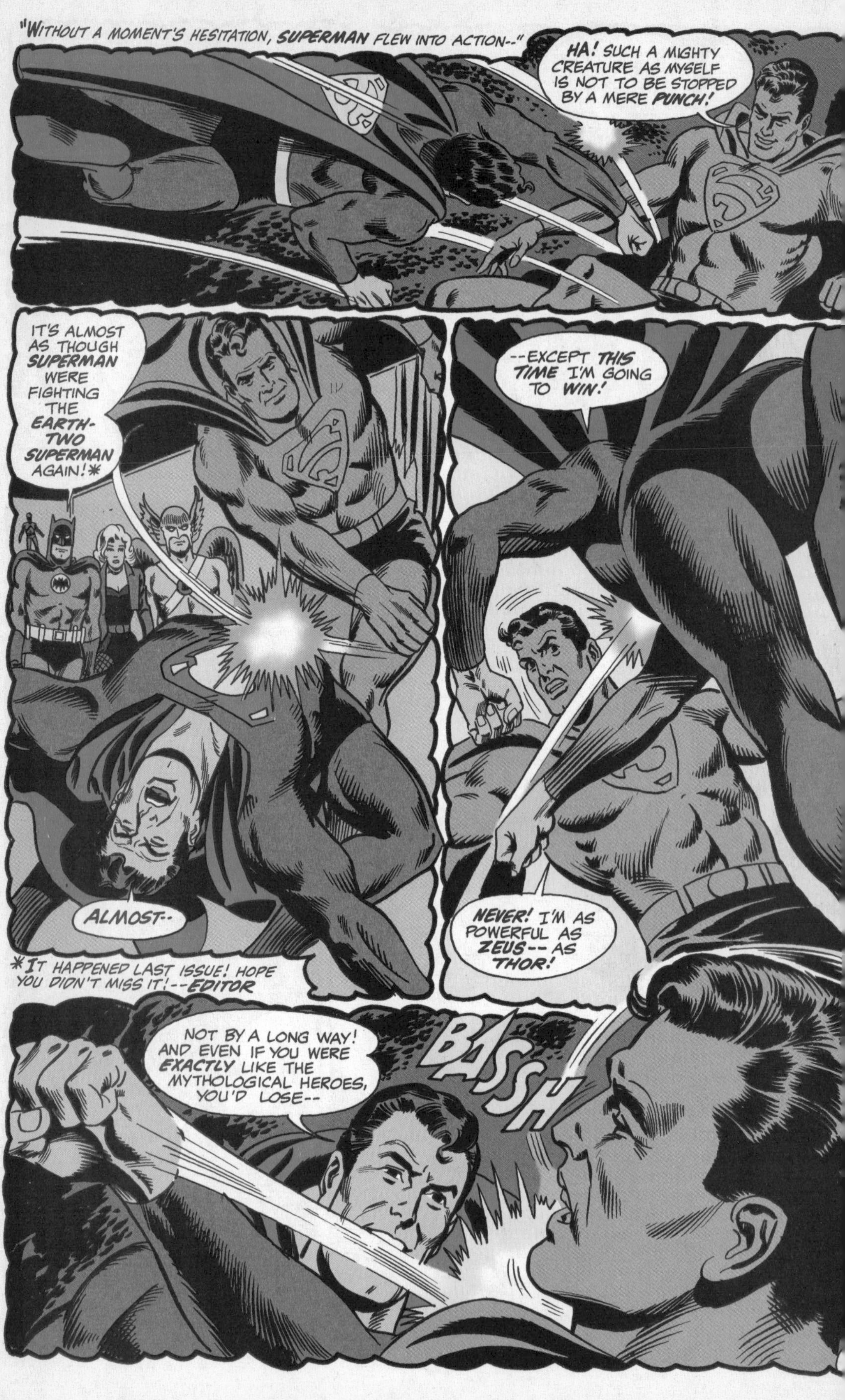
"WITHOUT A MOMENT'S HESITATION, SUPERMAN FLEW INTO ACTION--"
HA! SUCH A MIGHTY CREATURE AS MYSELF IS NOT TO BE STOPPED BY A MERE PUNCH!
IT'S ALMOST AS THOUGH SUPERMAN WERE FIGHTING THE EARTH-TWO SUPERMAN AGAIN!*
ALMOST--
--EXCEPT THIS TIME I'M GOING TO WIN!
NEVER! I'M AS POWERFUL AS ZEUS-- AS THOR!
*IT HAPPENED LAST ISSUE! HOPE YOU DIDN'T MISS IT!--EDITOR
NOT BY A LONG WAY! AND EVEN IF YOU WERE EXACTLY LIKE THE MYTHOLOGICAL HEROES, YOU'D LOSE--
BASSH

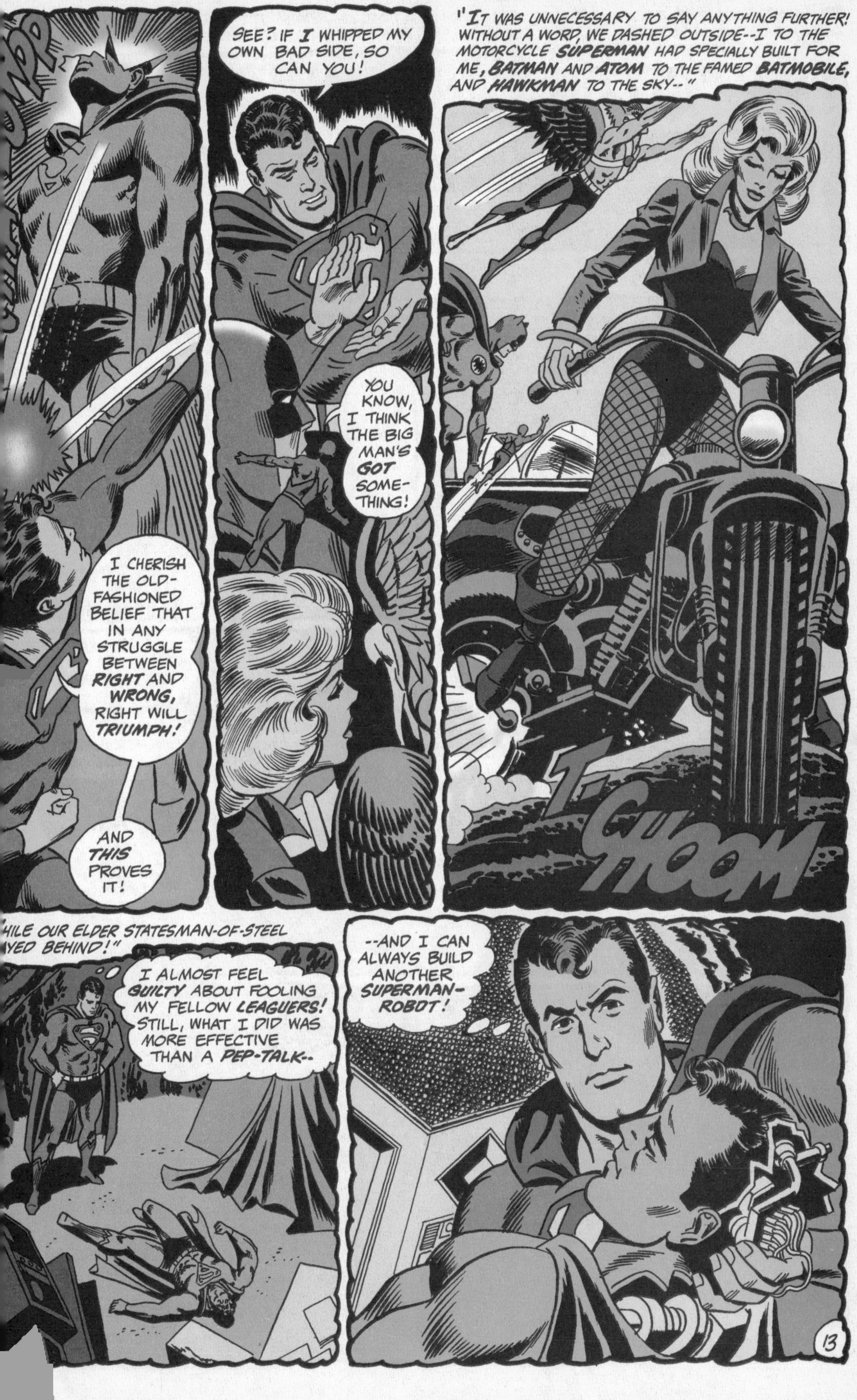
I CHERISH THE OLD-FASHIONED BELIEF THAT IN ANY STRUGGLE BETWEEN RIGHT AND WRONG, RIGHT WILL TRIUMPH!
AND THIS PROVES IT!
SEE? IF I WHIPPED MY OWN BAD SIDE, SO CAN YOU!
YOU KNOW, I THINK THE BIG MAN'S GOT SOME-THING!
"IT WAS UNNECESSARY TO SAY ANYTHING FURTHER! WITHOUT A WORD, WE DASHED OUTSIDE--I TO THE MOTORCYCLE SUPERMAN HAD SPECIALLY BUILT FOR ME, BATMAN AND ATOM TO THE FAMED BATMOBILE, AND HAWKMAN TO THE SKY--"
SHOOM
HILE OUR ELDER STATESMAN-OF-STEEL YED BEHIND!"
I ALMOST FEEL GUILTY ABOUT FOOLING MY FELLOW LEAGUERS! STILL, WHAT I DID WAS MORE EFFECTIVE THAN A PEP-TALK--
--AND I CAN ALWAYS BUILD ANOTHER SUPERMAN-ROBOT!
13

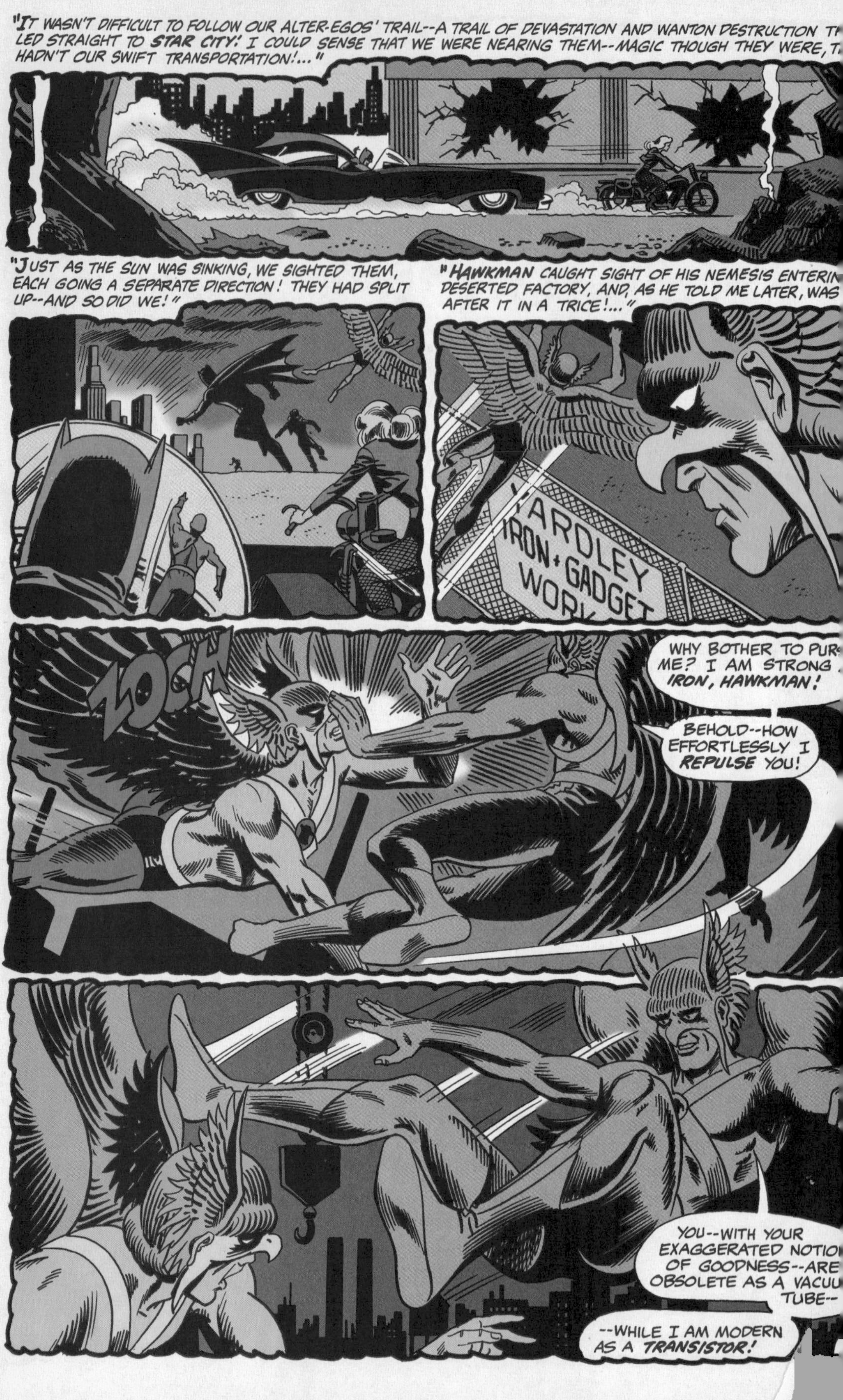
"IT WASN'T DIFFICULT TO FOLLOW OUR ALTER-EGOS' TRAIL--A TRAIL OF DEVASTATION AND WANTON DESTRUCTION TH
LED STRAIGHT TO STAR CITY! I COULD SENSE THAT WE WERE NEARING THEM--MAGIC THOUGH THEY WERE, T
HADN'T OUR SWIFT TRANSPORTATION!..."
"JUST AS THE SUN WAS SINKING, WE SIGHTED THEM, EACH GOING A SEPARATE DIRECTION! THEY HAD SPLIT UP--AND SO DID WE!"
"HAWKMAN CAUGHT SIGHT OF HIS NEMESIS ENTERIN
DESERTED FACTORY, AND, AS HE TOLD ME LATER, WAS
AFTER IT IN A TRICE!..."
YARDLEY IRON+GADGET WORK
ZOCH
WHY BOTHER TO PUR
ME? I AM STRONG
IRON, HAWKMAN!
BEHOLD--HOW EFFORTLESSLY I REPULSE YOU!
YOU--WITH YOUR EXAGGERATED NOTIO
OF GOODNESS--ARE
OBSOLETE AS A VACUU
TUBE--
--WHILE I AM MODERN AS A TRANSISTOR!

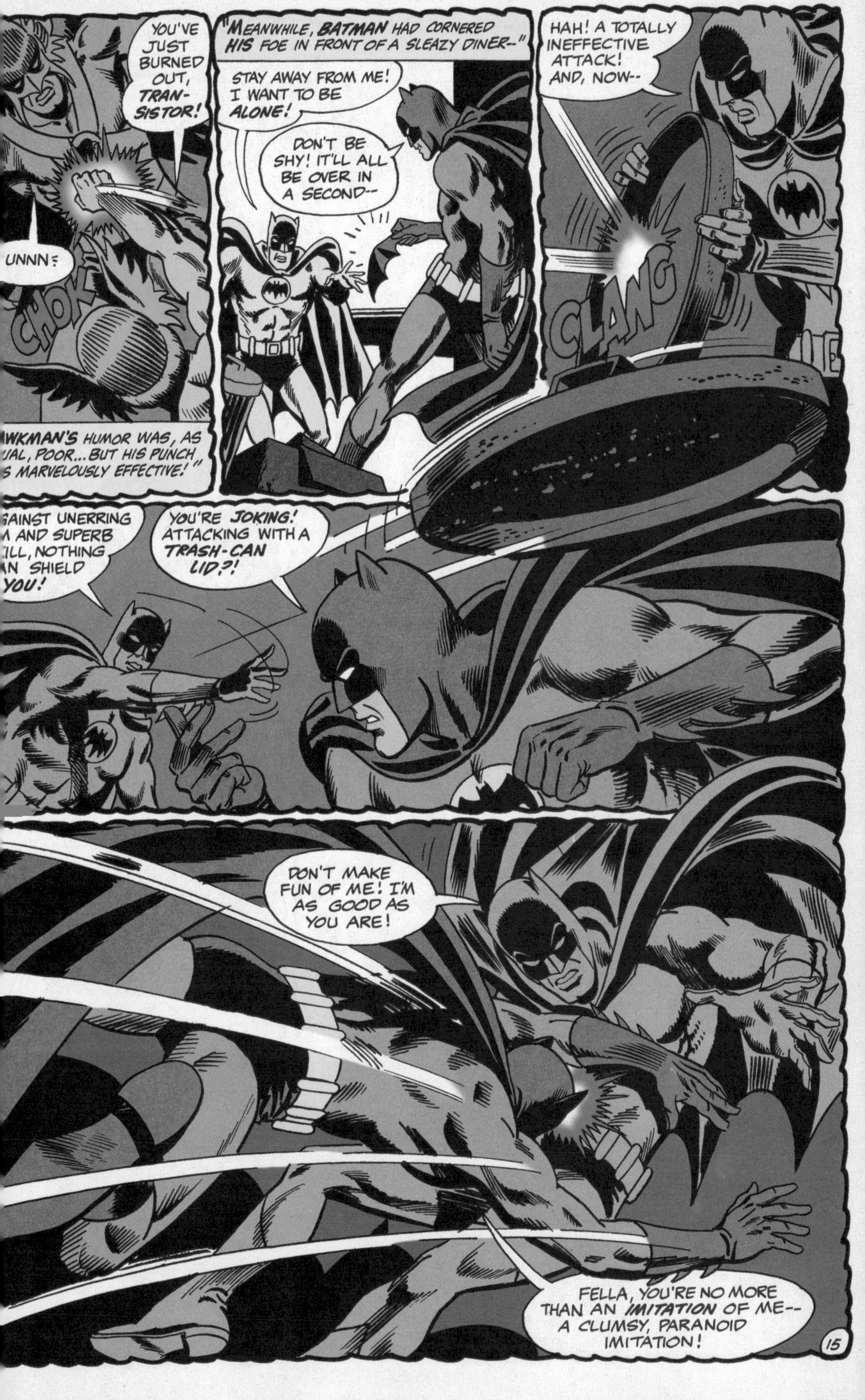

YOU'VE JUST BURNED OUT, TRAN-SISTOR!
UNNN
CHOK
WKMAN'S HUMOR WAS, AS IAL, POOR... BUT HIS PUNCH S MARVELOUSLY EFFECTIVE!"
"MEANWHILE, BATMAN HAD CORNERED HIS FOE IN FRONT OF A SLEAZY DINER--"
STAY AWAY FROM ME! I WANT TO BE ALONE!
DON'T BE SHY! IT'LL ALL BE OVER IN A SECOND--
HAH! A TOTALLY INEFFECTIVE ATTACK! AND, NOW--
CLANG
GAINST UNERRING M AND SUPERB ILL, NOTHING AN SHIELD YOU!
YOU'RE JOKING! ATTACKING WITH A TRASH-CAN LID?!
DON'T MAKE FUN OF ME! I'M AS GOOD AS YOU ARE!
FELLA, YOU'RE NO MORE THAN AN IMITATION OF ME-- A CLUMSY, PARANOID IMITATION!
15

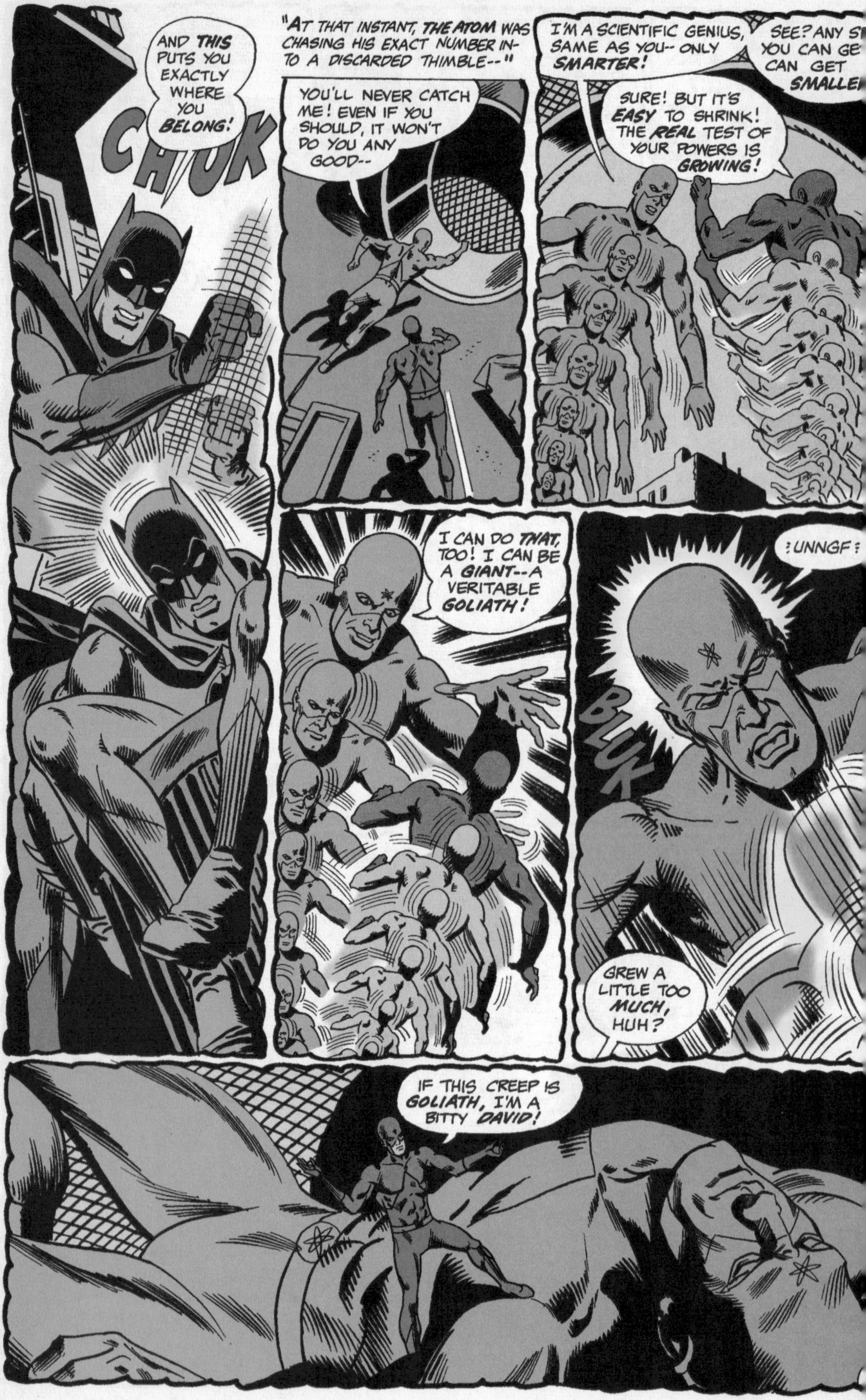

AND THIS PUTS YOU EXACTLY WHERE YOU BELONG!
CHUK
"AT THAT INSTANT, THE ATOM WAS CHASING HIS EXACT NUMBER INTO A DISCARDED THIMBLE--"
YOU'LL NEVER CATCH ME! EVEN IF YOU SHOULD, IT WON'T DO YOU ANY GOOD--
I'M A SCIENTIFIC GENIUS, SAME AS YOU-- ONLY SMARTER!
SURE! BUT IT'S EASY TO SHRINK! THE REAL TEST OF YOUR POWERS IS GROWING!
I CAN DO THAT, TOO! I CAN BE A GIANT--A VERITABLE GOLIATH!
:UNNGF:
BLUK
GREW A LITTLE TOO MUCH, HUH?
IF THIS CREEP IS GOLIATH, I'M A BITTY DAVID!

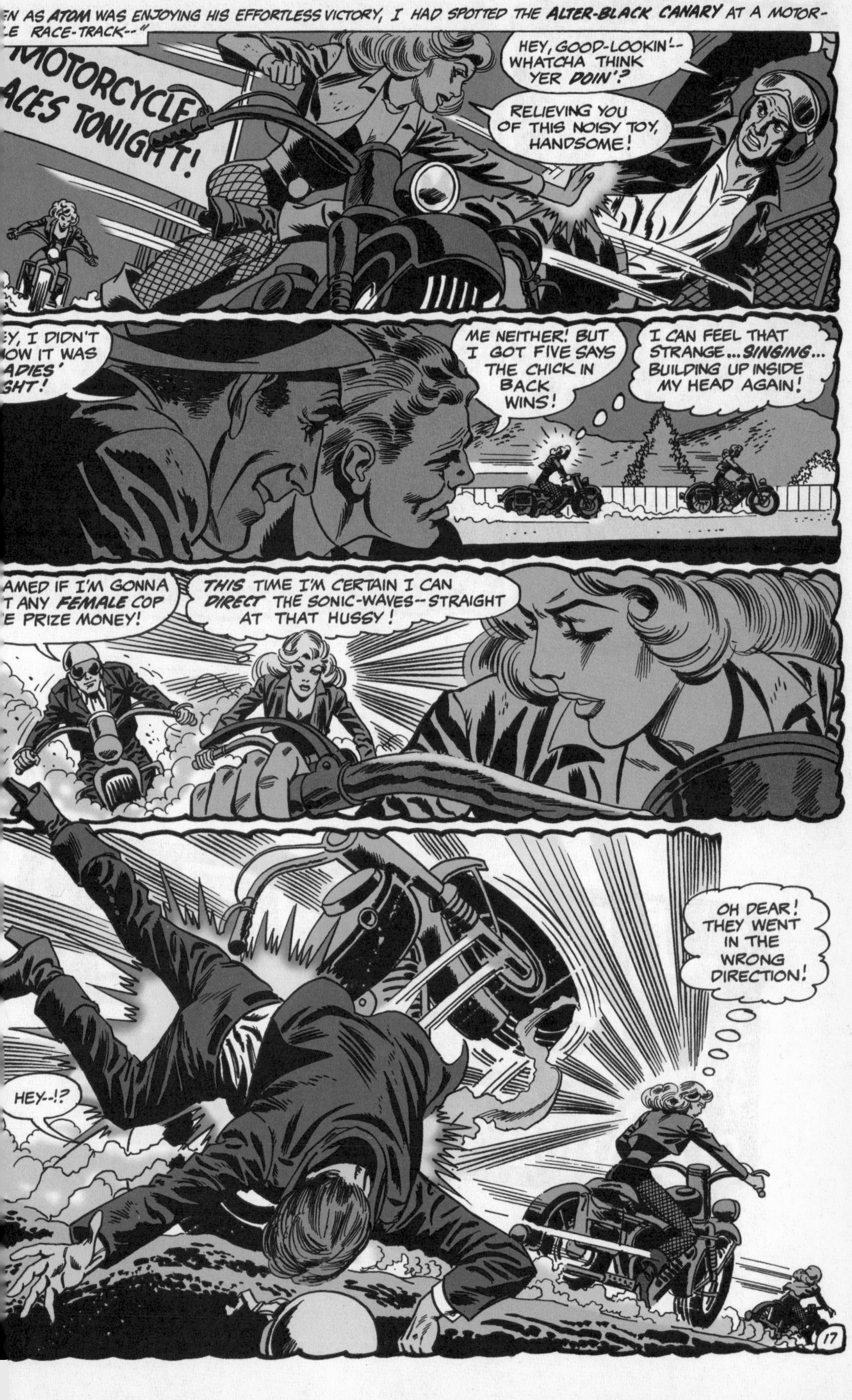
EN AS ATOM WAS ENJOYING HIS EFFORTLESS VICTORY, I HAD SPOTTED THE ALTER-BLACK CANARY AT A MOTOR-
LE RACE-TRACK--"
MOTORCYCLE
ACES TONIGHT!
HEY, GOOD-LOOKIN'-- WHATCHA THINK YER DOIN'?
RELIEVING YOU OF THIS NOISY TOY, HANDSOME!
EY, I DIDN'T
NOW IT WAS
ADIES'
GHT!
ME NEITHER! BUT I GOT FIVE SAYS THE CHICK IN BACK WINS!
I CAN FEEL THAT STRANGE...SINGING... BUILDING UP INSIDE MY HEAD AGAIN!
AMED IF I'M GONNA
T ANY FEMALE COP
E PRIZE MONEY!
THIS TIME I'M CERTAIN I CAN DIRECT THE SONIC-WAVES--STRAIGHT AT THAT HUSSY!
OH DEAR! THEY WENT IN THE WRONG DIRECTION!
HEY--!?
17

I'LL HAVE TO RELY ON MY *OLD* SKILLS--

"WE BOTH BROKE OUR FALLS EASILY! BEFORE THE OTHER ME CC RECOVER, HOWEVER, I APPLIED A 'SLEEPER' HOLD!--AND SHE IMMEDIATELY SLIPPED INTO UNCONSCIOUSNESS--"

JUSTICE LEAGUE of AMERICA

REST OF THE [JU]STICE LEAGUE [HA]D BEEN [SUC]CESSFUL--

BUT WITH ME, IT WAS DIFFERENT--

"COINCIDENTALLY, I FOUND THE EVIL CREATURE I HAD SPAWNED IN THE SAME SLUM WHERE EARLIER I'D STOPPED THE MUGGING..."

DROP THAT STUFF AND TURN AROUND!

AHHH... I WONDERED WHEN YOU'D GET HERE!

PUT IT BACK, OR SO HELP ME, I'LL...

DO *WHAT*, HYPOCRITE? HAVEN'T YOU REALIZED YET THAT *I* AM *YOU*?

I'M NO *CRIMINAL!*

[IT] WAS NEVER *CONVENIENT* FOR [YO]U TO COMMIT CRIME! INDEED, [YO]U'VE *FOUGHT* LAW-BREAKERS [B]UT NOT BECAUSE [YO]U'RE *GOOD!*

YOU MAINTAINED THE *GREEN ARROW* IDENTITY BECAUSE IT WAS *FUN!* YOU *ENJOYED* THE THRILL OF OUTSMARTING FOES-- YOU GLORIED IN THE *FAME* IT BROUGHT YOU!

Y-YES... YES...

BUT UNDERNEATH, YOU WERE ALWAYS OLIVER QUEEN--MUCH, *MUCH* MORE INTERESTED IN *WEALTH* THAN *HEROISM!* CAN YOU *DENY* IT?

N-NO... I CAN'T!

19

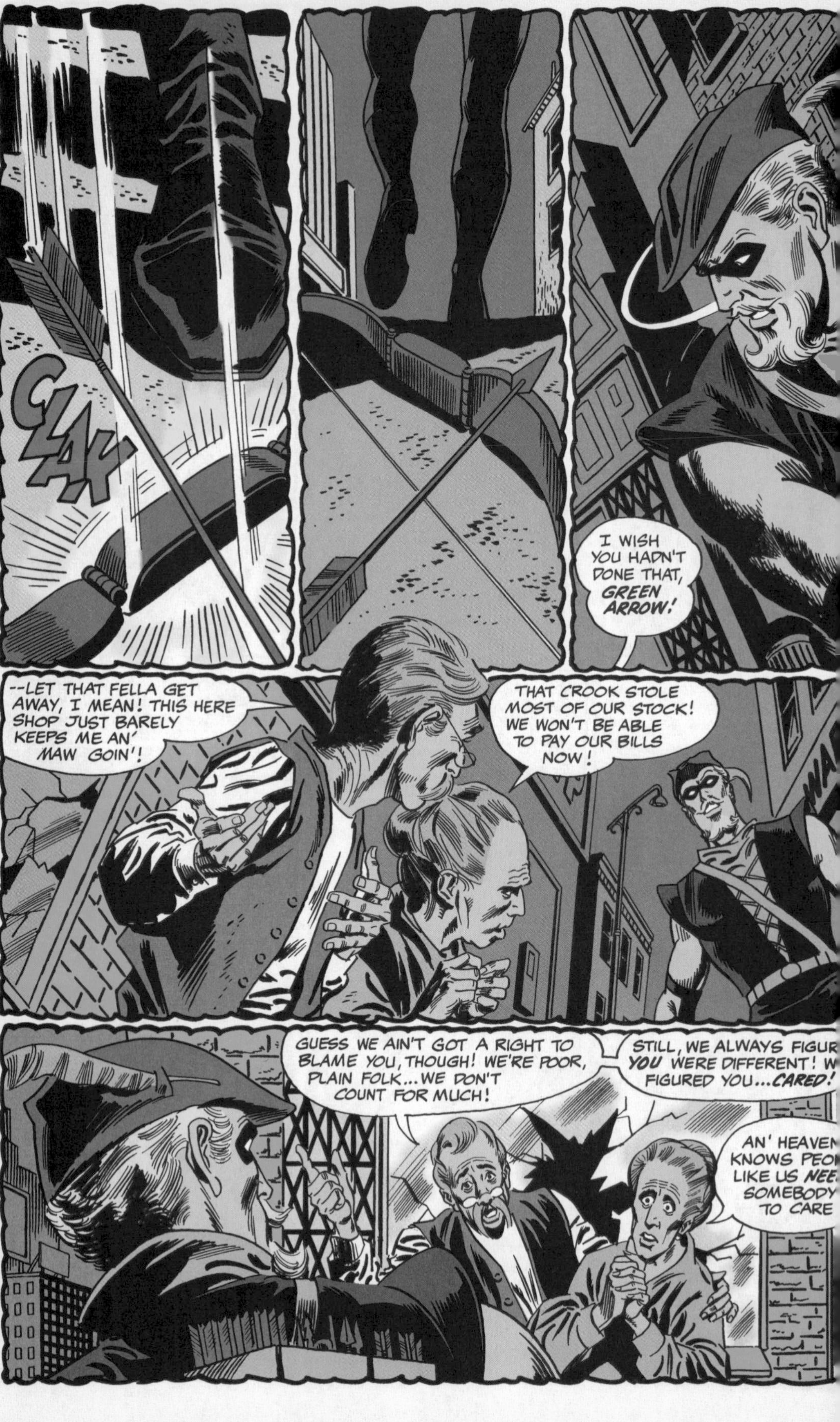
CLAK
I WISH YOU HADN'T DONE THAT, GREEN ARROW!
--LET THAT FELLA GET AWAY, I MEAN! THIS HERE SHOP JUST BARELY KEEPS ME AN' MAW GOIN'!
THAT CROOK STOLE MOST OF OUR STOCK! WE WON'T BE ABLE TO PAY OUR BILLS NOW!
GUESS WE AIN'T GOT A RIGHT TO BLAME YOU, THOUGH! WE'RE POOR, PLAIN FOLK...WE DON'T COUNT FOR MUCH!
STILL, WE ALWAYS FIGUR YOU WERE DIFFERENT! W FIGURED YOU...CARED!
AN' HEAVEN KNOWS PEO LIKE US NEE SOMEBODY TO CARE

DON'T MOVE!

--WAIT FOR ME!

I'LL BE BACK...

I SWEAR IT!

"THE HALTING, QUAVERY WORDS OF THOSE OLD FOLKS DID FOR ME WHAT THE PSYCHIATRIST COULDN'T...SHOWED ME WHAT I *SHOULD* BE-- WHAT I *HAD* TO BE!"

"I SIGHTED THAT DEMON-- THE CORRUPT MIRROR IMAGE OF MYSELF-- A BLOCK AWAY!"

YOU'VE GONE FAR ENOUGH! YOU'VE *EXISTED* TOO LONG!

THAT *MAY* BE TRUE! BUT THERE'S *ANOTHER* PART OF ME-- THE BETTER PART! THE HALF THAT *CONTROLS* VIOLENCE-- CHANNELS IT TOWARD BUILDING A DECENT WORLD!

THEN... ONE OF US MUST DIE!

SO... *GREEN ARROW* WAS NOT CONVINCED! HE STILL DOES NOT ADMIT THAT I AM HIM-- THE PART OF HIM THAT LOVES ACTION AND VIOLENCE!

"E WHIRLED, BOW DRAWN, AND LET RAZOR-SHARP SHAFT FLY--AT THE ME INSTANT I LOOSED A BLUNTED ARROW!"

21

"HIS AIM WAS OFF A TINY BIT! I TOOK THE BARB IN THE LEG--INSTEAD OF THE HEART..."

"...AND MINE? AS IT NEARED HIM, HE SHIMMERED... DISSOLVED..."

"ELSEWHERE, ALL OVER *STAR CITY*, THE SAME THING WAS HAPPENING! THE UGLINESS THAT FOR THE PAST T FYING HOURS HAD BEEN THREATENING THE SANITY OF THE *JUSTICE LEAGUERS* MELTED...DRAINED BACK INTO U

"ONCE MORE WE WERE CONTAMINATED WITH EVIL! AND ONCE MORE, WE WERE FULLY HUMAN-- NEITHER BETT NOR WORSE THAN THE OTHER 3 BILLION MEN AND WOMEN WHO WALK THE EARTH!"

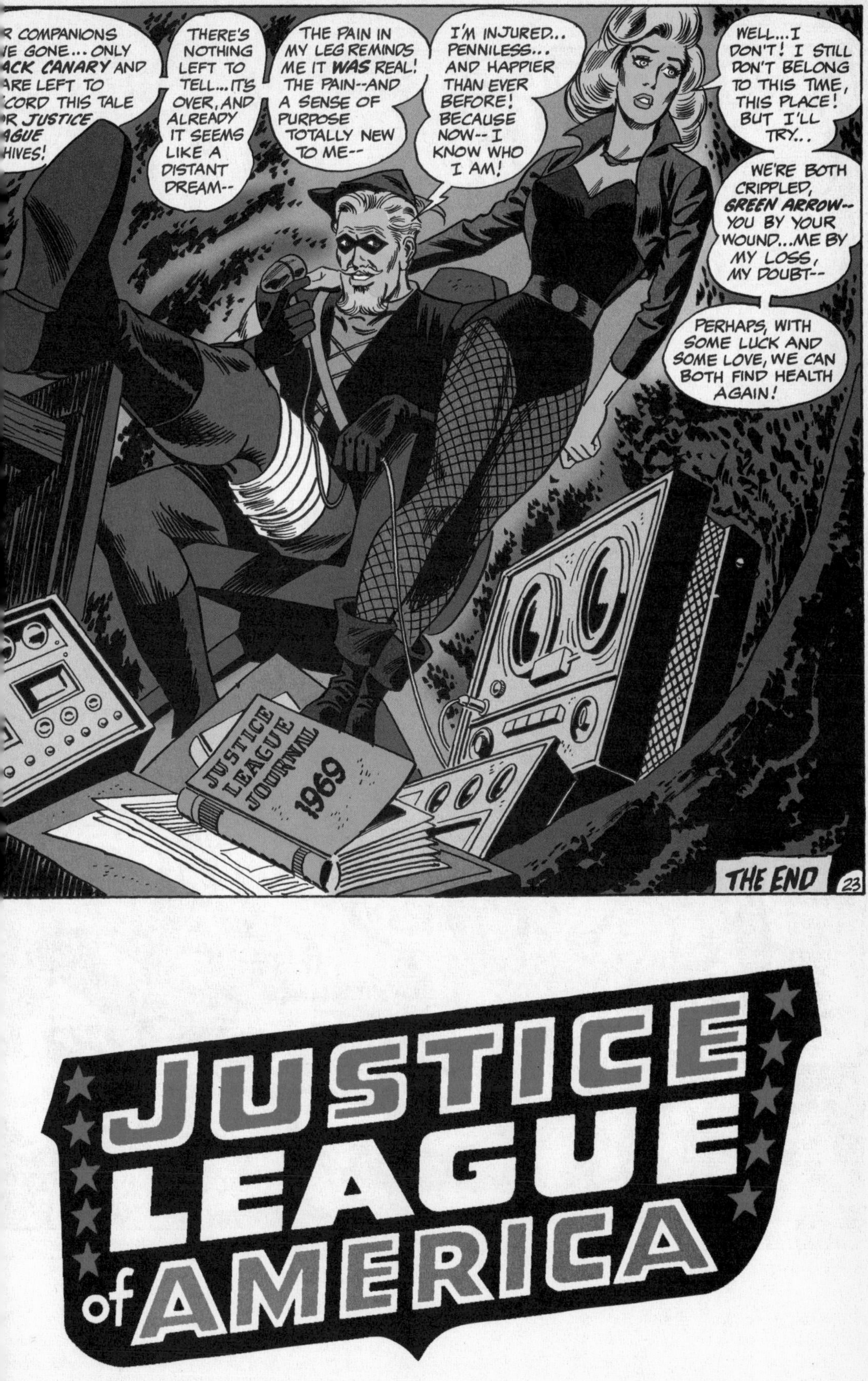

R COMPANIONS VE GONE... ONLY ACK CANARY AND ARE LEFT TO CORD THIS TALE R JUSTICE AGUE HIVES!
THERE'S NOTHING LEFT TO TELL... IT'S OVER, AND ALREADY IT SEEMS LIKE A DISTANT DREAM--
THE PAIN IN MY LEG REMINDS ME IT WAS REAL! THE PAIN--AND A SENSE OF PURPOSE TOTALLY NEW TO ME--
I'M INJURED... PENNILESS... AND HAPPIER THAN EVER BEFORE! BECAUSE NOW-- I KNOW WHO I AM!
WELL... I DON'T! I STILL DON'T BELONG TO THIS TIME, THIS PLACE! BUT I'LL TRY...
WE'RE BOTH CRIPPLED, GREEN ARROW-- YOU BY YOUR WOUND... ME BY MY LOSS, MY DOUBT--
PERHAPS, WITH SOME LUCK AND SOME LOVE, WE CAN BOTH FIND HEALTH AGAIN!
JUSTICE LEAGUE JOURNAL 1969
THE END
23

JUSTICE LEAGUE of AMERICA

"SPECTER in the SHADOWS!"

THE ROLL CALL

ATOM
BLACK CANARY
FLASH
GREEN ARROW
GREEN LANTERN
SUPERMAN
AND AT LONG LAST...
THE ELONGATED MAN!

WELCOME TO THE JUSTICE LEAGUE, ELONGATED MAN!

LEN WEIN: WRITER   DICK DILLIN & DICK GIORDANO: ARTISTS   JULIUS SCHWARTZ: EDITOR

A BALMY SPRING AFTERNOON-- AS TWO SURPRISINGLY FAMILIAR PEOPLE BROWSE LEISURELY THROUGH A PROMINENT ART MUSEUM...

HOW *BEAUTIFUL!* RALPH, DON'T YOU JUST ADORE *VAN GOGH?*

OH, I DON'T KNOW, SUE-- GIVE ME *GAUGUIN* ANY DAY!

ALL THOSE PAINTINGS OF TROPIC ISLANDS-- LOVELY SOUTH SEA GIRLS...

MR. DIBNY-- I'D CHOOSE MY *NEXT* PHRASE VERY *CAREFULLY!*

REMEMBER-- YOU'RE A *HAPPILY MARRIED MAN*-- AND IF YOU'D LIKE TO *STAY* THAT WAY...

...YOU'LL *WATCH* WHAT YOU...

EEEEE!

SPLURSHH

STUNNED, *SUE DIBNY* STAGGERS BACK-- AS A HANDFUL OF HUMANOID FORMS ERUPTS INTO ACTION...

DON'T KNOW *WHAT* THOSE CREATURES ARE-- BUT THEY'RE OBVIOUSLY NOT HERE TO *ADMIRE* THE DECOR--!

--AND IF *THAT* ISN'T A CUE FOR THE *ELONGATED MAN* TO TAKE AN *ELASTIC HAND*, I DON'T KNOW *WHAT* IS!

2

UH-UH, LUMPY--THAT'S WHAT YOU CALL YOUR *NO-NO!*

THE SIGNS SAY "PLEASE DO NOT TOUCH!"

BUT THOSE SIGNS *DON'T* APPLY TO *MY* TOUCHING YOU... *HUH?*

MY *FIST*--SINKING IN--AS IF THIS LUNATIC LOOTER WAS MADE OF *BREAD-DOUGH!*

NO--CHANGE THAT TO *SILLY PUTTY!*

THESE CREATURES REACT TO A PUNCH LIKE *NOTHING* I'VE EVER SEEN--!

FOR HEAVEN'S SAKE, *RALPH* *-- *LOOK OUT!*

*EDITOR'S NOTE: *E-MAN,* THE *ONLY* HERO TO PUBLICLY REVEAL HIS DUAL IDENTITY, GAINS HIS STRETCHING POWERS BY DRINKING AN ELIXIR DISTILLED FROM THE JUICE OF A TROPICAL FRUIT-- *GINGOLD!*

*B*UT BEFORE THE *DUCTILE DETECTIVE* CAN RESPOND TO HIS WIFE'S ANGUISHED SHOUT...

3 *UUNNNFF* THESE THINGS MAY *LOOK* SILLY-- BUT THEY *MOVE* AS FAST AS *THE FLASH!*

RESTRAINING MY ARMS AND LEGS-- MAKING IT ALMOST *IMPOSSIBLE* FOR ME--TO *STRETCH*--!

*H*ELPLESS IN THE SEMI-HUMANOIDS' GOOEY GRASP, THE *STRETCHABLE SLEUTH* IS BATTERED ABOUT MERCILESSLY...

--UNTIL HIS DARING LADY LEAPS TO HIS... *RESCUE?*

LET *GO* OF HIM, YOU LITTLE MONSTERS --LET *GO!* HARM ONE *HAIR* OF HIS PRECIOUS HEAD AND I'LL... *OOOOHHHH...*

MOMENTS LATER, THE *ELONGATED MAN* IS SENT SPRAWLING TO THE FLOOR-- AND THE PUTTY-MEN RETURN TO THEIR INTERRUPTED CRIME!

THEN, WITH SMASHING SUDDENNESS...

KWRASSH

TH-THEY'RE LEAPING OUT THE *WINDOW*--

--BUT... IT'S *FIVE STORIES* DOWN--!

G-GOT TO *STOP* THEM-- FROM *ESCAPING*--!

BUT BY THE TIME THE DAZED DETECTIVE CAN STRETCH TO THE SHATTERED WINDOW...

WHAT--? THEY'VE FORMED THEMSELVES INTO ONE BIG *BALL*-- BOUNCING AWAY FROM HERE *FASTER* THAN I COULD HOPE TO *FOLLOW*--!

AND SECONDS LATER...

OH, RALPH-- YOU *ALL RIGHT?* HOW DO YOU *FEEL?*

EMBARRASSED, MOSTLY! HOW DO I EXPLAIN BEING PUNCHED OUT BY A HALF-DOZEN GOOEY GUMDROPS?

BUT *THAT'S* NOT WHAT REALLY *BOTHERS* ME--!

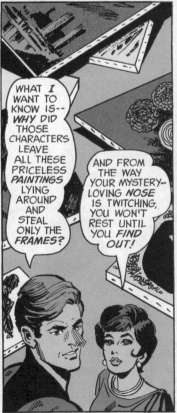

WHAT *I* WANT TO KNOW IS-- *WHY* DID THOSE CHARACTERS LEAVE ALL THESE PRICELESS *PAINTINGS* LYING AROUND AND STEAL ONLY THE *FRAMES?*

AND FROM THE WAY YOUR MYSTERY-LOVING *NOSE* IS TWITCHING, YOU WON'T REST UNTIL YOU *FIND OUT!*

NO, SUE-- I HAVE A FEELING THIS CASE IS *TOO BIG* FOR ME ALONE...

THIS IS A JOB FOR-- *THE JUSTICE LEAGUE OF AMERICA!*

WHAT'S THAT YOU SAY, GENTLE READER? *WHAT* IS THE *ELONGATED MAN* DOING WITH A *JUSTICE LEAGUE* SIGNAL DEVICE...?

4

FOR THE *ANSWER* TO THAT QUESTION, WE MUST TURN *TIME* BACK ONE BRIEF WEEK--TO A ROLLING COUNTRY ROAD ENJOYING THE REBIRTH OF SPRING--

--AND A SLEEK *SPORTS* CAR, LEAPING TO THE COMMAND OF A CONTENTED *RALPH DIBNY*...

WHAT A *GLORIOUS* DAY, SUE! AIR'S SO *FRESH* IT MAKES ME FEEL LIKE...

GREEN LANTERN!? W-WHAT ARE YOU DOING HERE?

FORGIVE THE SUDDEN *INTRUSION,* RALPH -- BUT I HAVE A VERY SPECIAL *INVITATION* TO EXTEND--!

AND MINUTES LATER, IN A SPECIAL SATELLITE ORBITING 22,300 MILES ABOVE THE EMERALD EARTH...

SINCE THE *MARTIAN MANHUNTER'S* RESIGNATION, THE JLA HAS BEEN OPERATING AT *LESS* THAN FULL STRENGTH! IT'S HIGH TIME WE VOTED IN A *NEW* MEMBER--

--AND *YOU*--RALPH *(ELONGATED MAN)* DIBNY-- ARE *IT!*

WELCOME TO THE *JUSTICE LEAGUE,* E-MAN--*CONGRATULATIONS!*

I--I'M *STUNNED*-- *SPEECHLESS*--! FOR THE FIRST TIME IN MY LIFE, I *DON'T* KNOW WHAT TO SAY--!

WELL, ALL I CAN SAY IS--IT'S *ABOUT TIME!*

SUE--YOU'RE *EMBARRASSING* ME! THAT'S A *TERRIBLE* THING TO SAY!

WHY? ISN'T A GIRL ENTITLED TO A LITTLE *WIFELY PRIDE* RIGHT ABOUT NOW?

NOW, BE STILL, SILLY -- AND LET EVERYONE *CONGRATULATE* YOU!

SMNACK

... AND THAT'S THE WHOLE *STORY,* GANG! I USUALLY HANDLE THIS KIND OF CRAZY CASE BY *MYSELF*--

--BUT THOSE FLUBBER-FREAKS HAVE ME *OUT-MATCHED* PHYSICALLY!

YOU CAN COUNT ON US TO *HELP,* RALPH--BUT I'M NOT SURE WHAT *SORT* OF HELP WE CAN GIVE!

OUR BEST CHANCE OF *FINDING* THOSE CREATURES IS--WAIT UNTIL THEY STRIKE *AGAIN*--BUT THAT'S...

PING PING PING PING

SOMETHING'S COMING IN ON THE *EARTH-MONITOR!*

AND WHEN THE INFORMATION HAS BEEN FULLY RECORDED...

THOSE PUTTY-PEOPLE *HAVE* STRUCK AGAIN--

IN *MOTOR CITY*--ON AN OIL RIG OFF THE *CALIFORNIA COAST*--AND IN THE SMALL NORTHEASTERN TOWN OF *DESOLATION!*

THEN WHAT ARE WE *WAITING* FOR? LET'S GET *AFTER* THEM!

MOTION CARRIED *UNANIMOUSLY!* SUPERMAN, WHY DON'T YOU AND I TAKE A QUICK TRIP TO *MOTOR CITY?*

CALIFORNIA'S *MY* OLD STOMPING GROUND, RALPH! SUPPOSE THE TWO OF US TACKLE *THAT* END?

WE'RE ALL THAT'S *LEFT,* GUYS--SO I GUESS *OUR* ASSIGNMENT IS *DESOLATION*--AND, BELIEVE ME--

--THERE WAS NEVER A PLACE MORE *APTLY* NAMED!

6

DESOLATION: AN *APTLY* NAMED TOWN, INDEED! LIFE IS MORE THAN *HARD* HERE-- IT IS A NEVER-ENDING STRUGGLE AGAINST THE VERY *EARTH* ITSELF-- TO PULL SOMETHING OF *VALUE* FROM ITS COLD, UNFEELING *HEART...*

INTO THIS UNSIGHTLY LITTLE SCAB ON THE LAND RACE THREE OF THE *JUSTICE LEAGUE'S* FINEST...

The **FLASH**
The **ATOM**
THE **GREEN ARROW**

AS THE SAYING GOES, GENTLEMEN-- THIS *MUST* BE THE PLACE!

THIS IS THE PLACE, ALL RIGHT-- I LOSE MY APPETITE JUST *LOOKING* AT IT!

BUT WE'RE HERE TO DO *MORE* THAN LOOKING, G.A.!

LET'S *SPLIT UP*-- HIT THOSE *SILLY* PUTTY-MEN FROM *THREE* SIDES!

OKAY BY *ME*, FLASH-- IF *GREEN ARROW* WILL GIVE ME A *LIFT!*

THEN HANG ON TO YOUR *HAIRLINE,* HALF-PINT-- I HAVEN'T HAD TIME TO INSTALL *SEAT-BELTS* ON THIS THING!

THWANGG

I'LL SEND YOU A *POST CARD* FROM PUTTY-LAND, ARCHER!

SOUND: A SHRILL WHISTLE AS *GREEN ARROW'S* GOOSE-FLETCHED SHAFT SLICES THE VALLEY AIR --

--THEN A SICKENING *SQUISH* AS 180 POUNDS OF 6-INCH *ATOM* SINK DEEP INTO A QUASI-HUMAN HIDE...

E-MAN WAS RIGHT! THESE THINGS *ARE* MADE OF *PUTTY!*

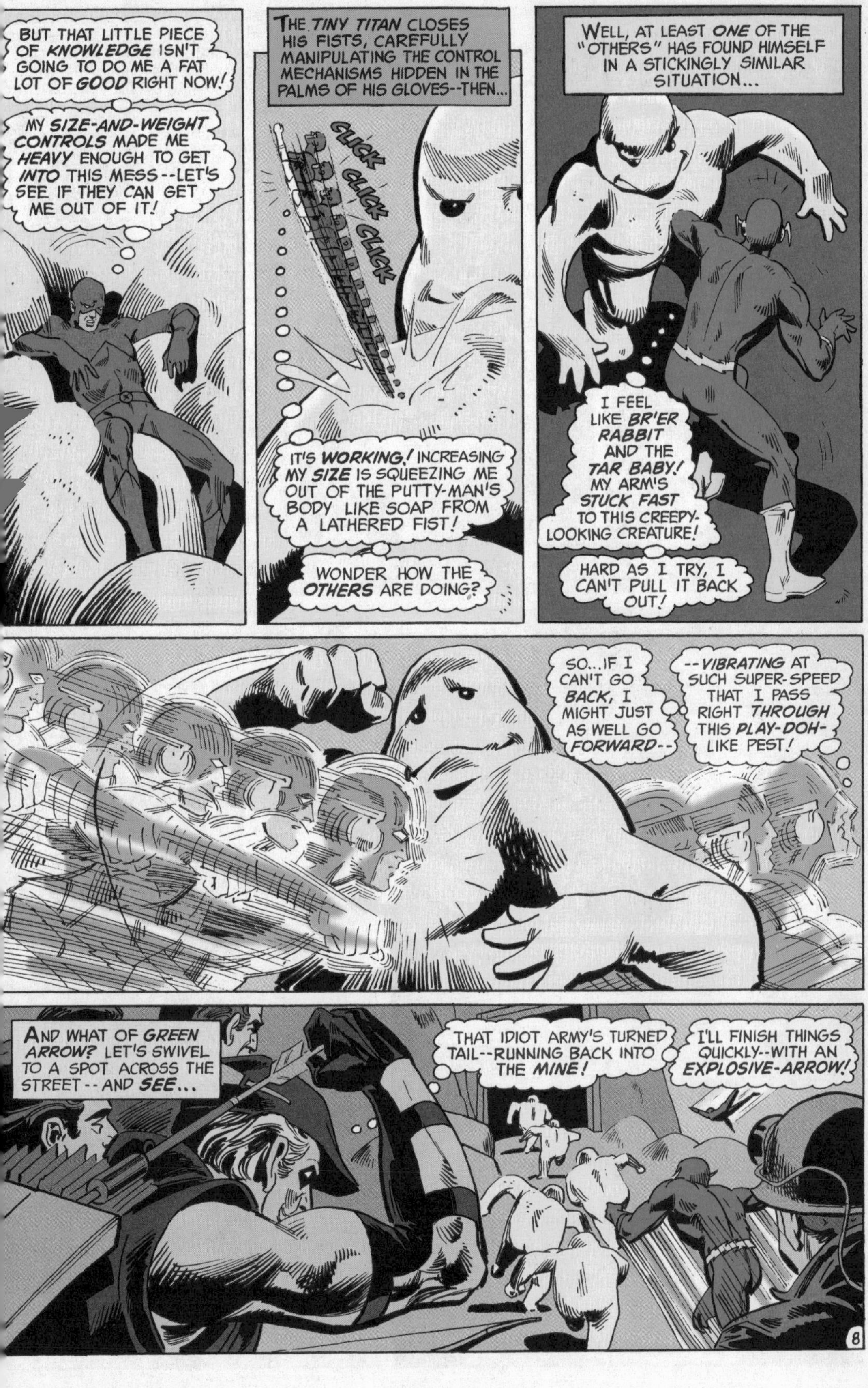
BUT THAT LITTLE PIECE OF KNOWLEDGE ISN'T GOING TO DO ME A FAT LOT OF GOOD RIGHT NOW!
MY SIZE-AND-WEIGHT CONTROLS MADE ME HEAVY ENOUGH TO GET INTO THIS MESS--LET'S SEE IF THEY CAN GET ME OUT OF IT!
THE TINY TITAN CLOSES HIS FISTS, CAREFULLY MANIPULATING THE CONTROL MECHANISMS HIDDEN IN THE PALMS OF HIS GLOVES--THEN...
CLICK CLICK CLICK CLICK
IT'S WORKING! INCREASING MY SIZE IS SQUEEZING ME OUT OF THE PUTTY-MAN'S BODY LIKE SOAP FROM A LATHERED FIST!
WONDER HOW THE OTHERS ARE DOING?
WELL, AT LEAST ONE OF THE "OTHERS" HAS FOUND HIMSELF IN A STICKINGLY SIMILAR SITUATION...
I FEEL LIKE BR'ER RABBIT AND THE TAR BABY! MY ARM'S STUCK FAST TO THIS CREEPY-LOOKING CREATURE!
HARD AS I TRY, I CAN'T PULL IT BACK OUT!
SO...IF I CAN'T GO BACK, I MIGHT JUST AS WELL GO FORWARD--
--VIBRATING AT SUCH SUPER-SPEED THAT I PASS RIGHT THROUGH THIS PLAY-DOH-LIKE PEST!
AND WHAT OF GREEN ARROW? LET'S SWIVEL TO A SPOT ACROSS THE STREET--AND SEE...
THAT IDIOT ARMY'S TURNED TAIL--RUNNING BACK INTO THE MINE!
I'LL FINISH THINGS QUICKLY--WITH AN EXPLOSIVE-ARROW!
8

WHAT THE--?

YOU *FIRE* THAT CONTRAPTION, *ARROW*--AN YOU'LL FINISH *EVERYTHING!*

THERE'S POCKETS OF *COAL GAS* IN THAT MINE! ONE *SPARK*-- AN' THEY'LL BE SCRAPIN' UP *PIECES* OF THIS TOWN FOR MONTHS!

THAT MIGHT NOT BE TOO *BAD* AN IDEA-- CONSIDERING--

--BUT I GUESS I'M GONNA HAVE TO HANDLE THIS THE *HARD* WAY--!

IT'S TIME I JOINED MY *BUDDIES* IN THE *MINE!*

MUSCLES FLEXING, THE *EMERALD ARCHER* SPRINTS ACROSS THE DUSTY STREET-- AND INTO THE GAPING MAW OF THE RUN-DOWN MINE!

...WHILE A SOMBER, TOP-COATED FIGURE STEPS SOUNDLESSLY FROM THE SHADOWS...

WELL--IT'S ABOUT *TIME* YOU GOT HERE, G.A.! WHAT *KEPT* YOU?

SORRY, SMALL FRY! WOULD YOU BELIEVE I GOT STOPPED FOR *JAY-WALKING*--?

ANYWAY, I'M HERE TO MAKE U FOR *LOST* TIME!

MAYBE I CAN'T USE MY *ARROWS* IN HERE--

--BUT LET'S SEE WHAT A *HUNK* OF PLAIN, UNADORNED *WOOD* WILL DO TO--!

N-O-T-H-I-N-G!

COAL GAS: NOXIOUS FUMES OF ACRID *METHANE*, RELEASED BY THE HURTLING SHARD OF WOOD, BILLOW INTO THE STALE MINE AIR--FILLING THE ROUGH-HEWN CHAMBER WITH RIPPLING CLOUDS OF-- *DEATH!*

HSSSSSSS SSS

PLUNKT

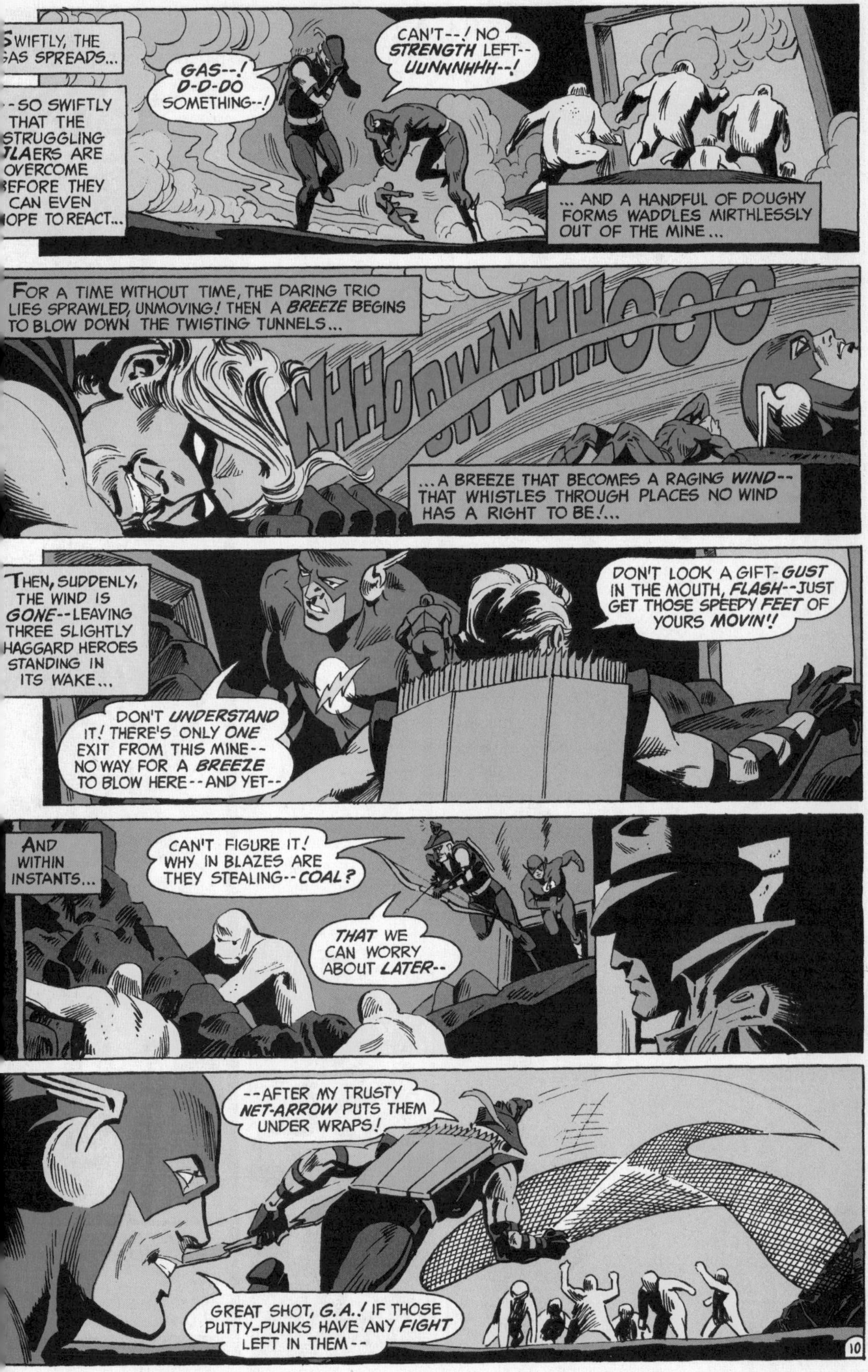
SWIFTLY, THE GAS SPREADS...
GAS--! D-D-DO SOMETHING--!
CAN'T--! NO STRENGTH LEFT-- UUNNNHHH--!
--SO SWIFTLY THAT THE STRUGGLING JLAERS ARE OVERCOME BEFORE THEY CAN EVEN HOPE TO REACT...
... AND A HANDFUL OF DOUGHY FORMS WADDLES MIRTHLESSLY OUT OF THE MINE...
FOR A TIME WITHOUT TIME, THE DARING TRIO LIES SPRAWLED, UNMOVING! THEN A BREEZE BEGINS TO BLOW DOWN THE TWISTING TUNNELS...
WHHOOWWHHOOO
...A BREEZE THAT BECOMES A RAGING WIND-- THAT WHISTLES THROUGH PLACES NO WIND HAS A RIGHT TO BE!...
THEN, SUDDENLY, THE WIND IS GONE--LEAVING THREE SLIGHTLY HAGGARD HEROES STANDING IN ITS WAKE...
DON'T UNDERSTAND IT! THERE'S ONLY ONE EXIT FROM THIS MINE-- NO WAY FOR A BREEZE TO BLOW HERE--AND YET--
DON'T LOOK A GIFT-GUST IN THE MOUTH, FLASH--JUST GET THOSE SPEEDY FEET OF YOURS MOVIN'!
AND WITHIN INSTANTS...
CAN'T FIGURE IT! WHY IN BLAZES ARE THEY STEALING--COAL?
THAT WE CAN WORRY ABOUT LATER--
--AFTER MY TRUSTY NET-ARROW PUTS THEM UNDER WRAPS!
GREAT SHOT, G.A.! IF THOSE PUTTY-PUNKS HAVE ANY FIGHT LEFT IN THEM--
10

--A LITTLE SUPER-COMPRESSED *AIR-PRESSURE* SHOULD SQUEEZE IT RIGHT *OUT* OF THEM!

AT BLINDING SPEED, THE *MODERN MERCURY* WHIRLS AROUND HIS NETTED FOES-- ALMOST OBSCURING THEM FROM SIGHT...

C'MON, *ARROW*-- LET'S GET IN ON THE *FINISH* OF THIS!

WAIT! SOMETHING'S *HAPPENING* TO THE *PUTTY-MEN*--!

SUDDENLY, THE BOUNDS OF *FLASH'S* SUPER-SPEED PRISON ARE SHATTERED--

--AS A GREAT BULBOUS SHAPE TAKES TO THE AZURE SKY...

HUH? THEY'VE TURNED INTO AN OLD-FASHIONED *BALLOON!*

USING MY *NET* TO CONTAIN THEMSELVES--

--AND MY *AIR-PRESSURE* TO GIVE THEM *BUOYANCY!*

WITH STUNNING SWIFTNESS, A FISTFUL OF GREEN-FLETCHED ARROWS IS LAUNCHED HEAVENWARD-- BUT...

FORGET IT, *G.A.*-- THEY'RE ALREADY OUT OF *RANGE!* NO WAY TO *CATCH* THEM NOW!

AT LEAST WE STOPPED THEM FROM *GETTING* WHAT THEY CAME FOR!

BY *WHY* WERE THEY SWIPING *COAL?* WHO COULD POSSIBLY HAVE *SENT* THEM?

AND AS THE *SCARLET SPEEDSTER* SPEAKS, A CERTAIN TOP-COATED FORM TURNS GRIMLY-- AND STEALS ONCE MORE INTO THE SHADOWS...

MOTOR CITY: AUTOMOTIVE CAPITAL OF A GREAT NATION. *DREAMS* ARE CONCEIVED HERE--SLEEK METALLIC FANTASIES THAT PULSE THROUGH THE COUNTRY'S CONCRETE ARTERIES--THE HALLMARKS OF A LIFE-STYLE...

INTO THE CITY'S LARGEST CAR FACTORY BURST THE *MAN OF STEEL* AND THE *BLONDE BOMBSHELL*...

SUPERMAN and the BLACK CANARY

THERE ARE THE *PUTTY-MEN*, BIRD-LADY, RIGHT WHERE MY *TELESCOPIC VISION* SPOTTED THEM--

--IN THE ACT OF STEALING... *TIRES?!*

OURS NOT TO REASON *WHY*, SUPERMAN--

--OURS BUT TO *WIN*-- OR *TRY!*

HEY--THESE THINGS REALLY *DO* STRETCH LIKE *TAFFY!*

SSKKWNURSHH

TWISTING HER LITHE BODY, THE *BLACK CANARY* LANDS ON HER FEET AND...

TAFFY--MEET *TIRE!* WOULDN'T BE SURPRISED IF YOU TWO WERE DISTANTLY *RELATED!*

BUT THE SMILE SWIFTLY FADES FROM THE CANARY'S LOVELY FACE AS...

THWUNGG

UUNNGHH--PUTTY-MAN'S STRETCHING HIS BODY-- SNAPPING THE TIRES *BACK* AT ME--!

AND HARDLY MORE THAN A WHISPER ESCAPES THE *GIRL GLADIATOR'S* LIPS-- AS SHE SINKS INTO OBLIVION...

÷SIGH÷

THWUMPA

THWUMA

12

AND ELSEWHERE IN THE SPRAWLING PLANT...

TOO BAD *BATMAN* ISN'T HERE! THIS IS THE KIND OF ACTION HE *THRIVES* ON!

STILL--*BLACK CANARY* MAKES A RATHER *ATTRACTIVE* SUBSTITUTE!

WONDER HOW SHE'S *DOING?*

A SHORT DISTANCE AWAY, THE SUBJECT OF *SUPERMAN'S* THOUGHTS LIES SENSELESS, MOVING SLOWLY, INEXORABLY, TOWARDS AN "IMPRESSIVE" FINISH...

THWUMPA THWUMPA THWUMPA

...WHILE THE *ONLY BEING* WHO MIGHT POSSIBLY *SAVE* HER MEETS WITH AN UNEXPECTED *DELAY*...

THEY'RE *DOWN*--BUT NOT *OUT!*

DROPPING EMPTY AUTO BODIES ON ME!

K--RUMMPCH

...OR *IS* HE THE "ONLY BEING"?

THUMPA THUMPA THUMPA

A MANUFACTURING PLANT IS A COMPLEX CONSTRUCTION OF CONCRETE AND STEEL, COMPLETELY ENCLOSED FROM THE OUTSIDE WORLD...

HOW, THEN, DOES ONE EXPLAIN THE SUDDEN *WIND* THAT WHISTLES THROUGH THE STRUCTURE, SNATCHING A "SLEEPING BEAUTY" FROM THE POUNDING JAWS OF *DEATH?*...

THWUMPA THWUMPA THWUMPA THWUMPA

... A WIND THAT PUTS A REAWAKENED *BLACK CANARY* ON HER FEET ONCE MORE--WHILE A CERTAIN *METROPOLIS MARVEL* REGAINS HIS FOOTING IN SPECTACULAR STYLE...

THANKS, *SUPERMAN*--THAT BLAST OF *SUPER-BREATH* SAVED ME FROM BECOMING A VERY *FLAT* YOUNG LADY!

HUH? BUT *I* HAVEN'T USED ANY *SUPER-BREATH*, CANARY--!

IF *YOU* DIDN'T-- WHO *DID?*

THAT'S A QUESTION FOR A *LATER* DATE--LIKE *AFTER* WE'VE FINISHED THE *PUTTY-MEN!*

HIS UNEARTHLY MUSCLES WORKING AT INCREDIBLE SPEED, THE *KRYPTONIAN COLOSSUS* BEGINS RESHAPING THE DAMAGED AUTO BODIES...

... INTO A GARBAGE SCOOP OF STUNNING PROPORTIONS...

MY OWN LITTLE *CLEAN-UP* CAMPAIGN--TO GET THIS *TRASH* OFF THE FLOOR--AND INTO THE *CAN* WHERE IT BELONGS!

NO TRASH-CANS AROUND--GUESS I'LL HAVE TO SETTLE FOR THIS *DISPOSAL VAT!*

LAY YOU ODDS THESE CHARACTERS AREN'T EVEN *BIO-DEGRADABLE!*

AND BEFORE THE *MAN OF STEEL* CAN IMPRISON THE PUTTY-MEN MORE SECURELY...

WHA--? THEY'RE OOZING THROUGH THE DRAINHOLE LIKE *TOOTHPASTE!*

GOT TO GRAB THEM BEFORE--

--*TOO LATE!* THEY'RE *GONE*-- INTO THE PLANT'S LEAD-PIPE SYSTEM!

I'D HAVE TO *TEAR THE PLACE APART* TO FIND THEM *NOW!*

IT'S OKAY, *SUPERMAN*-- AT LEAST WE STOPPED THEM FROM STEALING THE *TIRES!*

ACROSS THE PLANT, A CERTAIN TOP-COATED FIGURE SMILES GRIMLY BEFORE HE TURNS AWAY...

14

THE *CALIFORNIA COAST:* 840 MILES OF LOW, SANDY BEACHES AND ROCK-DIRT HEADLANDS, DOTTED BY A HANDFUL OF NATURAL ISLANDS--AND A COUPLE OF *MAN-MADE* ONES.

HERE AND THERE, GREAT *OIL DRILLS* PUMP A MURKY BLACK FLUID FROM THE DEPTHS OF THE SUN-STREAKED SEA--THE LIFE-BLOOD OF A NATION.

A GLEAM OF JADE-LIGHT-- AND TWO FORMS COME SLICING THROUGH THE HUMID PACIFIC SKY...

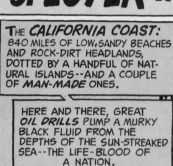

GREEN LANTERN and The ELONGATED Man

JACKPOT, RALPH --WE'VE *FOUND* 'EM!

I CLAIM *FIRST LICKS,* GL!

I OWE THESE CHARACTERS *PLENTY* FROM THE *LAST* TIME WE TANGLED!

IN YOUR CASE, PAL-- *TANGLED* IS EXACTLY THE RIGHT WORD!

BLAST! SHOULD'VE KNOWN MY *POWER RING* WOULDN'T AFFECT PAST *YELLOW* PUTTY-MEN--!

STILL, THERE'S *EFFECT*--AND THERE'S *CAUSE*--

--AND THE *RING* CAN DEFINITELY *CAUSE* THESE OIL DRUMS TO *POUND* MY POINT HOME!

THAT SHOULD HOLD 'EM FOR A FEW SECONDS! HOW *YOU* MAKING OUT--?

RALPH--? RALPH--?!

NO-OOOH!

GO GET HIM, *JUSTICE LEAGUER!*

TIME STANDS STILL AS AN ANXIOUS *GREEN LANTERN* PEERS DOWN INTO THE VIOLENTLY FROTHING WATERS--

--WAITING-- WAITING...

...UNTIL A SIMPLE DOUGHY FORM BURSTS FROM THE INKY DEPTHS--*ALONE*...

GREAT GUARDIANS! RALPH'S STILL *DOWN* THERE!

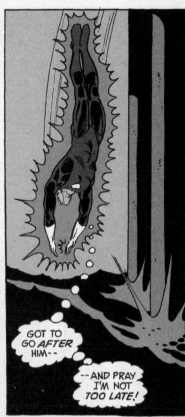

GOT TO GO *AFTER* HIM--

--AND PRAY I'M NOT *TOO LATE!*

LIKE A JADE JAVELIN, THE *POWER-RINGED PALADIN* PLUNGES BENEATH THE WAVES--

--LEAVING A SHADOWY SPECTATOR TO CONTINUE HIS SILENT VIGIL...

NO *TRACE* OF HIM-- BUT THE RIP-TIDES ARE *STRONG* HERE!

COULD THEY HAVE *CARRIED* AWAY RALPH'S *BODY...?*

HUH? A FIELD OF *GOLDEN SEAWEED*-- AND I *STUMBLED* BLINDLY INTO IT--!

16

THIS YELLOW *MENACE* TIGHTENING AROUND ME--

SEARING VELVET FILLS THE SPACES BEHIND THE *GREEN GLADIATOR'S* EYES AS THE WRITHING VEGETATION TIGHTENS ITS EMBRACE--

THE UNDERSEA CURRENT RIPPLES AND ROLLS--

--AND SUDDENLY COMES *ALIVE!*...

...BUT IT IS A LIFE WHICH *GIVES* LIFE--

--AS THE SWIFTLY-SWIRLING MAELSTROM PULLS *GREEN LANTERN* FREE OF THE GREEDILY GRASPING GROWTH...

...AND HURLS HIM TO THE SURFACE ONCE MORE!...

PUTTY-MEN *GONE*--NOT A CHANCE OF TRACKING THEM *NOW*--!

I COULDN'T EVEN GET *THAT* RIGHT!

POOR *RALPH*-- ALL THIS POWER AT MY COMMAND-- AND I STILL COULDN'T *SAVE* HIM--!

WHO'D HAVE THOUGHT THE *ELONGATED MAN'S FIRST* CASE WITH THE *JUSTICE LEAGUE* WOULD ALSO BE HIS *LAST?*

HOW WILL I BREAK THIS TO THE *OTHERS?*

IN A MOMENT, THE *EMERALD CRUSADER* IS GONE-- AND THE MYSTERIOUS FIGURE WHO HAS BEEN WATCHING FROM THE SHADOWS TURNS AWAY AS WELL...

"SPECTER IN THE SHADOWS!" CHAPTER 5

IN THE *JUSTICE LEAGUE'S* ORBITING HEAD-QUARTERS--AFTER *GREEN LANTERN* HAS RECOUNTED THE WHOLE SORROWFUL STORY...

I CAN'T BELIEVE RALPH'S GONE--! WH-WHAT WILL WE TELL HIS *WIFE?*

WE'LL TELL *SUE* WHAT SHE'D *WANT* TO HEAR--

--THAT RALPH DIED WITH *HONOR* AND *DIGNITY--* FIGHTING FOR WHAT HE BELIEVED--!

--AND THAT WE WON'T REST--TILL THE ONES *RESPONSIBLE* HAVE PAID... *HUH?*

PLING PLING PLING PLING PLING

THE JLA EMERGENCY *HOMING* SIGNAL! BUT I *CAN'T* GET A READING ON THE MEMBER WHO'S *SENDING* IT--!

RIGHT, *GREEN ARROW--*LET'S TRACE THOSE SIGNALS BACK TO THEIR *SOURCE!*

THERE'S A SIMPLE ENOUGH SOLUTION TO *THAT,* HALF-PINT...

AND SHORTLY, A HANDFUL OF GAUDILY-COSTUMED FORMS HURTLES RELENTLESSLY THROUGH THE STAGNANT AIR THAT HANGS HEAVILY OVER A SPRAWLING *SWAMPLAND...*

THE *EVERGLADES--!?* WHAT WOULD ONE OF *US* BE DOING DOWN *THERE?*

LET'S GO IN FOR A *CLOSER* LOOK-- AND *FIND OUT!*

WE MUST BE GETTING *NEARER,* GANG-- THAT EMERGENCY SIGNAL IS SOUNDING OFF LIKE A YEAR'S SUPPLY OF *FIRE ALARMS!*

WOW!

DOUBLE WOW!

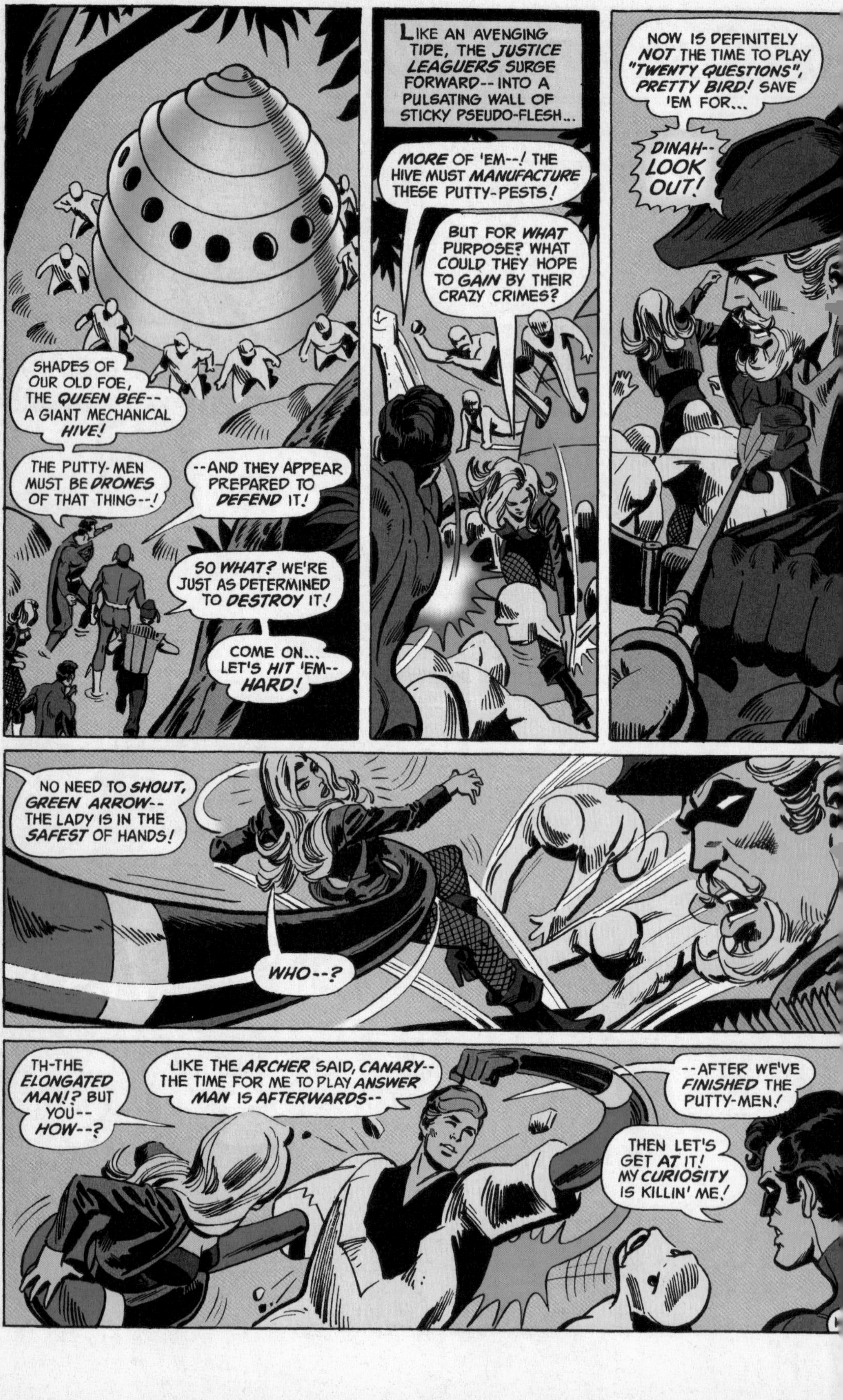

SHADES OF OUR OLD FOE, THE QUEEN BEE-- A GIANT MECHANICAL HIVE!
THE PUTTY-MEN MUST BE DRONES OF THAT THING--!
--AND THEY APPEAR PREPARED TO DEFEND IT!
SO WHAT? WE'RE JUST AS DETERMINED TO DESTROY IT!
COME ON... LET'S HIT 'EM-- HARD!
LIKE AN AVENGING TIDE, THE JUSTICE LEAGUERS SURGE FORWARD-- INTO A PULSATING WALL OF STICKY PSEUDO-FLESH...
MORE OF 'EM--! THE HIVE MUST MANUFACTURE THESE PUTTY-PESTS!
BUT FOR WHAT PURPOSE? WHAT COULD THEY HOPE TO GAIN BY THEIR CRAZY CRIMES?
NOW IS DEFINITELY NOT THE TIME TO PLAY "TWENTY QUESTIONS", PRETTY BIRD! SAVE 'EM FOR...
DINAH-- LOOK OUT!
NO NEED TO SHOUT, GREEN ARROW-- THE LADY IS IN THE SAFEST OF HANDS!
WHO--?
TH-THE ELONGATED MAN!? BUT YOU-- HOW--?
LIKE THE ARCHER SAID, CANARY-- THE TIME FOR ME TO PLAY ANSWER MAN IS AFTERWARDS--
--AFTER WE'VE FINISHED THE PUTTY-MEN!
THEN LET'S GET AT IT! MY CURIOSITY IS KILLIN' ME!

...AS AWESOME *EMERALD ENERGY* CARVES A YAWNING *PIT* INTO THE MARSHLAND FLOOR...

...A PIT SWIFTLY FILLED TO CAPACITY AT THE IRRESISTIBLE URGING OF THE *FASTEST MAN ALIVE*...

...AND FUSED FOREVER SHUT BY THE *MAN OF STEEL'S* SEARING HEAT VISION...

THEN--AND *ONLY* THEN--IS THERE TIME FOR QUESTIONS--AND-ANSWERS...

WHY DIDN'T YOU LET *US* IN ON YOUR PUTTY-MAN MASQUERADE, RALPH--?

WE WERE *BROKEN-HEARTED--!*

SORRY, GANG-- BUT THERE WASN'T *TIME!*

THE IDEA DIDN'T OCCUR TO ME TILL I HAD ONE OF THOSE CHARACTERS UNDER-WATER--!

IT WAS THE ONLY WAY I COULD THINK OF TO *DISCOVER* THEIR HIDE-OUT--

HUMMMMMMM

HUH? WHAT IN BLAZES IS *THAT?*

I'M NO *EXPERT* ON THAT HIVE--BUT I *HAVE* LEARNED A LITTLE BIT!

THE SOUND YOU HEAR IS THE *ACTIVATION* OF THE HIVE'S *SELF-DESTRUCT MECHANISM!*

A MATTER OF MOMENTS --AND THIS WHOLE NEIGHBORHOOD WILL BE IN ITTY-BITTY *PIECES!*

HUMMMMMMM

20

THE ONLY WAY TO *PREVENT* THE EXPLOSION IS TO *DEFUSE* THE DETONATOR--BUT...

SKIP THE *BUTS!* LET'S TAKE THAT BIG GOLD BLISTER APART AT THE SEAMS!

BUT AS THE DARING DEFENDERS BULLDOZE FORWARD...

UNNF! THERE'S AN INVISIBLE *FORCE-FIELD* SURROUNDING IT-- STRONGER THAN EVEN *I* CAN PENETRATE!

THAT'S WHAT I WAS TRYING TO *TELL* YOU! THERE'S *NO* WAY INTO THAT GIZMO!

BELIEVE ME--I'VE *TRIED!*

MAYBE *YOU* TRIED, RALPH-- BUT YOU DIDN'T HAVE *HELP* THEN!

I BETCHA OUR COMBINED POWER CONCENTRATED ON A SINGLE SPOT WILL *CRACK* THAT FIELD!

BUT EVEN SO-- THE PASSAGEWAYS IN THERE ARE TOO *SMALL* FOR ANYONE TO MOVE THROUGH!

BOY, RALPH--DO *YOU* HAVE THINGS TO *LEARN!*

AND THE *ELONGATED MAN'S* NEXT LESSON IS QUICKLY TAUGHT--AS HIS FELLOW *JLAERS* COMBINE THEIR AMAZING ABILITIES IN A DESPERATE EFFORT TO BREACH THE HIVE'S DEFENSES--

--AND TO A SMALL DEGREE *SUCCEED...*

THAT'S MY *CUE!* SEE YOU SOON!

THEN--DEEP WITHIN THE MECHANICAL LABYRINTH...

HUMMING'S GROWING *LOUDER*-- MUST BE GETTING CLOSER TO MY GOAL!

SUDDENLY...

WHA--? MUST'VE STUMBLED INTO ONE OF THE PUTTY-MAN PRODUCTION CENTERS!

STUFF'S WRAPPING AROUND ME--MESSING UP MY SIZE-AND-WEIGHT CONTROLS!

I'M *TRAPPED!*

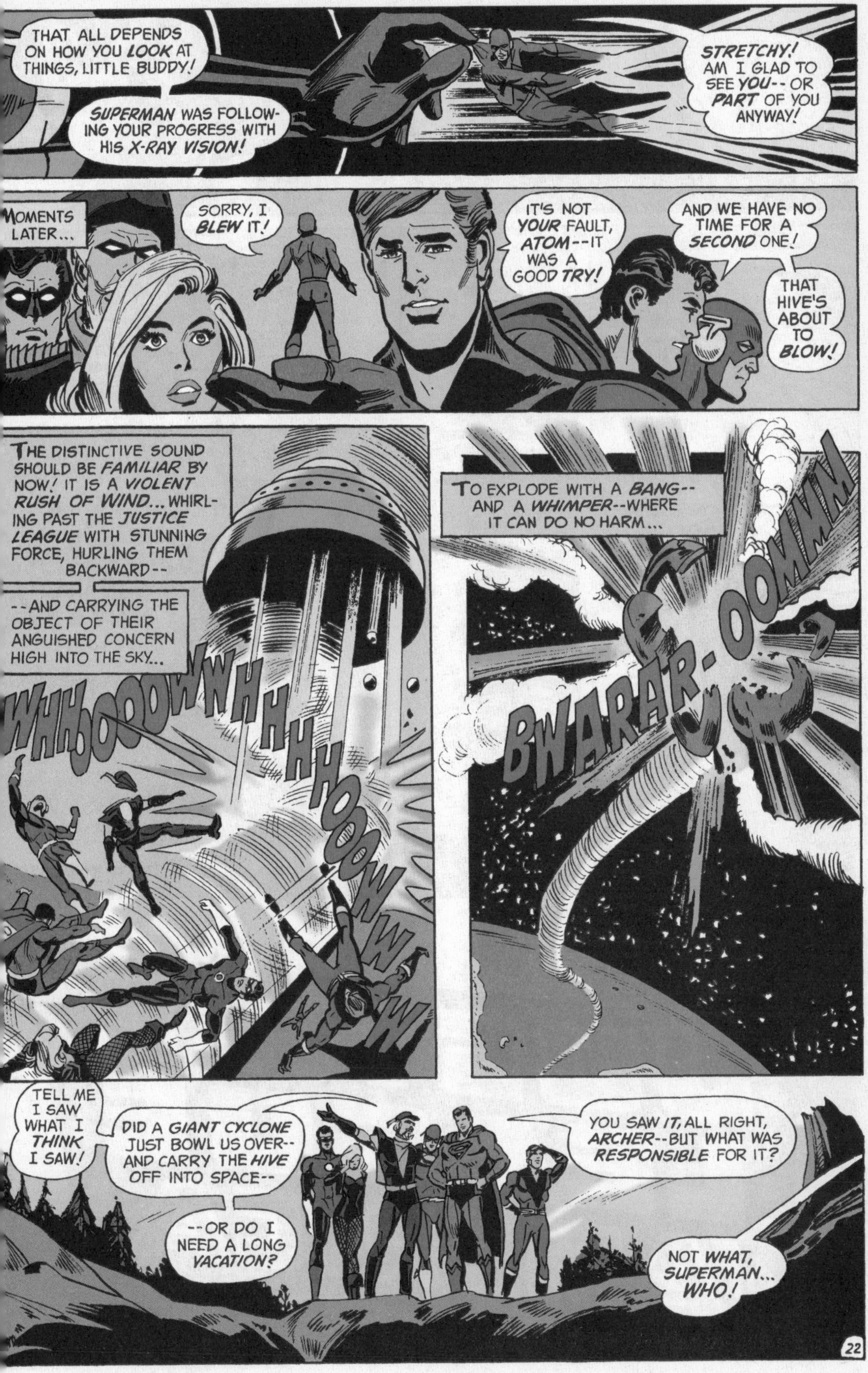
THAT ALL DEPENDS ON HOW YOU LOOK AT THINGS, LITTLE BUDDY!
SUPERMAN WAS FOLLOWING YOUR PROGRESS WITH HIS X-RAY VISION!
STRETCHY! AM I GLAD TO SEE YOU-- OR PART OF YOU ANYWAY!
MOMENTS LATER...
SORRY, I BLEW IT!
IT'S NOT YOUR FAULT, ATOM--IT WAS A GOOD TRY!
AND WE HAVE NO TIME FOR A SECOND ONE!
THAT HIVE'S ABOUT TO BLOW!
THE DISTINCTIVE SOUND SHOULD BE FAMILIAR BY NOW! IT IS A VIOLENT RUSH OF WIND... WHIRLING PAST THE JUSTICE LEAGUE WITH STUNNING FORCE, HURLING THEM BACKWARD--
--AND CARRYING THE OBJECT OF THEIR ANGUISHED CONCERN HIGH INTO THE SKY...
WHHOOOOWWHHHHHOOOWWWW
TO EXPLODE WITH A BANG-- AND A WHIMPER--WHERE IT CAN DO NO HARM...
BWARAR-OOMMM
TELL ME I SAW WHAT I THINK I SAW!
DID A GIANT CYCLONE JUST BOWL US OVER-- AND CARRY THE HIVE OFF INTO SPACE--
--OR DO I NEED A LONG VACATION?
YOU SAW IT, ALL RIGHT, ARCHER--BUT WHAT WAS RESPONSIBLE FOR IT?
NOT WHAT, SUPERMAN... WHO!
22

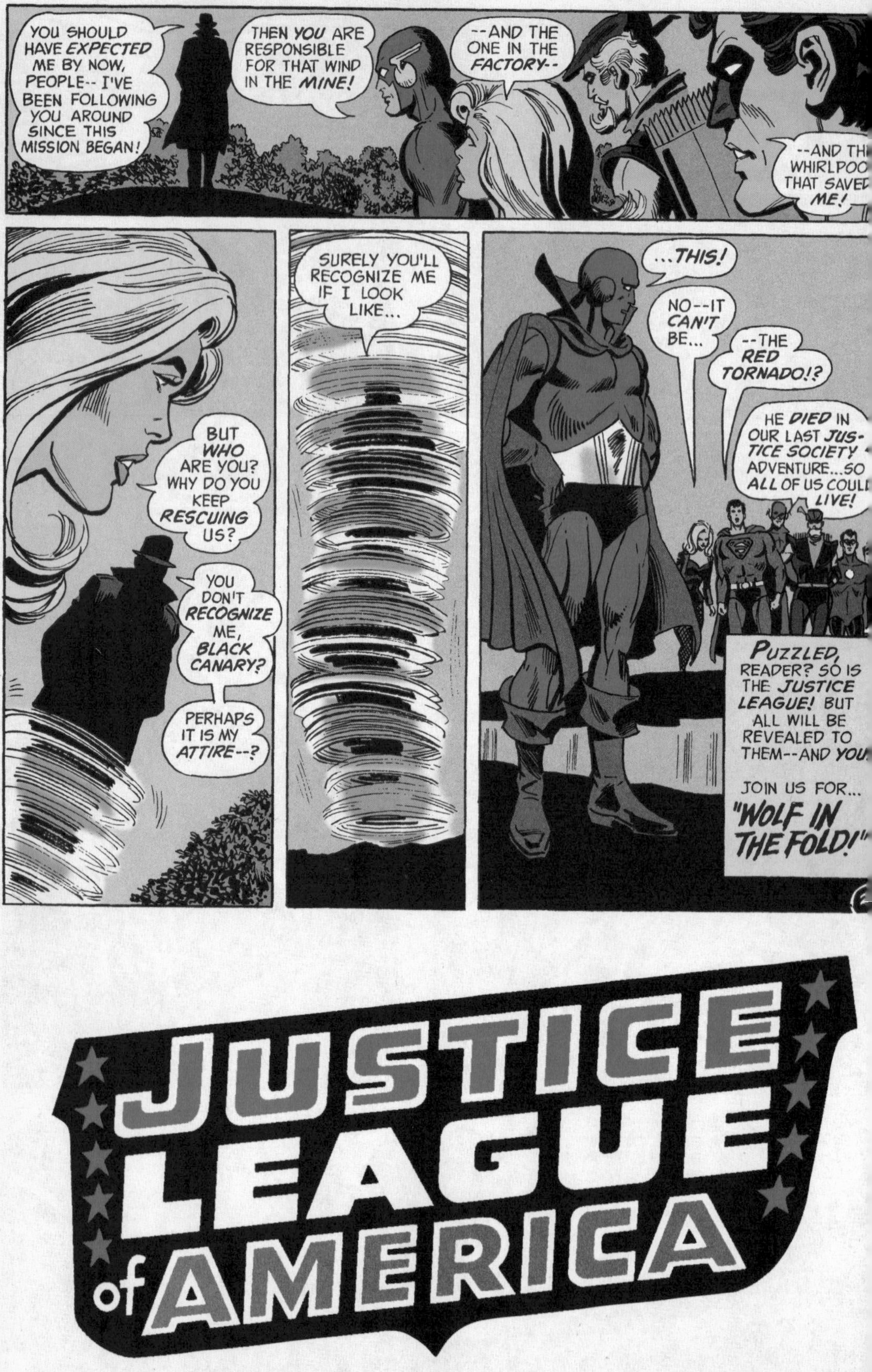
YOU SHOULD HAVE EXPECTED ME BY NOW, PEOPLE-- I'VE BEEN FOLLOWING YOU AROUND SINCE THIS MISSION BEGAN!
THEN YOU ARE RESPONSIBLE FOR THAT WIND IN THE MINE!
--AND THE ONE IN THE FACTORY--
--AND TH WHIRLPOO THAT SAVE ME!
BUT WHO ARE YOU? WHY DO YOU KEEP RESCUING US?
YOU DON'T RECOGNIZE ME, BLACK CANARY?
PERHAPS IT IS MY ATTIRE--?
SURELY YOU'LL RECOGNIZE ME IF I LOOK LIKE...
...THIS!
NO--IT CAN'T BE...
--THE RED TORNADO!?
HE DIED IN OUR LAST JUS-TICE SOCIETY ADVENTURE...SO ALL OF US COUL LIVE!
PUZZLED, READER? SO IS THE JUSTICE LEAGUE! BUT ALL WILL BE REVEALED TO THEM--AND YOU
JOIN US FOR... "WOLF IN THE FOLD!"

JUSTICE LEAGUE of AMERICA

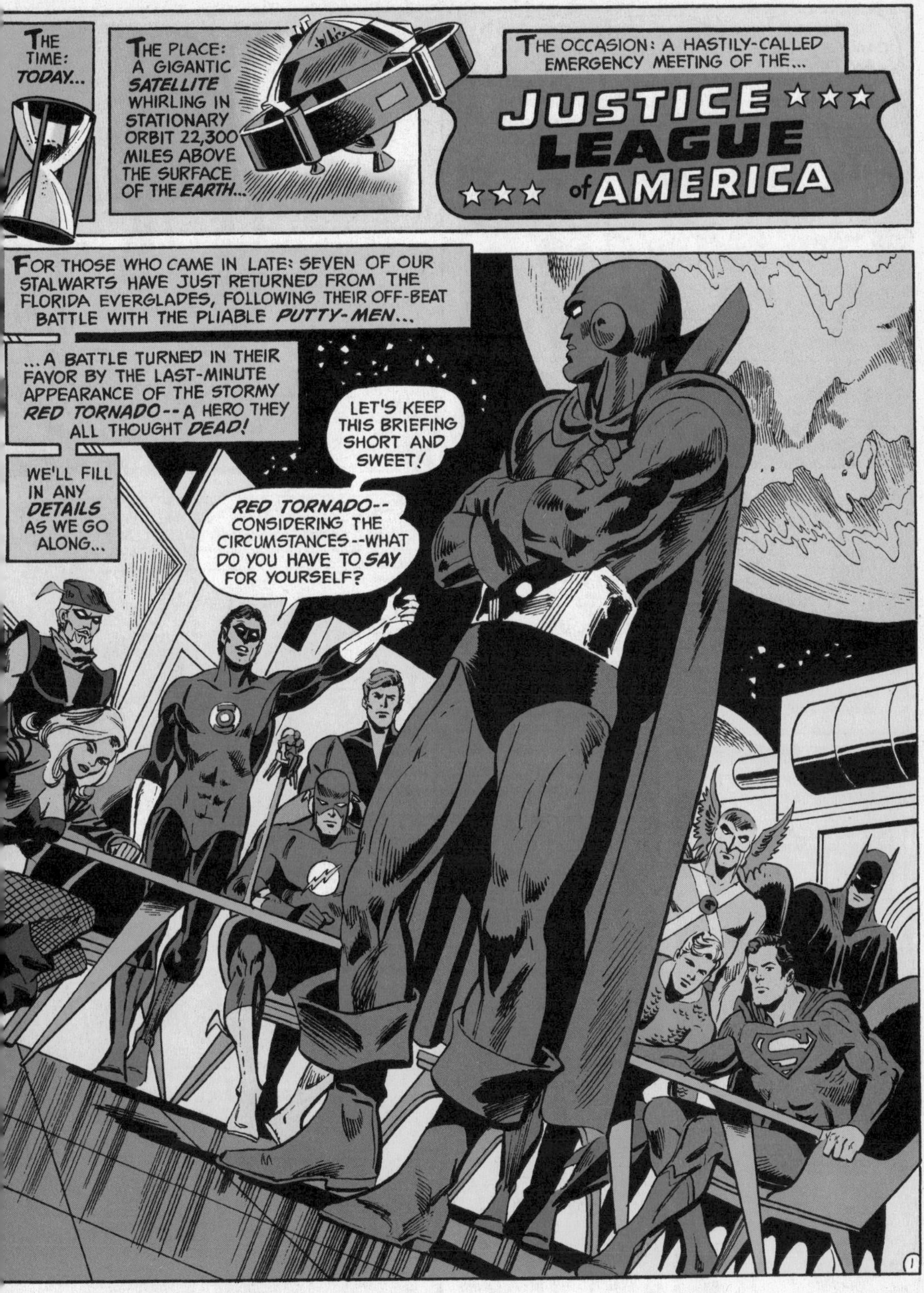
THE TIME: TODAY...
THE PLACE: A GIGANTIC SATELLITE WHIRLING IN STATIONARY ORBIT 22,300 MILES ABOVE THE SURFACE OF THE EARTH...
THE OCCASION: A HASTILY-CALLED EMERGENCY MEETING OF THE...
JUSTICE LEAGUE of AMERICA
FOR THOSE WHO CAME IN LATE: SEVEN OF OUR STALWARTS HAVE JUST RETURNED FROM THE FLORIDA EVERGLADES, FOLLOWING THEIR OFF-BEAT BATTLE WITH THE PLIABLE PUTTY-MEN...
...A BATTLE TURNED IN THEIR FAVOR BY THE LAST-MINUTE APPEARANCE OF THE STORMY RED TORNADO--A HERO THEY ALL THOUGHT DEAD!
WE'LL FILL IN ANY DETAILS AS WE GO ALONG...
LET'S KEEP THIS BRIEFING SHORT AND SWEET!
RED TORNADO--CONSIDERING THE CIRCUMSTANCES--WHAT DO YOU HAVE TO SAY FOR YOURSELF?
1

NOT MUCH *CAN I SAY, GREEN LANTERN*--THERE'S NOT A GREAT DEAL I *KNOW!*

COME ON, PAL--WE *ALL* WATCHED YOU *DIE!*

HOW DID YOU PULL YOUR *LAZARUS* BIT--AND WHEN DID YOU GROW A *FACE?*

YOU *JEST, GREEN ARROW*--BUT THIS IS *NOT* A LAUGHING MATTER!

MY MEMORY CIRCUITS ARE *UNCLEAR* ON THE SUBJECT-- MOSTLY PROJECTION AND CONCLUSION--

--BUT I WILL *ENLIGHTEN* YOU AS BEST I CAN!

"AS YOU REMEMBER, I STOLE THE *NEBULA-ROD* WHEN YOU AND THE *JUSTICE SOCIETY* COMBINED FORCES AGAINST THE *HAND THAT HELD THE EARTH*..."

"THE *EXPLOSION* OCCURRED AS EXPECTED--AND YOU THOUGHT ME *DESTROYED!*"

"*O*BVIOUSLY, I WAS *NOT!*"

"*H*OW LONG I LAY AS ONE DEAD I DO NOT KNOW-- BUT EVENTUALLY, MY *DAMAGED* BODY WAS *DISCOVERED*..."

"...BY A *BLIND* SCULPTOR LIVING ALONE DEEP IN YOUR *ROCKY MOUNTAINS*..."

"...IN THE HOPE THAT MY *ANDROID* BODY MIGHT SURVIVE THE ERUPTING INTERSTELLAR ENERGIES WHERE YOUR *HUMAN* FORMS WOULD *NOT*..."

"*I*NSTEAD, IN A ONE-IN-A-BILLION CHANCE, THE ERUPTION TORE A *HOLE* IN THE DIMENSIONAL FABRIC-- AND HURLED ME FROM *MY EARTH* INTO *YOURS*..."

"THE OLD MAN TOOK ME INTO HIS HOME-- TENDED ME..."

"...AND WHAT PROMPTED HIM TO SCULPT *FEATURES* UPON MY EMPTY ANDROID FACE I WILL NEVER KNOW..."

"EVENTUALLY, MY INTERNAL REPAIR MECHANISMS RETURNED ME TO *CONSCIOUSNESS*..."

WHERE... *AM I?* WHAT HAS ...*HAPPENED* TO ME?

BE *CALM*, FRIEND-- *RELAX!* YOU ARE IN *SAFE* HANDS!

"*CONVERSATIONS* WITH THE OLD MAN DURING MY *RECOVERY* CONVINCED ME I WAS ON THE *WRONG EARTH!*"

"WHEN I WAS *WELL* ENOUGH, I THANKED MY BLIND FRIEND--AND SET ABOUT TO *CORRECT* THE SITUATION..."

"BUT THAT WAS EASIER *PLANNED* THAN *ACCOMPLISHED!*"

"TO MY SURPRISE, I FOUND I COULD NOT *PIERCE* THE DIMENSIONAL BARRIER..."

"SOME SIDE EFFECT OF THE *NEBULOID* DESTRUCTION PREVENTED ME FROM EVER *RETURNING* TO MY HOME WORLD!"

I CAME SEARCHING FOR *YOU* THEN--BUT KNOWING YOUR *LOW* OPINION OF ME--I HELPED YOUR CAUSE IN *SECRET*--

--DECIDING THAT THE *SOONER* YOU DEFEATED THE *PUTTY-MEN*, THE *SOONER* YOU'D HAVE TIME FOR *ME!*

TORNADO, THAT'S NOT *FAIR!* JUST BECAUSE WE FAILED TO LISTEN TO YOU *ONCE*--

YES--AND THAT FAILURE CAUSED THE *DEATH* OF *BLACK CANARY'S* HUSBAND! BUT *ENOUGH* OF SUCH GRIM THINGS!

SUFFICE IT THAT I *DESTROYED* THE *PUTTY-MAN-PRODUCING HIVE-DEVICE*--AND YOU FINALLY BROUGHT ME *HERE!*

3

YOU'RE *RIGHT*, TORNADO -- WE'VE TREATED YOU *UNJUSTLY!* IT'S TIME WE *MADE UP* FOR IT!

SINCE YOU'RE *TRAPPED* ON *OUR* WORLD -- AND IN RECOGNITION OF YOUR CRACKING THE *PUTTY-MEN* CASE...

...I NOMINATE YOU FOR *MEMBER-SHIP* IN THE *JUSTICE LEAGUE!*

WAITAMINNIT! WHAT'S THIS GROUP *BECOMING...?*

A *REFUGEE CAMP* FOR *EARTH-TWO* OUTCASTS?

I DON'T REMEMBER YOU COMPLAINING SO *LOUDLY* WHEN *BLACK CANARY* WAS PROPOSED FOR MEMBERSHIP, *GREEN ARROW!*

RED TORNADO HAS *EARNED* HIS NOMINATION! THE QUESTION IS -- WILL HE *ACCEPT* IT?

YES, HAWKMAN -- I WILL *ACCEPT!*

I HAVE *NOWHERE ELSE* TO GO!

THE VOTING IS FAST AND FURIOUS -- AND WHEN IT IS *DONE...*

PASSED... UNANIMOUSLY!

CONGRATULATIONS, *RED TORNADO* -- YOU HAVE JUST BECOME A MEMBER OF THE *JUSTICE LEAGUE OF AMERICA!*

EXCELLENT! NOW I CAN *DESTROY* THEM ALL!

THUS, A *NEW* FIGURE JOINS THE FAMOUS RANKS -- BUT HAVE THE *WORLD'S GREATEST HEROES* MADE A *FATAL ERROR?* HAVE THEY ALLOWED A...

"WOLF IN THE FOLD!"

LEN WEIN
WRITER

DICK DILLIN
&
DICK GIORDANO
ARTISTS

FOR *PART* OF THE ANSWER, LET US TURN *ELSEWHERE*-- TO A *HIDDEN LABORATORY* DEEP IN THE *ROCKY MOUNTAINS*...

--AND THE *ORIGINATOR* OF THE *RED TORNADO'S MURDER-FILLED* THOUGHT...

EXCELLENT! NOW I CAN *DESTROY* THEM ALL!

HIS NAME IS *MORROW, THOMAS OSCAR*--BUT HIS FRIENDS, IF HE HAD ANY, WOULD CALL HIM *TOMORROW*...

T.O. MORROW--WHO, INSPIRED BY HIS NAME, HAS DEDICATED HIMSELF TO DELVING INTO THE WORLD OF THE *FUTURE*...

T.O. MORROW --HE WHO FIRST *CREATED* THE AMAZING *RED TORNADO*...

...ONLY TO HAVE HIS CREATION TURN *AGAINST* HIM IN THE CAUSE OF *JUSTICE!*

T.O. MORROW--WHO PAUSES IN HIS BUSINESS TO *GLOAT*...

MY TEMPORARY *CONTROL* OVER THE *TORNADO* IS *GONE*-- BUT IT NO LONGER *MATTERS!*

SOON THE *JUSTICE LEAGUE* WILL BE *FINISHED*-- AND I'LL SLEEP *PEACEFULLY* AT LAST!

NOT THAT I HOLD ANY *GRUDGES* AGAINST THEM! THEY DO *THEIR* THING--I DO *MINE!* IT'S JUST A MATTER OF *SELF-PRESERVATION!*

IF MY COMPUTER HADN'T MADE THIS *PREDICTION*, I'D PROBABLY HAVE LEFT THEM *ALONE!*

IN PRECISELY 28 DAYS, THE COSMIC BALANCE WILL SHIFT-- AND EITHER T.O. MORROW OR THE JUSTICE LEAGUE OF AMERICA WILL CEASE TO EXIST

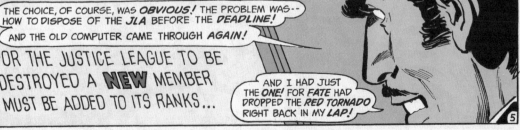

THE CHOICE, OF COURSE, WAS *OBVIOUS!* THE PROBLEM WAS-- HOW TO DISPOSE OF THE *JLA* BEFORE THE *DEADLINE!*

AND THE OLD COMPUTER CAME THROUGH *AGAIN!*

FOR THE JUSTICE LEAGUE TO BE DESTROYED A *NEW* MEMBER MUST BE ADDED TO ITS RANKS...

AND I HAD JUST THE *ONE!* FOR *FATE* HAD DROPPED THE *RED TORNADO* RIGHT BACK IN MY *LAP!*

5

I *REPAIRED* HIM--GAVE HIM HIS NEW *FACE*-- THEN *ALTERED* HIS MEMORY CIRCUITS TO *REMEMBER* ME AS A *BLIND OLD MAN!*

THAT ACCOMPLISHED *PART* OF IT--BUT I STILL HAD TO GIVE HIM *CAUSE* TO *JOIN* THE *JUSTICE LEAGUE!*

MY MONITORS HAD DISCOVERED THE *QUEEN BEE'S* HIDDEN *HIVE!* I ACTIVATED IT-- INVOLVED THE *JLA* WITH ITS *PUTTY-DRONES*--

--AND *ARRANGED* THE SITUATION SO THE *RED TORNADO* WOULD COME OUT LOOKING *GOOD!*

YOU *SAY* SOMETHIN', BOSS?

NO, ROSCOE-- JUST CHECKING TO BE CERTAIN EVERYTHING IS *SET!*

IT'S ALL *READY,* BOSS-- JUST LIKE YOU *SAID!*

WE'LL TAKE THESE *FUTURE-WEAPONS* AND USE 'EM WHERE THE *RED TORNADO* IS CERTAIN TO *SEE!*

SPLENDID! ANYTHING AT ALL TO MAKE HIM USE HIS NEWLY-GAINED *JLA SIGNAL DEVICE!*

FOR I'VE PLANTED A SMALL *MECHANISM* INSIDE THE *TORNADO'S* BODY THAT *ALTERS* THE DEVICE'S *FREQUENCY!*

THE *FIRST* TIME HE *PRESSES* THAT TRANSMITTER--

--THE *JUSTICE LEAGUE* OF *AMERICA* WILL *DIE!*

TURN TIME AHEAD TWENTY-FOUR HOURS TO THE BUSY STREETS OF *NEW YORK CITY*-- AS THE *RED TORNADO* ATTEMPTS TO ESTABLISH A NEW LIFE...

...A *HUMAN* LIFE...

NO *LUGGAGE?* I'M *SORRY,* SIR!

NO *IDENTIFICATION,* EH? WELL, WE'RE ALL *FILLED UP!*

NO *DRIVER'S LICENSE?* NO *CREDIT CARDS?*

I'M AFRAID YOU'LL HAVE TO TRY SOMEPLACE *ELSE!*

HOW *IRONIC!* FOR ALL OF MY EXISTENCE, I HAVE WANTED TO BE *HUMAN*--AND NOW THAT THE OPPORTUNITY PRESENTS ITSELF--

--NO ONE WILL GIVE ME THE *CHANCE!*

TOTALLY DEJECTED, THE TOP-COATED *TORNADO* SHUFFLES DOWN THE STREET, OBLIVIOUS TO EVERYTHING AROUND HIM...

...LIKE THE MINIATURE *TANK* WHIRRING PAST HIM IN THE OPPOSITE DIRECTION...

A TOY-LIKE CONTRAPTION THAT GROWS *LARGER* WITH EVERY PASSING INCH...

...ITS MECHANISMS UNFOLDING FROM SOME DEEP INNER RECESS...

...UNFOLDING... LARGER... EVER *LARGER*... *LARGER*...

...UNTIL IT ERUPTS INTO FULL MATURITY-- WITH A SOUND LIKE MUFFLED *THUNDER*...

WHAT--?!

BW A-ROOOM

BANK

⑦

TO BORROW A LINE FROM ONE OF MY NEWLY-GAINED *PARTNERS*...

THIS IS A JOB...

...FOR...

...*RED TORNADO!*

HIS ALREADY-ANGUISHED MIND RAGING FOR BATTLE, THE *CRIMSON CYCLONE* WHIRLS ACROSS THE STREET...

YOU ARE ALL *UNDER ARREST!* SURRENDER QUIETLY-- AND YOU WILL NOT BE *HURT!*

WHO IN BLAZES IS *THAT?!*

BEATS *ME*--BUT IT SURE AIN'T *SUPERMAN!*

YOU WILL LEARN, FELONS--MUCH TO YOUR CHAGRIN--THAT ONE NEED NOT BE A *MAN OF STEEL*--

--TO CONQUER MEN OF *TIN!*

YOUR SUPER-STRENGTH-GIVING *EXOSKELETONS* WILL AVAIL YOU *NOTHING*--

--IF YOU CANNOT *UNTANGLE* YOURSELVES TO *USE* THEM!

WE DON'T NEED *MUSCLE* TO FINISH *YOU* OFF, WHIRLY-BIRD!

THIS HERE *ENERGY-TRANSVERTER* OUGHT'A DO THE JOB UP *FINE!*

APPARENTLY, I DID NOT CLEARLY MAKE MY *POINT...*

BUT BEFORE THE *WHIRLWIND WONDER* CAN COMPLETE HIS SENTENCE...

THAT *DEVICE*-- TURNING MY POWERS *AGAINST* ME!

I'M *CAUGHT*-- A *PRISONER* OF MY OWN TORNADO!

I HATE TO *DO* THIS-- HATE TO PROVE THAT THE *JLA* WAS *RIGHT*--

--THAT I *AM* INCAPABLE OF HANDLING THINGS ON MY *OWN*--

--BUT THE TRIUMPH OF GOOD OVER EVIL IS THE *LEAGUE'S* PRIMARY CONCERN, SO...

FANTASTIC! IN ONE MORE MOMENT, *RED TORNADO* WILL *PRESS* HIS SIGNAL-- AND MY WORRIES --AND THE *JUSTICE LEAGUE'S* -- WILL BE *OVER!*

ONLY *THEIRS* WILL BE OVER-- *PERMANENTLY!*

BUT AS THE *RUBY REVOLVER'S* FINGER STREAKS TO HIS *BELT-BUCKLE...*

UH UH UH-- DON'T TOUCH THAT *DIAL!*

WHO--?

9

HI, *REDDY!* HOPE YOU DON'T MIND MY DROPPING IN UNEXPECTEDLY-- BUT I HAPPENED TO BE IN THE *NEIGHBORHOOD* AND...

--YOU THOUGHT YOU'D MAKE *CERTAIN* I DID NOT *FOUL UP* MY FIRST TIME IN THE FIELD, RIGHT?

YOU CAN'T *BLAME* A GUY FOR WANTING TO HELP A FRIEND-- AND THAT'S WHAT YOU *ARE,* TORNADO-- A *FRIEND!* I'LL PROVE...

≥UUNNNH!≤ MACHINE THREW MY *POWER-RING* BLAST *BACK* AT ME!

WELL, *TWO* CAN PLAY AT *THAT* GAME!

THIS *MIRROR* WILL REDIRECT MY *POWER-RING* BOLTS BACK TO WHERE THEY WERE *INTENDED!*

FOR SEVERAL TENSION-FILLED MOMENTS, THE EMERALD ENERGY PLAYS BACK AND FORTH BETWEEN MIRROR AND MACHINE...

...POWER RESTRAINED AND STRAINING...

...UNTIL IT FINDS *RELEASE* IN THE CHAIN'S WEAKEST LINK...

THE TRANSVERTER IS *DESTROYED*-- BUT THE FORCE OF THE EXPLOSION HAS *STUNNED GREEN LANTERN!*

I'LL HAVE TO DEFEAT THE REST OF THIS GANG-- *ALONE!*

FWOOM

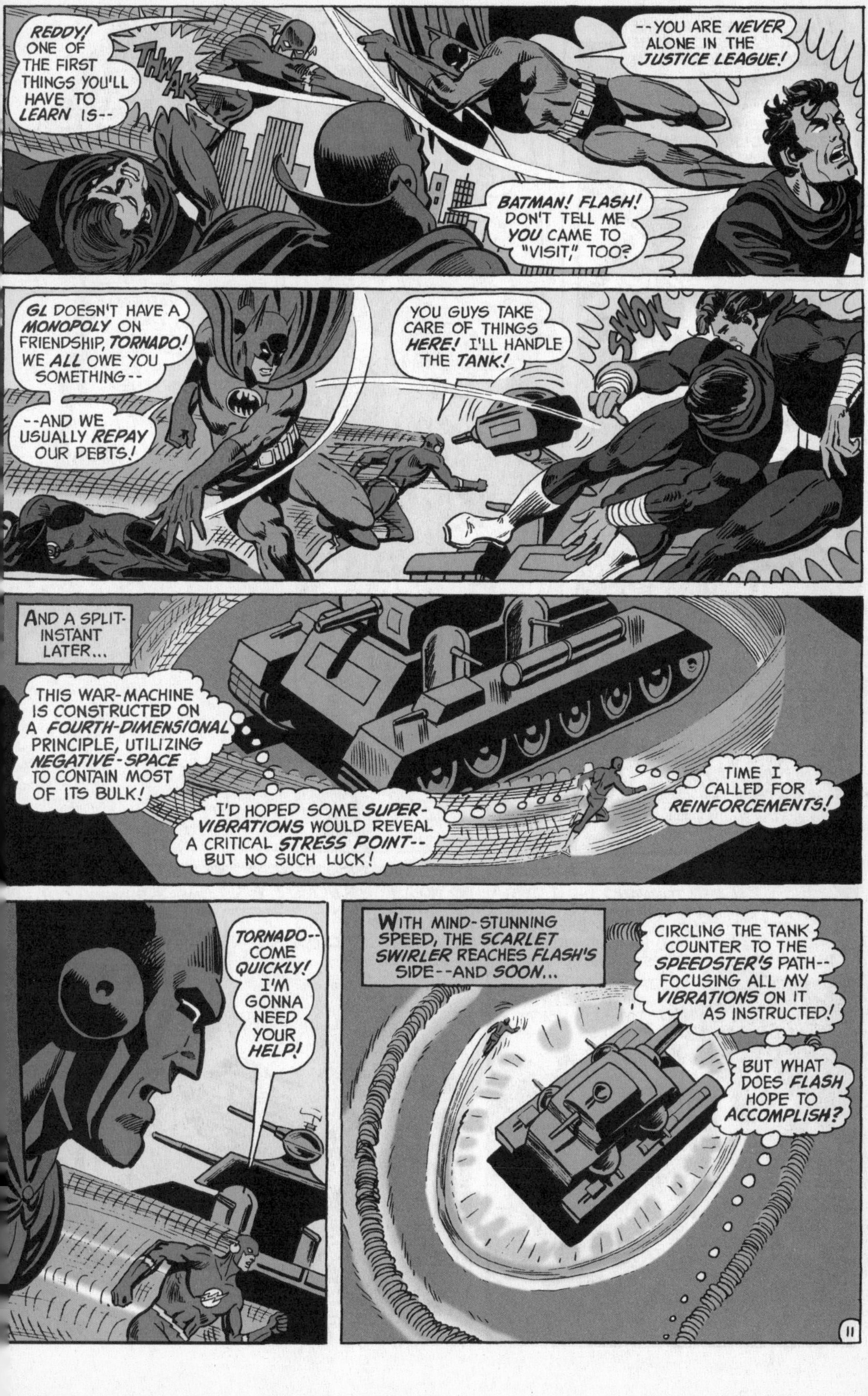
REDDY! ONE OF THE FIRST THINGS YOU'LL HAVE TO LEARN IS--
THWAK
--YOU ARE NEVER ALONE IN THE JUSTICE LEAGUE!
BATMAN! FLASH! DON'T TELL ME YOU CAME TO "VISIT," TOO?
GL DOESN'T HAVE A MONOPOLY ON FRIENDSHIP, TORNADO! WE ALL OWE YOU SOMETHING--
--AND WE USUALLY REPAY OUR DEBTS!
YOU GUYS TAKE CARE OF THINGS HERE! I'LL HANDLE THE TANK!
SMOK
AND A SPLIT-INSTANT LATER...
THIS WAR-MACHINE IS CONSTRUCTED ON A FOURTH-DIMENSIONAL PRINCIPLE, UTILIZING NEGATIVE-SPACE TO CONTAIN MOST OF ITS BULK!
I'D HOPED SOME SUPER-VIBRATIONS WOULD REVEAL A CRITICAL STRESS POINT--BUT NO SUCH LUCK!
TIME I CALLED FOR REINFORCEMENTS!
TORNADO--COME QUICKLY! I'M GONNA NEED YOUR HELP!
WITH MIND-STUNNING SPEED, THE SCARLET SWIRLER REACHES FLASH'S SIDE--AND SOON...
CIRCLING THE TANK COUNTER TO THE SPEEDSTER'S PATH--FOCUSING ALL MY VIBRATIONS ON IT AS INSTRUCTED!
BUT WHAT DOES FLASH HOPE TO ACCOMPLISH?
11

WHILE, ACROSS THE STREET, A CERTAIN *CAPED CRIME-BUSTER* IS ACCOMPLISHING *PLENTY...*

HOPE THE *TORNADO* DOESN'T *RESENT* OUR PRESENCE-- BUT HE'D *NEVER* HAVE BEEN ABLE TO CONTROL THIS SITUATION BY *HIMSELF!*

EVEN *GREEN LANTERN* COULDN'T HANDLE IT *SOLO!*

THWRACK

BATMAN!--I'M *SURPRISED* AT YOU! THE NUMBER ONE *RULE* IN THE *SUPER-HERO* BUSINESS IS-- ALWAYS *WATCH YOUR BACK!*

I *WAS* WATCHING, *GL*--BUT I DECIDED TO LEAVE THE LAST ONE FOR *YOU!*

REMIND ME TO RETURN THE "*FAVOR*" SOME DAY!

SO--I SEE YOU PEOPLE HAVE *TIED UP* THINGS ON *YOUR* END!

NATURALLY, *FLASH*-- WE ONLY...

HEY--WHAT HAPPENED TO THE *TANK?*

OH, *THAT*-- A *SIMPLE* THING, REALLY!

RED TORNADO AND I JUST KEPT *BOMBARDING* IT WITH *CONFLICTING* VIBRATIONS TILL WE HIT THE PRIME STRESS POINT--

--AND *REVERSED* THE EXPANSION PROCESS!

WOULD ANYONE CARE FOR A VERY *DEADLY* WIND-UP TOY?

BLAST! I WAS *SO CLOSE*--!

TIME IS RUNNING *OUT*-- BUT I STILL HAVE A FEW *GAMBITS* LEFT TO *PLAY!*

SOON AFTER, IN *JLA* HEADQUARTERS...

GREEN LANTERN, I *RESENT* YOUR INTRUSION IN MY BATTLE! I DEMAND TO BE TREATED AS AN *EQUAL* MEMBER OF THE *JUSTICE LEAGUE*, OR...

AWW...COME ON, *TORNADO*--YOU WERE JUST ABOUT TO *CALL* US WHEN WE SHOWED!

THAT IS A MISTAKE I WILL *NOT* MAKE AGAIN!

ENOUGH *BICKERING!* WE HAVE A PROBLEM BEFORE US THAT NEEDS A *SOLUTION!*

THE *UNIFORMS* THEY WORE WERE *FAMILIAR!* IF ONLY...

GOT IT!--T.O. MORROW! HIS FACELESS MINIONS WORE THAT OUTFIT THE *FIRST* TIME WE MET...

--THE *RED TORNADO!* INTERESTING THAT HE AND *MORROW* SHOULD REAPPEAR AT THE *SAME* TIME! SORT OF MAKES ONE *WONDER*--!

WHAT--!?

ENOUGH! I HAVE *BETTER* THINGS TO DO THAN STAND HERE AND TOLERATE YOUR VEILED *ACCUSATIONS!*

TORNADO --WAIT! WE DIDN'T *MEAN*...

NO, FLASH-- LET HIM *GO!* IT'S *SIMPLER* THIS WAY!

I HAVE MATTERS TO DISCUSS THAT ARE *NOT* FOR THE *RED TORNADO'S* EARS!

13

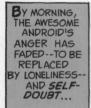

BY MORNING, THE *AWESOME ANDROID'S* ANGER HAS FADED--TO BE REPLACED BY *LONELINESS*-- AND *SELF-DOUBT*...

I *DISLIKE* DOING THIS--BUT SINCE I CAN'T FIND *ACCOMMODATIONS* WITHOUT FIRST FINDING *EMPLOYMENT*...

NEW YORK JOB OPPORTUNITIES, INC.

NEXT, PLEASE!

SILENTLY, THE *RED TORNADO* TAKES HIS SEAT--THE INEVITABLE FORMS ARE PRODUCED AND...

NAME?

UH... *SMITH!* JOHN SMITH!

ADDRESS?

GENERAL DELIVERY!

UH-HUH! *AGE?*

AT THE MOMENT I FEEL LIKE THE *OLDEST* MAN ALIVE!

PLEASE--JUST ANSWER THE QUESTIONS! *PREVIOUS EMPLOYMENT?*

FREE-LANCE LAW OFFICER!

FREE-LANCE...? ER--*REASON* FOR APPLICATION?

SURVIVAL!

HEY--ARE YOU *PUTTING ME ON,* MISTER... SMITH--?

NO, YOU'RE *NOT,* ARE YOU? I CAN SEE IT IN YOUR *EYES!*

TELL ME, SIR-- WHEN WAS THE *LAST* TIME YOU HAD A *DECENT* MEAL?

WHY, I...

NEVER MIND--I CAN *IMAGINE!* C'MON--I'LL TREAT YOU TO *LUNCH!*

BUT--!

NO *BUTS!* THE NAME'S *KATHY SUTTON--* GIRL-SAMARITAN-- AND I HAVEN'T *LOST* A CLIENT YET!

FOR A GUY WHO HASN'T EATEN LATELY, YOU SURE DON'T SEEM HUNGRY!

SOMETHING WRONG?

NO--I WAS MERELY WONDERING WHY YOU ARE SO GENEROUS TO A STRANGER!

YOU'RE NO STRANGER, SMITH--I SEE YOUR TYPE EVERY DAY! NEW TO THE BIG CITY--FULL OF DREAMS--IDEALS--BUT WITH NO MONEY--NO PLACE TO STAY!

HECK--I WAS LIKE THAT MYSELF ONCE!

YOU'RE QUITE A WOMAN, KATHY SUTTON!

SURE--THE LAST OF THE SOFT TOUCHES, THAT'S ME!

STILL--IF YOU NEED A PLACE TO STAY I THINK I CAN FIND YOU ONE!

THAT WOULD BE APPRECIATED!

IT'S A NICE ROOM, MR. SMITH--YOU'LL LIKE IT! NEVER WOULD'VE RENTED IT TO A STRANGER IF MISS SUTTON HADN'T PUT IN A GOOD WORD FOR YA--

--AND ADVANCED ME THE FIRST WEEK'S RENT!

SHE'S A DARLIN' GIRL, KATHY IS!

YES--SHE'S A "DARLIN'" GIRL, INDEED!

15

IN THE DAYS THAT FOLLOW, THE BOND OF *FRIENDSHIP* GROWS STRONGER BETWEEN THE VIBRANT *KATHY SUTTON* AND THE SOMBER-FACED ANDROID WHO CALLS HIM-SELF *JOHN SMITH*...

...FOR IT IS A BOND FORGED OF MUTUAL ENJOYMENT AND PERHAPS, THE FIRST SAD, STINGING FLAMES OF--*LOVE*...

BUT, MILES AWAY, A SINISTER, WHITE-GARBED FIGURE CONSIDERS THAT BOND THE *WEAKEST* LINK IN A FAR MORE DANGEROUS *CHAIN*...

SO--THE *RED TORNADO* HAS FOUND HIMSELF A *GIRL FRIEND!* DIDN'T THINK HE HAD IT *IN* HIM!

NO MATTER, THOUGH-- FOR HE'S PROVIDED ME WITH NUMEROUS NEW POSSIBILITIES--

--AND TIME IS *RUNNING OUT* FOR ME!

AND THE FOLLOWING MORNING...

JOHN! JOHN-- I'VE *GOT* SOME-THING FOR YOU--!

I'VE *FOUND* YOU A *JOB!*

THAT'S *SPLENDID*, KATHY!

WELL...IT'S NOT *MUCH* OF A JOB, REALLY--JUST A *LAB ASSISTANT* TO A DOCTOR *GORDON*-- BUT...

KATHY--DO YOU HEAR AN ODD *SOUND?*

AND IT IS *QUITE* AN *ODD* SOUND--LIKE THE FURIOUS BUZZING OF A BILLION ANGRY *BEES* MINGLED WITH THE PLAINTIVE HOWL OF A THOUSAND *WOLVES*...

...A SOUND THAT PULLS JOHN *(RED TORNADO)* SMITH'S EYES SKYWARD TO SEE...

--*MORROW'S MEN*-- WITH *NEW* FUTURISTIC WEAPONS!

KATHY, YOU MUST GET *AWAY* FROM HERE BEFORE...

--THOSE *RAYS!* THEY'VE TURNED KATHY--AND EVERYONE *ELSE* ON THE STREET-- INTO *STONE!*

THE RAYS MUST ONLY AFFECT *HUMAN* TISSUE-- FOR THEY HAD *NO* EFFECT ON MY *SYNTHETIC* FLESH!

MUST CAPTURE THOSE FLYING SLEDS QUICKLY--FIND A WAY TO *REVERSE* THE *MEDUSA* PROCESS--BEFORE IT'S *TOO LATE!*

A PAIR OF WELL-PLACED *WHIRLWINDS* SHOULD... *HUH?*

THEY'RE PASSING RIGHT *THROUGH* THE SLEDS--AS IF THEY WERE NOT EVEN *THERE!*

⑰

THAT'S 'CAUSE WE *WEREN'T* THERE, WISE GUY! THESE SHIPS ARE PROTECTED BY *IMAGE-DISTORTERS--* LITTLE DODADS THAT MAKE YA SEE US WHERE WE *AIN'T!*

BUT WE CAN SEE *YOU* PERFECT-LIKE!

UUHHNN-- ENERGY BOLTS DISRUPTING MY CIRCUITS! CAN'T *MOVE--!*

BANK

BZZAATTT

BUT THE SCARLET-CLAD FORM HAS SCARCELY HIT THE SIDEWALK WHEN ANOTHER POWERFUL FORM STREAKS IN TO TAKE ITS PLACE...

EASY, *TORNADO! I'LL* HANDLE THIS!

SUPERMAN!

I'VE HEARD OF MAKING *LARGE* WITHDRAWALS-- BUT THERE'S A *LIMIT--*

LET *GO* OF THAT *BANK,* SUPERMAN--

BANK

-- OR WOULD'JA LIKE US TO DROP *HER* INSTEAD?

YOU WOULDN'T *DARE--!*

WOULDN'T *WE?*

KATHY-- *NOOOOO!*

NO!

WHO IN--?

HANG ON TO YOUR PROPELLER-BEANIE, *TORNADO* -- THE LADY IS IN *GOOD* HANDS!

THE *ELONGATED MAN!* HAVE *YOU* BEEN TRAILING ME, TOO?

ANYTHING FOR A *PAL*, PAL! RALPH-- ONCE-AN-*OUTFIELDER*-ALWAYS-AN-*OUTFIELDER*-- DIBNY, AT YOUR SERVICE--

--AND I *DIDN'T* COME ALONE!

HAWKMAN! BUT THAT *MACE* WILL DO HIM NO GOOD! HE CANNOT ATTACK SOMETHING THAT IS *NOT* WHERE ONE SEES IT!

THOSE DEVICES AREN'T REALLY *INVISIBLE!* THEY JUST DEFLECT THEIR IMAGES AGAINST AN EMPTY SKY!

BUT WHAT IF THAT SKY WERE *NOT* EMPTY?

WHEET WHEET

Suddenly, THE AIR IS ALIVE WITH THE BEATING OF WINGS-- AS AN AVIAN ARMY RESPONDS TO *HAWKMAN'S* WHISTLED CALL...

·;WHEET!;· ·;WHEET!;· FILL THE SKY, MY BROTHERS! TURN IT BLACK AS *NIGHT!*

WITHIN INSTANTS...

I'VE "*FOULED UP*" THE AIR-SPACE SO MUCH, WE CAN MAKE OUT THE *TRUE* LOCATIONS OF THE THREE FLYERS AS OPPOSED TO THE *PROJECTED* IMAGES!

ENOUGH *EXPLANATION*, HAWKMAN! LET'S *HIT* 'EM!

19

AND WHEN THE *MAN OF STEEL* SAYS *"HIT 'EM,"* THAT'S EXACTLY WHAT HE *MEANS!...*

IT APPEARS I'VE MESSED UP THEIR *IMAGE-DISTORTERS!* THESE SKY-BUGGIES HAVE STOPPED PLAYING *"HIDE-AND-GO-SEEK"!*

MAYBE IT'S BECAUSE YOU ASKED THEM SO *SWEETLY!*

A BIT OF *GENTLE CARNAGE* LATER...

OKAY, CHUM-- YOU GUYS ARE GONNA TELL US HOW TO TURN THESE PEOPLE BACK TO *NORMAL*-- OR WE'RE GOING TO TURN *YOU* INTO *ABSTRACT ART!*

OKAY, STRETCH-SOCKS!--TAKE IT *SLOW!* WE'LL TELL *EVERYTHIN'!*

ALL YOU GOTTA DO TO *REVIVE* THEM FOLKS IS...

...THIS! G-GAS! THEIR UNIFORMS ARE *FILLED* WITH IT!

GREAT SCOTT!--IT'S *STRONGER* THAN ANY I'VE EVER *KNOWN* BEFORE--AFFECTING *ME* AS WELL!

WHA--? MUST *STOP* THOSE FUMES!

BUT BEFORE THE *SCARLET SWIRLER* CAN EVEN MOVE, THE NOXIOUS VAPORS HAVE DONE THEIR WORK AND...

WE'RE *BEATEN*-- UNLESS I CAN SUMMON *HELP*--

BUT THOSE THUGS HAVE TAKEN OUR *SIGNAL DEVICES!*

GOT TO REACH THE *TORNADO*--

--PRESS *HIS* SIGNAL *DEVICE*-- WHILE THERE'S STILL TIME!

ANXIOUS EYES WATCH AS A BLACK-GLOVED HAND PRESSES A SILVER BELT PIECE AND...

EEEAAARRGGHHHH

I'VE DONE IT--*DONE IT!* THE *JUSTICE LEAGUE OF AMERICA* IS DEAD-- BY ITS OWN HAND!

I DIDN'T IMAGINE MY GAS WOULD AFFECT THE *RED TORNADO!* WANTED HIM *CONSCIOUS* TO PRESS HIS SIGNAL--BUT THAT DOESN'T MATTER *NOW!*

EXACTLY *TWO* HOURS BEFORE THE DEADLINE TIME --AND THE JLA HAS CEASED TO *EXIST!* I'M *SAFE!*

I'VE BEEN COOPED UP IN THIS LAB FOR ALMOST A *MONTH!* TIME I WENT TO GET SOME *FRESH AIR*-- AND *CELEBRATE!*

GOING SOMEWHERE, T.O. MORROW?

NO! IT CAN'T BE!

YOU'RE *DEAD*-- YOU'RE *ALL DEAD!!*

A GROSS *EXAGGERATION,* MORROW! *NONE* OF US IS *DEAD!* WE JUST WANTED TO MAKE YOU *THINK* SO!

RIGHT! *SUPERMAN* DISCOVERED THAT *EXTRA* CIRCUIT INSIDE *R.T.* DAYS AGO-- AND BURNED IT OUT WITH HIS *SUPER-VISION!*

BUT WHAT I SAW ON MY *SCREEN*--?!

JUST A LITTLE *SHOW* PUT ON FOR YOUR BENEFIT--WITH THE HELP OF MY *POWER RING!*

WE WANTED TO MAKE SURE YOU HAD NO *OTHER* HOLD ON THE *TORNADO* THAT WE *DIDN'T* KNOW ABOUT!

21

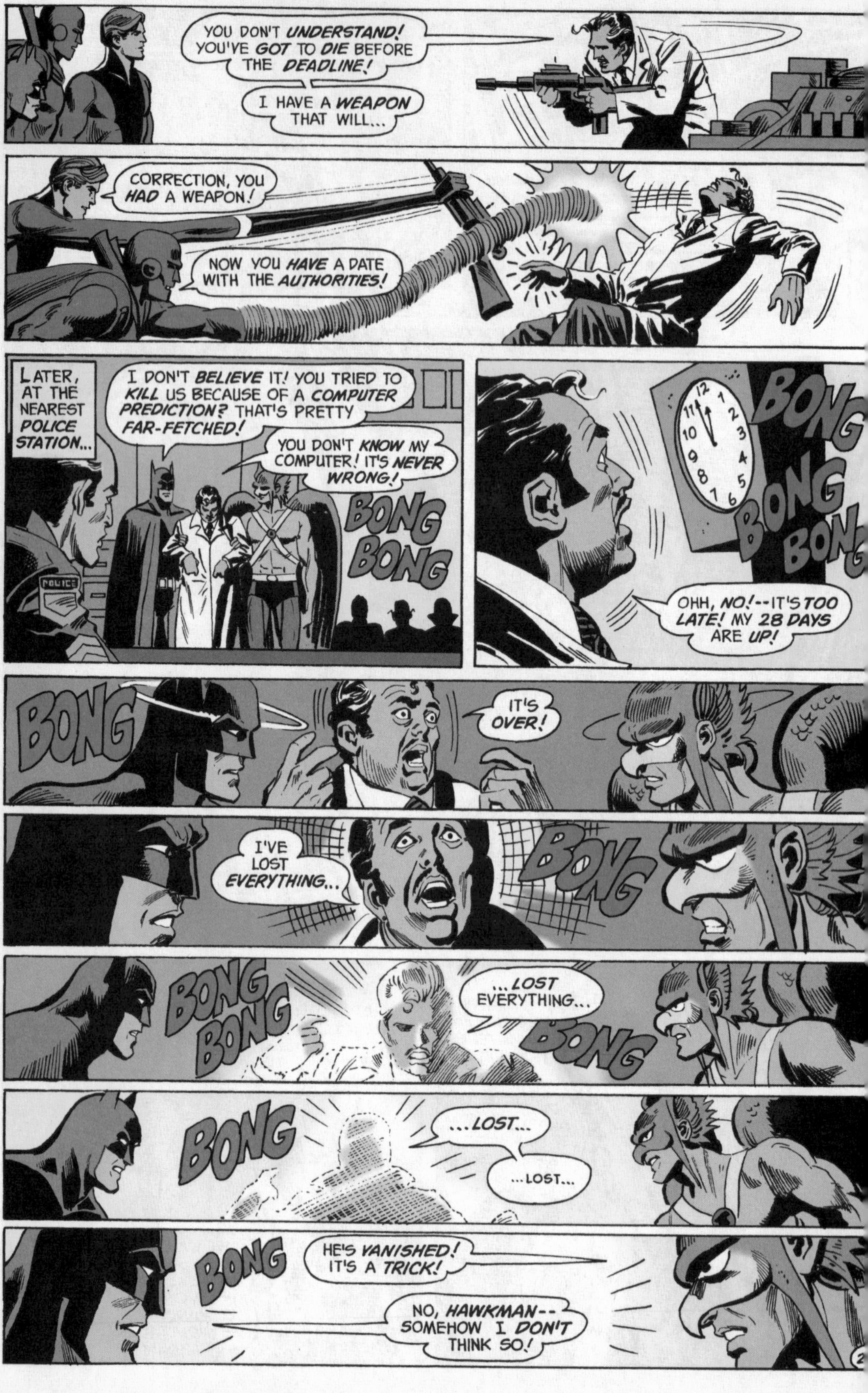

YOU DON'T UNDERSTAND! YOU'VE GOT TO DIE BEFORE THE DEADLINE!
I HAVE A WEAPON THAT WILL...
CORRECTION, YOU HAD A WEAPON!
NOW YOU HAVE A DATE WITH THE AUTHORITIES!
LATER, AT THE NEAREST POLICE STATION...
I DON'T BELIEVE IT! YOU TRIED TO KILL US BECAUSE OF A COMPUTER PREDICTION? THAT'S PRETTY FAR-FETCHED!
YOU DON'T KNOW MY COMPUTER! IT'S NEVER WRONG!
POLICE
BONG
BONG
BONG
BONG
BONG
OHH, NO!--IT'S TOO LATE! MY 28 DAYS ARE UP!
BONG
IT'S OVER!
I'VE LOST EVERYTHING...
BONG
BONG
BONG
...LOST EVERYTHING...
BONG
BONG
...LOST...
...LOST...
BONG
HE'S VANISHED! IT'S A TRICK!
NO, HAWKMAN--SOMEHOW I DON'T THINK SO!

SORRY IF WE SEEMED TO *USE* YOU, TORNADO-- BUT WE HAD *NO* IDEA HOW MUCH *CONTROL* MORROW HAD OVER YOU!

AN *UNDERSTANDABLE* REACTION, *BATMAN*-- WHEN THE PERSON YOU ARE DEALING WITH IS A--*MACHINE!*

BUT YOU'RE *NOT* A MACHINE, *TORNADO*-- JUST A BIT MORE *VULNERABLE* TO CERTAIN THINGS THAN *MOST* PEOPLE ARE!

MY OWN THOUGHTS EXACTLY, *GREEN LANTERN!* NOW-- IF YOU FELLOWS WILL *EXCUSE* ME--?

RED TORNADO, WHERE ARE YOU *GOING?* IS IT SOMETHING WE *SAID?*

IN A WAY, RALPH DIBNY... *IN A WAY!*

I'M GOING TO DISCOVER IF AN ANDROID IS *VUNERABLE* TO-- *LOVE!*

THE END

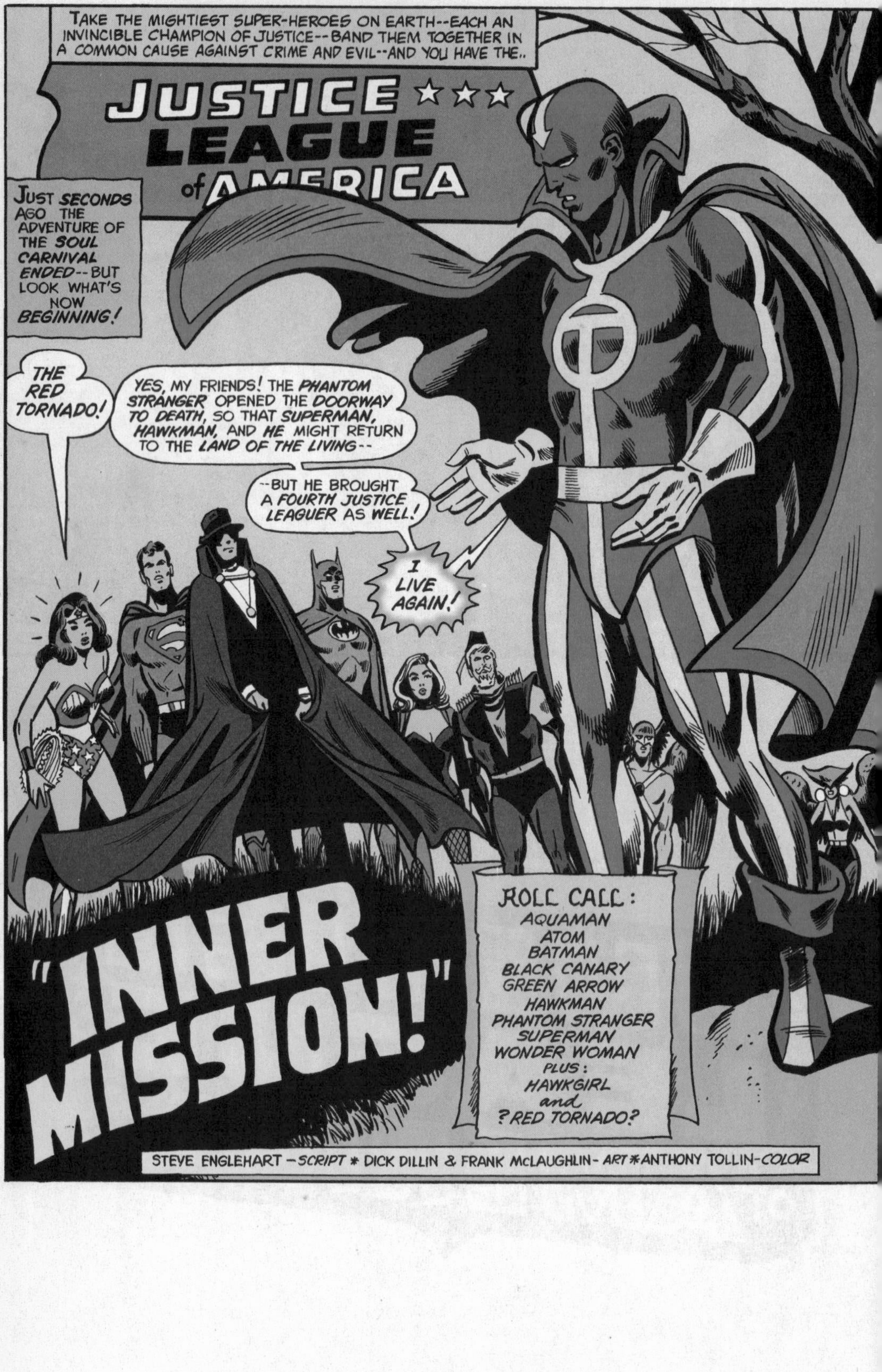

TAKE THE MIGHTIEST SUPER-HEROES ON EARTH--EACH AN INVINCIBLE CHAMPION OF JUSTICE--BAND THEM TOGETHER IN A COMMON CAUSE AGAINST CRIME AND EVIL--AND YOU HAVE THE..
JUSTICE LEAGUE of AMERICA
JUST SECONDS AGO THE ADVENTURE OF THE SOUL CARNIVAL ENDED--BUT LOOK WHAT'S NOW BEGINNING!
THE RED TORNADO!
YES, MY FRIENDS! THE PHANTOM STRANGER OPENED THE DOORWAY TO DEATH, SO THAT SUPERMAN, HAWKMAN, AND HE MIGHT RETURN TO THE LAND OF THE LIVING--
--BUT HE BROUGHT A FOURTH JUSTICE LEAGUER AS WELL!
I LIVE AGAIN!
"INNER MISSION!"
ROLL CALL: AQUAMAN ATOM BATMAN BLACK CANARY GREEN ARROW HAWKMAN PHANTOM STRANGER SUPERMAN WONDER WOMAN PLUS: HAWKGIRL and ?RED TORNADO?
STEVE ENGLEHART–SCRIPT * DICK DILLIN & FRANK McLAUGHLIN-ART * ANTHONY TOLLIN-COLOR

REDDY! WE THOUGHT YOU WERE GONE FOREVER!

THIS HAS BEEN A NIGHT OF MIRACLES! THE JUSTICE LEAGUE CAN OVERCOME ANYTHING!

WELCOME BACK, RED TOMATO!

WHEN WE SAW YOU BLOWN TO BITS, WHILE FIGHTING NEKRON--!

I KNOW, BATMAN... BUT I WONDER IF IT IS TRULY POSSIBLE TO COMPLETELY DESTROY AN ANDROID SUCH AS MYSELF! BOTH MIND AND BODY HAVE BEEN RE-FORMED!

I HAVE "DIED" AND "RETURNED" ONCE BEFORE, YOU REMEMBER!

YES, I DO REMEMBER! AND, NOT TO BE UNKIND, REDDY...

...I REMEMBER YOU WERE RETURNED AS PART OF A SCHEME BY YOUR CREATOR, T.O. MORROW--TO DESTROY US!

I ALSO REMEMBER AZGORE, THE DEMON OF DEATH, TELLING ME THAT NO ONE CAN HOLD HIS SOUL TO-GETHER ON THE "OTHER SIDE" FOR VERY LONG--

--CERTAINLY NOT THE MONTHS THAT YOU'VE BEEN MISSING!

SUPERMAN--!

WAIT, CANARY! HE MAY HAVE SOMETHING THERE!

I DO NOT KNOW HOW TO ANSWER YOU, SUPERMAN! MY MEMORY-CIRCUITS ARE UNCLEAR ON THE SUBJECT--

EXCUSE ME! THOSE ARE THE VERY WORDS I USED WHEN RELATING MY FALSE STORY THE LAST TIME I RETURNED! BUT I SWEAR I AM SPEAKING THE TRUTH NOW!

I WILL SUBMIT TO *ANY TESTS YOU DESIRE*, TO *PROVE* MYSELF! I WISH, MORE THAN *ANYTHING*, TO ABIDE ONCE MORE WITH *YOU*-- MY *FRIENDS*!

THAT SOUNDS FAIR TO *ME*!

WHAT ARE YOU *DOING*, SUPERMAN?

JUST FOLLOWING UP MY *FIRST THOUGHT*, HAWKMAN--BUT MY *TELESCOPIC VISION* SHOWS *NO SIGN* OF *T.O. MORROW* ANYWHERE ON EARTH!

OF COURSE, HE *COULD* BE *BEHIND LEAD*--OR WORKING THROUGH A *PARALLEL DIMENSION*--

--OR HE *COULD* HAVE *NOTHING TO DO* WITH THIS MIRACLE AT *ALL*! HE *COULD* BE *REALLY DEAD*!

AS *ONE MAN* WHO CAME BACK FROM THE *DEAD* TO *ANOTHER*, SUPERMAN, WE SHOULD BE THE *LAST* TO DOUBT THE *RED TORNADO'S* STORY!

I'M ONLY TRYING TO *PROTECT* THE *LEAGUE*--

WHAT DO *YOU* SAY, *STRANGER*? YOU'RE THE *EXPERT* ON THESE MATTERS!

BUT THE *PHANTOM STRANGER* SAYS *NOTHING*--NOT UNLIKE THE *USUAL HABIT* OF THE MAN WHO *QUESTIONED* HIM! INSTEAD, HE STEPS *FORWARD*--

--AND GAZES FROM THE SHADOWS OF HIS *HIDDEN EYES* INTO THE SHADOWS OF THE *ANDROID'S SLITS*!

THEN--

I CAN REACH *NO CONCLUSION*, BATMAN! MY REALM IS THAT OF *SORCERY* AND THE *SUPER-NATURAL*-- NOT *SCIENCE*!

I CANNOT MAKE THE *CONTACT* I WOULD LIKE WITH THE *RED TORNADO'S* MIND! ITS *COMPUTERIZED CIRCUITS* ELUDE MY *GRASP*!

OH, GREAT!

3

I *UNDERSTAND!* YOU *DARE NOT* ACCEPT ME ON *FAITH*-- NOR SHOULD I *ASK* YOU TO, AFTER MY *PREVIOUS BETRAYAL!*

I SHOULD HAVE *KNOWN* THAT...BUT WHEN I FOUND MYSELF IN *FRONT* OF YOU AGAIN, AFTER *SO LONG...*

BUT YOU ARE *RIGHT!* I WILL *GO!*

WAIT--!

YES--?

LET'S NOT LEAVE THIS *UNSETTLED!* I WANT TO ASK YOU SOME *QUESTIONS*--

--QUESTIONS ONLY THE *REAL RED TORNADO* WOULD BE ABLE TO *ANSWER!*

OF *COURSE!* ANYTHING YOU *SAY!*

THEN *TELL* ME--WHO WAS THE *ORIGINAL RED TORNADO?*

SHE WAS *MA HUNKLE*-- A WOMAN WITH *DELUSIONS OF GRANDEUR* WHO TRIED TO JOIN THE *JUSTICE SOCIETY!*

CORRECT! AND WHERE HAVE YOU MET *HAWKGIRL* BEFORE?

I MET HER IN *MIDWAY CITY*-- WHEN *HAWKMAN* WAS TURNED TO *SALT!*

CORRECT! AND WHAT IS THE *SECRET ORIGIN* OF THE *JLA?*

THE *MARTIAN MANHUNTER* WAS *UNDER ATTACK* AND YOU MISTOOK THAT FOR AN *ALIEN INVASION!*

4

SUPERMAN! WHY-- WHY ARE YOU *LOOKING* AT ME LIKE THAT? IS THAT NOT *CORRECT*?

QUITE CORRECT!

--EXCEPT THAT THE *REAL RED TORNADO* NEVER *KNEW* IT! THAT "ORIGIN" STORY HAS BEEN *KEPT SECRET* FROM ALL *LATER* MEMBERS!

THOUGH HIS FORM *APPEARS HUMAN,* IT CAN CHANGE AT *ANY INSTANT* INTO A *RAGING WHIRLWIND!*

YOU ARE *VERY CLEVER!* I WAS *CERTAIN* I COULD PLAY MY PART TO *PERFECTION*--

--AND, AT THE VERY *LEAST,* THAT MY RUSE WOULD APPEAL TO YOUR *SICKENING SENTIMENTALITY!*

HEY, THAT'S NOT *REDDY'S* VOICE!

SOMEBODY ELSE IS USING HIS *BODY!*

MEANING-- *YOU ARE A FRAUD!*

BUT THE ENIGMATIC ANDROID IS *QUICKER* THAN HIS HANG-DOG DEMEANOR HAS LED *SUPERMAN* TO *SUSPECT!*

GREAT MOONS OF KRYPTON! HE'S WHIPPING UP A *REAL TORNADO!*

HARD, EVEN FOR *ME* TO GET *AT* HIM--!

THE LIGHT *DAWNS,* EH? BUT I'LL *DESTROY* YOU *YET!*

5

NOT IF YOU COME IN FROM *ABOVE THE STORM!*

THIS ISN'T *"THE EXORCIST"*! HIS *HEAD* DOESN'T SPIN!

BUT THE *REST OF HIM DOES*-- FASTER AND FASTER-- TILL *TALL TREES TOPPLE* AND THE VERY *SKY* SEEMS *TORN ASUNDER!*

HOLD ON, HONEY! HOLD ON!

THEN, FINALLY--

DEUS EX MACHINA! THIS CURSED *ANDROID BODY* CAN NO LONGER STAND THE *STRAIN!*

IT WILL *DISINTEGRATE* IF I CONTINUE!

BUT *HEAR* ME, YOU TWO--

--AND ALL THE *REST OF YOU!* THE *BODY* MAY FAIL ME, BUT *THE SPIRIT* CAN *NEVER BE DESTROYED!*

MY *MIND*, AND MY *HATRED*, WILL LIVE *FOREVER!*

NONE OF *YOU* WILL LIVE OUT THE *DAY!*

6

HE'S GONE *LIMP!* IT IS A *TRICK!*

I DO NOT *THINK* SO, KATAR! I HAVE BEEN A POLICEWOMAN *TOO LONG* TO MISTAKE *TRUE DEATH!*

THIS FORM IS NO LONGER *OCCUPIED!*

POOR *REDDY!* HE CAN'T EVEN *REST IN PEACE!*

YOU WERE *RIGHT, SUPERMAN!* HE *COULDN'T* HAVE COME BACK TO LIFE--BUT WE WANTED TO *BELIEVE* HE COULD!

FIRST, I GET IN TROUBLE BY BEIN' *TOO HOT-HEADED--*

--AND *NOW* WHEN I TRY TO *COOL* IT, I GET SUCKERED BY MY *BLEEDING HEART!*

YOU CAN'T *WIN!*

OH, *YES,* WE *CAN!* WE *HAVE* TO--AND *THIS TIME,* WE HAVE TO WIN *ONCE AND FOR ALL!*

YOU KNOW WHO THAT *WAS,* CONTROLLING *REDDY'S* BODY... *RIGHT?*

THE *CONSTRUCT!*

WHO IS *THE CONSTRUCT?*

ALL WE KNOW IS WHAT *AQUAMAN, ATOM,* AND THE *ELONGATED MAN* TOLD US AFTER *MEETING* HIM, AND EVEN *THEY* DIDN'T GET THE *FULL STORY!*

APPARENTLY, IT'S A *MIND* THAT LIVES IN *MACHINES!*

WONDER WOMAN--? WHAT IS THE MATTER?

I--DON'T *KNOW!* A SUDDEN *NAUSEA*--WHEN THE CONSTRUCT WAS MENTIONED--

I *WONDER*--! IF *THE CONSTRUCT* COULD USE *REDDY'S* BODY AS AN *AUTOMATON*--

--WELL, *SOMEONE* USED *ME* THE *SAME WAY* WHEN I TURNED AGAINST THE *JLA!* WE HAD *NO CLUES* THAT HE WAS BEHIND THAT--

THIS IS *TOTAL WAR,* THEN-- AND WE'LL NEED *EVERYONE* TO *WIN* IT!

I'D LIKE TO *PROPOSE* THAT WE GRANT HAWKGIRL FULL *OFFICIAL STATUS* FOR IT, AND ENROLL *HER* IN THE LEAGUE!

WHAT DO YOU *MEAN,* KATAR? YOU KNOW OUR RULE AGAINST *DUPLICATING POWERS!*

WHA--? WHAT DO *YOU* MEAN, *SUPERMAN?* SHE SAVED US FROM *COUNT CRYSTAL*-- SAVED US *AGAIN* JUST *NOW*--!

I KNOW THAT! WE'VE *ALWAYS* WELCOMED HER *HELP!* BUT THE JLA IS *ALREADY* CLOSE TO BEING AN *ARMY!*

WE *HAVE* TO HAVE SOME *LIMITS!* I'M *SORRY!*

AND I AM SORRY, *TOO*-- BUT I STAND WITH MY *WIFE!*

THE JLA CAN HAVE *BOTH* OF US-- OR *NEITHER!*

DON'T THREATEN ME, KATAR! I WANT THE *LEAGUE* TO REMAIN *INTACT,* BUT *NOT THAT WAY!*

WHY NOT *DEFER* THE PROBLEM FOR SOME *HAPPIER MOMENT?* IT CAN BE SETTLED AFTER THE *DANGER* IS SETTLED!

DID YOU *SAY* SOMETHING... *STRANGER?*

I *AM* A MEMBER OF THE *JUSTICE LEAGUE,* AM I *NOT?*

I PROPOSE THAT *HALF* OF YOU SEEK THOSE WHO HAVE *ENCOUNTERED* THE *CONSTRUCT,* AND THE *OTHER HALF* FOLLOW *WONDER WOMAN'S* LEAD!

8

THAT'S THE *FIRST TIME* YOU'VE *EVER* TAKEN PART IN A *MEETING*, PHANTOM STRANGER--BUT IT'S A *GOOD BEGINNING!*

I'LL TAKE *BOTH* OF THE *HAWKS* WITH ME!

ALL RIGHT! I CHOOSE OLLIE AND DINAH!

SORRY, SUPERMAN! OLLIE AND I DON'T ALWAYS COME AS *BOOKENDS!*

I'M GOING WITH *SHIERA* AND *DIANA!*

I'LL GO WITH YOU, SUPERMAN!

WHAT ABOUT *YOU*, STRANGER--?

AS I SAID BEFORE, MY REALM IS THAT OF *SORCERY* AND THE *SUPERNATURAL*--NOT *SCIENCE!* I CAN BE OF *NO FURTHER USE* TO YOU IN THIS!

UNTIL WE MEET AGAIN-- *FAREWELL!*

LET'S GET *MOVING!* WE CAN GIVE *REDDY* A *PROPER BURIAL* LATER!

GOODBYE, RED TORNADO! REST IN PEACE *THIS TIME*--WHEREVER YOU ARE!

AND SO, WITH SCARCELY A *PAUSE* FROM THEIR *CLASH* WITH *COUNT CRYSTAL,* THE *JUSTICE LEAGUE* LEAVES THE *VALLEY OF THE SHADOW* FOR *NEW DANGERS!*

EACH ONE CASTS A *FINAL GLANCE* AT THE LIFELESS REMAINS OF THEIR *FALLEN COMRADE,* AND THEN TURNS *RESOLUTELY* TOWARD THE *FUTURE!*

DID WE SAY... *LIFELESS?!?*

9

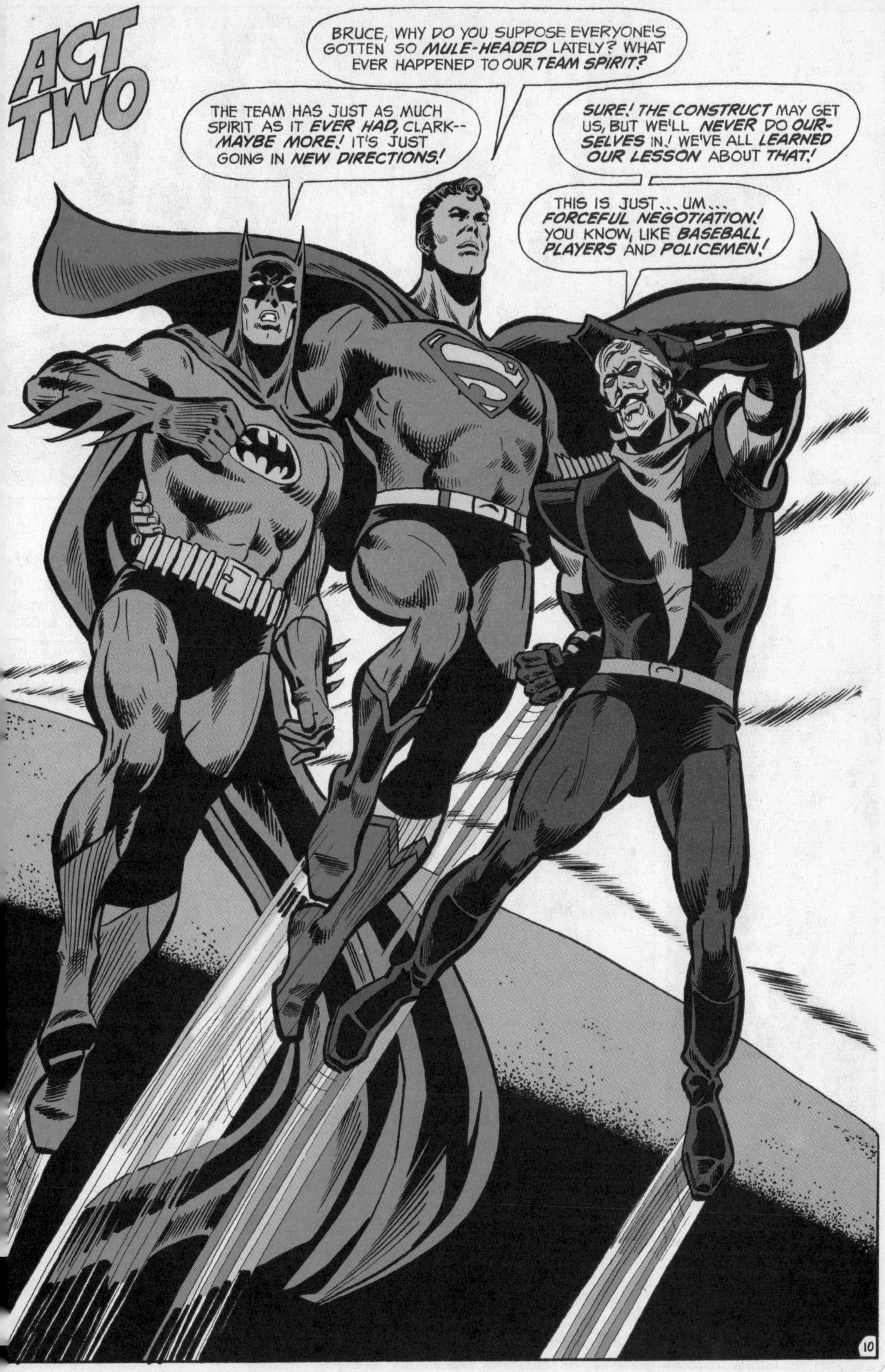
ACT TWO
BRUCE, WHY DO YOU SUPPOSE EVERYONE'S GOTTEN SO MULE-HEADED LATELY? WHAT EVER HAPPENED TO OUR TEAM SPIRIT?
THE TEAM HAS JUST AS MUCH SPIRIT AS IT EVER HAD, CLARK-- MAYBE MORE! IT'S JUST GOING IN NEW DIRECTIONS!
SURE! THE CONSTRUCT MAY GET US, BUT WE'LL NEVER DO OURSELVES IN! WE'VE ALL LEARNED OUR LESSON ABOUT THAT!
THIS IS JUST... UM... FORCEFUL NEGOTIATION! YOU KNOW, LIKE BASEBALL PLAYERS AND POLICEMEN!
10

I HOPE IT'S NOT *TOO LONG* BEFORE WE CAN DO A LITTLE "*NEGOTIATING*" WITH *THE CONSTRUCT!* I KEEP THINKING HOW HE... *USED* POOR OLD *REDDY!*

WHEN ARE WE GONNA GET TO *AQUAMAN* AND *ATOM?*

RIGHT NOW!

HEY! EASY, PAL--!

BUT THE *MAN OF STEEL* WHIRLS HIS *CAPE* AROUND HIS FRIENDS' HEADS IN THE *WINK OF AN EYE,* TRAPPING *AIR* INSIDE WITH THEM--

--AND BEFORE THEY'VE *BREATHED TWICE,* THEY'RE PRESENTED WITH *SYNTHETIC AIR* FROM THE *LAND OF LEGEND--ATLANTIS!*

WELCOME!

WELCOME, MY FRIENDS!

HI, GUYS!

ATOM! WHAT ARE YOU DOING INSIDE THAT *BUBBLE?*

THIS IS MY *UNDERSEA SHIP--* DESIGNED *ESPECIALLY* FOR ME BY THE *BEST MINDS* HERE!

THERE'S NO SENSE WORKING UP A *MASK* FOR ME, WHEN I CAN GET *COMPLETE TRANSPORTATION* IN A *SMALLER PACKAGE!*

HUNH!-- DIG THE *SCIENTIST!*

WHAT BRINGS YOU DOWN TO SEE US, LEAGUERS?

WELL, I KNEW RAY HAD BEEN *VISITING* YOU SINCE YOUR RUN-IN WITH *THE CONSTRUCT*-- AND THE CONSTRUCT IS BACK AGAIN!

WHAT?! IMPOSSIBLE!

I DESTROYED HIM *MYSELF*!

OR-- *DID* I?

PERHAPS *ANOTHER* MECHANICAL CONSCIOUSNESS MAY ONE DAY EXIST, BUT IT WILL NOT KNOW OF *WILLOW* AND HER *ISLAND*!

IF *CONSTRUCT'S* BACK, BOYS, HE'S *NOT* THE SAME ONE I FOUGHT! IT'S *ANOTHER* ONE, VERY *SIMILAR*!

HE'LL ONLY KNOW WHAT HE'S LEARNED IN *THIS* "LIFETIME"!

BUT *EMOTIONS* ARE AS ETERNAL AS THE *SEAS*, RAY! I *TALKED* WITH THE *ORIGINAL*-- HE WAS *ALREADY DRUNK WITH POWER* AND *QUITE MAD*!

HE'LL BE--LIKE A *NEW PROGRAM* ON THE *SAME OLD WAVELENGTH*! HE WON'T *REMEMBER* FIGHTING US BEFORE--BUT--

--HE'LL *HATE* US *JUST THE SAME*!

THAT'S WHAT WE WANT TO *TALK* TO YOU ABOUT, *AQUAMAN*! WE NEED *INFORMATION*!

ALL RIGHT! I'LL HELP ANY WAY I *CAN*! WE'RE READY---

HOLD IT A MINUTE!

LET ME SLIP OUT OF THIS *HOTROD* BEFORE WE SAY ANYTHING *MORE*!

CONSTRUCT CAN LIVE IN *ANY MACHINE*, YOU KNOW! LET'S GO SOMEWHERE *ELSE*!

ARE YOU *SERIOUS*?

LET'S *GO*, OLLIE!

I CAN BREATHE INSIDE OLLIE'S HELMET-- GET INSIDE BY MAKING MYSELF SMALL ENOUGH TO PASS BETWEEN ITS MOLECULES!

DEUS EX MACHINA! THAT *LITTLE ONE* IS *CLEVER*!

12

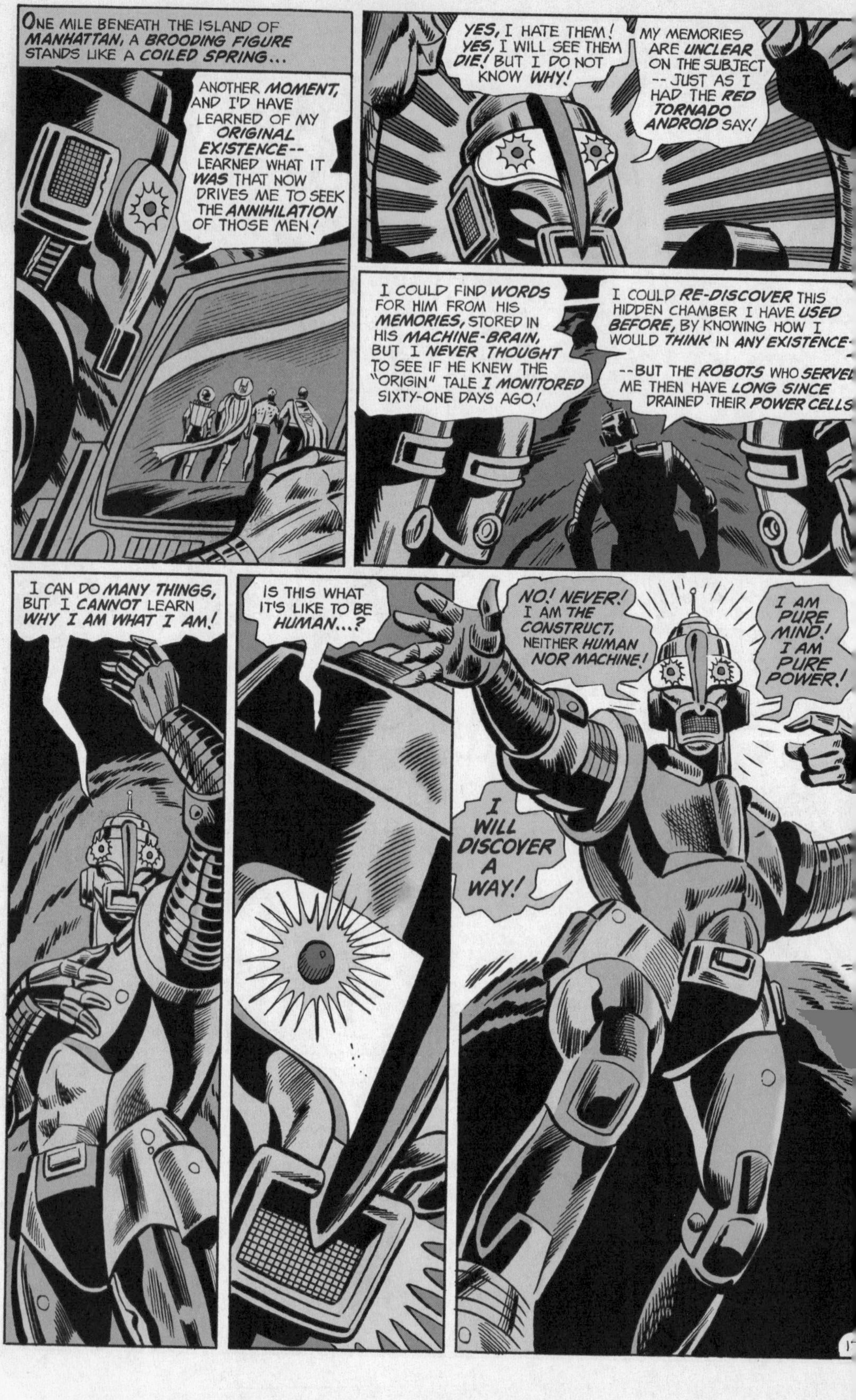

ONE MILE BENEATH THE ISLAND OF MANHATTAN, A BROODING FIGURE STANDS LIKE A COILED SPRING...
ANOTHER MOMENT, AND I'D HAVE LEARNED OF MY ORIGINAL EXISTENCE-- LEARNED WHAT IT WAS THAT NOW DRIVES ME TO SEEK THE ANNIHILATION OF THOSE MEN!
YES, I HATE THEM! YES, I WILL SEE THEM DIE! BUT I DO NOT KNOW WHY!
MY MEMORIES ARE UNCLEAR ON THE SUBJECT -- JUST AS I HAD THE RED TORNADO ANDROID SAY!
I COULD FIND WORDS FOR HIM FROM HIS MEMORIES, STORED IN HIS MACHINE-BRAIN, BUT I NEVER THOUGHT TO SEE IF HE KNEW THE "ORIGIN" TALE I MONITORED SIXTY-ONE DAYS AGO!
I COULD RE-DISCOVER THIS HIDDEN CHAMBER I HAVE USED BEFORE, BY KNOWING HOW I WOULD THINK IN ANY EXISTENCE-
--BUT THE ROBOTS WHO SERVED ME THEN HAVE LONG SINCE DRAINED THEIR POWER CELLS
I CAN DO MANY THINGS, BUT I CANNOT LEARN WHY I AM WHAT I AM!
IS THIS WHAT IT'S LIKE TO BE HUMAN...?
NO! NEVER! I AM THE CONSTRUCT, NEITHER HUMAN NOR MACHINE!
I AM PURE MIND! I AM PURE POWER!
I WILL DISCOVER A WAY!

BUT FOR *NOW*, THE *ATLANTEAN WAR CHAMBER* WHEREIN THE JLA'S COUNCIL IS CONVENED REMAINS *INSCRUTABLE*!

NO MACHINE -- NO *COMPUTER*, *HEATER*, OR *LAMP* -- HAS BEEN LEFT "*LIVE*"!

AT *LENGTH*, HOWEVER--

I CAN STAND IT *NO LONGER*! I WILL *NEVER* LEARN WHAT I WANT FROM *THEM*!

FAL OOMP

THEN... THEY MUST NOT LIVE TO OPPOSE ME!

14

FA-LAMM

GREAT FATHER NEPTUNE! OUR MOST POTENT DEFENSE WEAPON, AT POINT-BLANK RANGE!

WE'LL BE ALL RIGHT, AQUAMAN! GET IT!

FLUID GRACE AND RIPPLING POWER: CROWNED OR NOT, THIS IS THE KING OF THE SEAS!

FA-LAM

FALAM

15

WE'RE BRINGING *DANGER* TO *ATLANTIS!* WE MUST *LEAVE!*

I KNOW JUST WHERE TO GO!

YOU *DO--?*

YOU *BET!* WHILE YOU *BIG GUYS* WERE *FLEXING YOUR MUSCLES,* I WAS HOLDING MY BREATH AND TAKING A CHANCE ON THE *WAR-COMPUTER* IN THERE!

NOTHING *ZAPPED* ME, SINCE HE WAS BUSY WITH *YOU* -- SO I WAS ABLE TO *TRIANGULATE* HIS *BROADCASTING BEAM!*

I MAKE HIM IN *MANHATTAN!*

WE'RE ON OUR WAY!

WHILE BACK IN *VERMONT...*

16

AND WHILE YOU PONDER *THAT* ONE, WE'LL SKIP BACK OUT TO *SEA*...

PARADISE ISLAND!

THIS IS WHERE WE'LL FIND OUR *ANSWERS!*

CAREFUL, *KATAR!* NO MAN MUST EVER *SET FOOT* ON OUR *SACRED GROUND!*

DO NOT *WORRY*, DIANA.! I *KNOW* YOUR *AMAZON RULES!*

HOLA, MOTHER!

DIANA!

KATAR, I MUST *SPEAK* WITH YOU-- OVER *HERE!*

KATAR, PERHAPS YOU SHOULD NOT HAVE *MENTIONED* MY *MEMBERSHIP!*

I, *TOO*, FEEL THE *JUSTICE LEAGUE'S* RULE TO BE *UNFAIR*, BUT I HAVE NO WISH TO *DIVIDE THEM* OVER IT!

NONSENSE, MY DARLING! YOU ARE *TOO GENEROUS* WITH THESE *PEOPLE!*

TRADITIONS GROW THROUGH *INERTIA*-- NOT *PROGRESS!* THE TRADITION AGAINST *DUPLICATING POWERS* EXISTS BECAUSE NO ONE HAS EVER *CHALLENGED* IT!

WE ARE *ALIENS* HERE, SHAYERA! IN THE *FINAL ANALYSIS*, DESPITE MY *JLA FRIENDSHIPS*, YOU ARE MY *ONE TRUE COMPANION* IN LIFE--AS I AM *YOURS!*

I SHALL CHALLENGE *ANYTHING* THAT SERVES TO COME *BETWEEN US!*

17

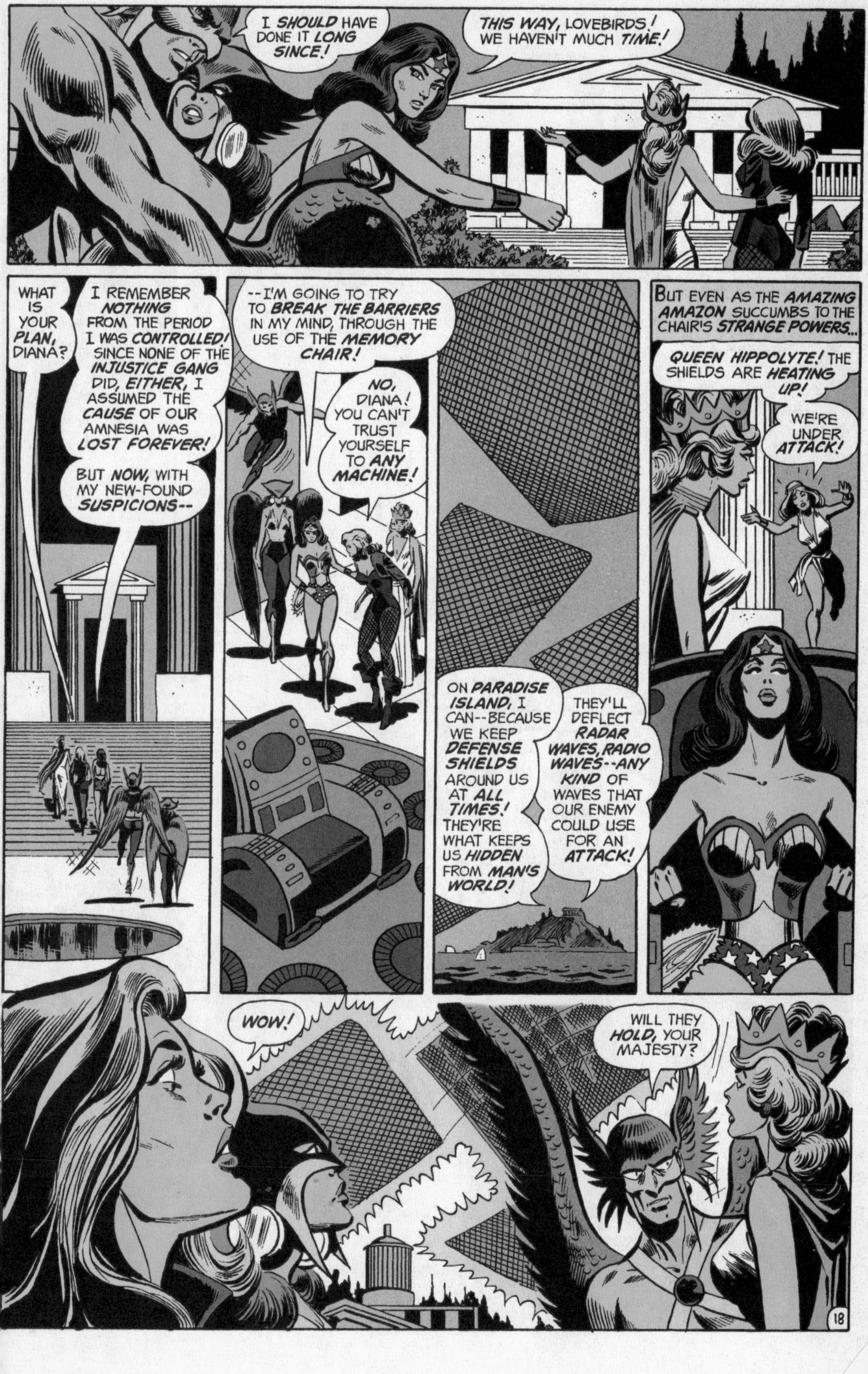
I SHOULD HAVE DONE IT LONG SINCE!
THIS WAY, LOVEBIRDS! WE HAVEN'T MUCH TIME!
WHAT IS YOUR PLAN, DIANA?
I REMEMBER NOTHING FROM THE PERIOD I WAS CONTROLLED! SINCE NONE OF THE INJUSTICE GANG DID, EITHER, I ASSUMED THE CAUSE OF OUR AMNESIA WAS LOST FOREVER!
BUT NOW, WITH MY NEW-FOUND SUSPICIONS--
--I'M GOING TO TRY TO BREAK THE BARRIERS IN MY MIND, THROUGH THE USE OF THE MEMORY CHAIR!
NO, DIANA! YOU CAN'T TRUST YOURSELF TO ANY MACHINE!
ON PARADISE ISLAND, I CAN--BECAUSE WE KEEP DEFENSE SHIELDS AROUND US AT ALL TIMES! THEY'RE WHAT KEEPS US HIDDEN FROM MAN'S WORLD!
THEY'LL DEFLECT RADAR WAVES, RADIO WAVES--ANY KIND OF WAVES THAT OUR ENEMY COULD USE FOR AN ATTACK!
BUT EVEN AS THE AMAZING AMAZON SUCCUMBS TO THE CHAIR'S STRANGE POWERS...
QUEEN HIPPOLYTE! THE SHIELDS ARE HEATING UP!
WE'RE UNDER ATTACK!
WOW!
WILL THEY HOLD, YOUR MAJESTY?
18

THEY WILL HOLD, *HAWKMAN!* THEY *MUST!*

WHILE IN VERMONT...

THUD

BUT *NOW,* A PALE AND SHAKEN *WONDER WOMAN* HAS RISEN FROM HER *TRANCE...*

HERA HELP ME LAY MY *HANDS* ON HIM, JUST *ONCE!* GREAT *APHRODITE,* LET IT BE *SO!*

DIANA! WHAT *IS* IT?

I *REMEMBER* THE *CONSTRUCT,* MOTHER! I REMEMBER--THE *DOMINATION!*

YET *MORE* THAN THAT, I REMEMBER THE *UNSPEAKABLY INHUMAN MIND ITSELF,* AS IT CRAWLED THROUGH MY *BRAIN!*

I KNOW HOW IT *THINKS*-- AT LEAST, IN *SOME* WAYS!

19

MY CAPTOR WAS *CONSTRUCT II,* THE *SECOND* IN AN APPARENT *SERIES* OF *MIND-MONSTERS* BORN FROM THE SPECTRUM OF WAVES IN THE *ETHER!*

IT INHABITED THE *INJUSTICE GANG SATELLITE* UNTIL FATE *DESTROYED* IT! THE ONE WHO USED *RED TORNADO'S* BODY MUST BE *CONSTRUCT III!*

THEN EVEN IF WE DEFEAT *HIM,* THERE'LL BE *MORE?*

NO, DINAH! BECAUSE EVEN THOUGH EACH *NEW ONE* LACKS THE *PREVIOUS ONES'* MEMORIES, THEIR MINDS THINK *EXACTLY ALIKE!*

KNOWING *ONE,* I KNOW THEM *ALL*-- AND I KNOW HOW TO *FIND* THEM! MORE-OVER, I KNOW HOW TO *DESTROY* THEM FOREVER!

CONSTRUCT III IS THE *LAST* OF HIS KIND!

BUT PRINCESS DIANA MIGHT NOT BE SO *CERTAIN,* IF SHE COULD SEE THE TWISTED FIGURE WHIRLING SLOWLY *SOUTHWARD,* OUT OF *VERMONT*--

--ON A *DIRECT COURSE* FOR--

-- MANHATTAN, NEW YORK!

ACT THREE

I CAN'T FIND A *SINGLE CLUE,* CLARK! IF *THE CONSTRUCT* IS HERE! HE'S NOT *ADVERTISING* IT!

TOO BAD THIS ISN'T *GOTHAM!* HE COULDN'T HIDE FROM ME THERE!

DON'T BE SO *SURE,* BRUCE! THIS IS NO *HUMAN* VILLAIN WE'RE DEALING WITH!

20

THE LATEST REPORTS FROM *OLLIE*, *RAY*, AND *AQUAMAN* ARE *NO BETTER!*

DON'T YOU THINK WE SHOULD *COOL IT* WITH THE *TRANSCEIVERS?*

UH-OH! LOOK *THERE!*

THE *ROBOT PLANE!* I WONDER HOW *THEY'VE* DONE!

NO--THE BOYS ARE ONLY REPORTING THEIR *FAILURES!* A *SUCCESS* THEY'LL REPORT IN *PERSONALLY*, SO THERE'S NO DANGER OF *THE CONSTRUCT CATCHING ON!*

LIKE *GHOSTS* IN THEIR *INVISIBLE* CONVEYANCE, THE RETURNING MEMBERS *SWOOP DOWN* ON A LONG, FLAT *ROOF-TOP*, AND IMMEDIATELY *LEAP FREE!*

YOU HAVEN'T *FOUND* HIM YET, HAVE YOU?

NO, KATAR-- YOU'RE IN *LUCK!*

BUT HE *IS* IN *NEW YORK!* WE HEARD YOUR *SCOUTING REPORTS!*

THAT BEING *SO,* I CAN FIGURE *JUST* WHERE HE'D CHOOSE TO *HIDE!*

YOU *CAN?* HOW--?

I'LL FILL YOU IN AS WE GO, BRUCE--

--TO THE WORLD'S MOST EXTENSIVE COMPUTER COMPLEX, IN THE *BASEMENT* OF THE *WORLD TRADE CENTER!*

FIVE YEARS AGO, THESE *MAMMOTH MONOLITHS* WERE BUT AN *ARCHITECT'S DREAM!* TODAY, THEY MARK THE *HEART* OF *WORLD COMMERCE!*

ALL RIGHT, DIANA-- I'VE ROUNDED UP THE *OTHERS* TO *HELP* US!

BUT *HEAVEN* HELP US IF WE BARGE IN THERE AND YOU'RE *WRONG!*

I'M *NOT* WRONG! I *KNOW* HOW *CONSTRUCT* THINKS!

21

YES... WE'VE HAD *SOME* TROUBLE WITH OUR COMPUTERS LATELY! THEY PRINT *GIBBERISH* AT TIMES, FOR NO REASON WE CAN *DETERMINE!*

BUT WE COULD *NEVER* ALLOW YOU TO TAKE THEM *APART,* LOOKING FOR SOME--SOME *MONSTER!*

NO NEED FOR *THAT,* SIR--UNLESS YOU KNOW WHERE THESE *AUXILIARY CABLES* SPLICED *INTO* YOUR *LINES* LEAD TO!

WHY, *NO!* THOSE SHOULDN'T *BE* THERE!

THEN WHAT WE'RE *LOOKING* FOR IS *BEHIND* THAT WALL-- AND UNLESS I MISS BOTH MY *GUESS* AND MY *MARK*--

CREEK

--WE'VE *FOUND* IT! THE *GIZMO* I PUT IN THE ARROW'S HEAD HOMED IN ON THE DOOR'S OPENING CONTROL!

ATOM! LOOK! THE *CONSTRUCT'S* CANNONS!

AND *THERE*-- IN THE *DARK*--

--THE *CONSTRUCT HIMSELF!*

22

CLANG

EMPTY! THIS BODY'S AS EMPTY AS THE *RED TORNADO'S!*

NO! IT CAN'T BE!

I'M VERY MUCH AFRAID IT *CAN,* PRINCESS!

YOU WERE *RIGHT* ABOUT THIS *HIDE-OUT* --BUT WHAT'S A *HIDE-OUT* TO A CREA-TURE THAT CAN *TRANSFER HIS MIND* ANYWHERE ON EARTH?

WE'RE CHASING A *WILL-O'-THE-WISP!*

DEEP SILENCE SETTLES UPON THEM NOW, LIKE A HEAVY BLANKET OF CHILLING SNOW, AS THE BATMAN'S SEPULCHRAL SENTENCE SINKS IN!

THEY'VE USED UP ALL THEIR CLUES! THEY'VE OVERCOME SEEMINGLY IMPOSSIBLE ODDS--LEARNED SECRETS THEY WERE NEVER MEANT TO KNOW--AND STILL THEY'VE COME UP EMPTY!

NOW WHAT? WE'LL HAVE TO CONTINUE OUR SEARCHING--THOUGH WE CAN'T EVEN BE SURE HE'S IN NEW YORK ANY LONGER!

LET'S START AGAIN AT SEVEN! IT'S NEARLY FOUR NOW, AND CLARK KENT HAS TO GET BACK FOR HIS SIX O'CLOCK NEWSCAST!

THE REST OF YOU GRAB SOME FOOD, AND MAYBE A NAP--

MY FRIENDS--! I HAVE FOUND YOU!

OOHHH--!

SWIFTER THAN MERCURY--

--AND FASTER THAN A SPEEDING BULLET--

--THE JUSTICE LEAGUE SURGES FORWARD TO CATCH THIS INCREDIBLE INTRUDER!

24

AND ALTRUISM HAS *NOTHING* TO DO WITH IT!

ALL RIGHT, ANDROID-- *TALK!* WHAT GAME ARE YOU PLAYING *THIS TIME?*

NO GAME-- *SUPERMAN!* I'M-- *REALLY ME*-- AGAIN!

THE CONSTRUCT USED ME-- AND *DISCARDED* ME--BUT IN *SO DOING,* SOMETHING WAS *REKINDLED* INSIDE!

MY CONSCIOUSNESS IS *NOT* LIKE A HUMAN'S! NEITHER IS IT LIKE *THE CONSTRUCT'S!* THERE IS A *PERMANENT RECORD* OF IT, STORED IN MY *COMPUTER-BRAIN*--

--AND THOUGH MY LIFE WAS *EXTINGUISHED* IN BATTLING *NEKRON,* THE *FOCUS OF ENERGY* THE *CONSTRUCT* BROUGHT TO MY BODY WHEN HE *REASSEMBLED ITS PARTS* REACTIVATED MY *CIRCUITS!*

EVEN AS HE *USED ME* TO *SPEAK* WITH YOU, I WAS *COMING BACK* TO MYSELF! AFTER HE *LEFT ME,* I SLOWLY REGAINED MY *STRENGTH!*

IT IS AS I'VE *ALWAYS* SAID: AN ANDROID CAN *NEVER TRULY DIE!*

WELL, NOW! THAT'S THE *BEST* ONE YET!

C'MON, CREEP! WHAT DO *YOU* THINK?

YOU-- YOU DO *NOT BELIEVE* ME?

ATOM, RUN A *TRIANGULATION* ON HIM!

I JUST *DID,* SUPERMAN, BUT IT'S *NO GOOD!* I STILL MAKE *THE CONSTRUCT'S* POWER IN THIS CITY--

BUT THERE'S JUST *TOO MUCH* ENERGY IN THE BIG APPLE TO GET A *PRECISE FIX!* HE *COULD* BE IN THE ANDROID, BUT HE MIGHT BE *ANYWHERE ELSE,* TOO!

ENIGMATIC AS *EVER*, EH?

WONDER WOMAN, YOU AND YOUR *CREW* TAKE THIS *WOLF* IN SHEEP'S CLOTHING AND HAVE HIM *LOCKED UP!*

IF THIS *IS* THE *CONSTRUCT*, HIS *MIND* WILL PROBABLY LEAVE THE *BODY*, BUT AT LEAST WE'LL HAVE GUARDED OUR *FLANK!*

SEE YOU AT *SEVEN!*

COME ON, *BOYS!* I'LL FLY YOU TO *METROPOLIS* AND SPRING FOR A *MEAL!*

WAIT! YOU MUST *BELIEVE* ME!

I WANT TO *HELP!*

WONDER WOMAN!! BLACK CANARY! HAWKMAN! I'VE COME SO *FAR--!*

DON'T WASTE YOUR *ACT* ON *ME*, ANDROID! I *CRIED* FOR *REDDY* ONCE, AND *ONCE* IS *ENOUGH!*

HAWKGIRL! WHAT CAN I DO TO *CONVINCE* YOU?

PLEASE! THERE MUST BE *SOMETHING!* YOU *HAVE* TO *UNDERSTAND!*

I AM ONLY AN *ANDROID!* I AM NOT "*REAL*"-- NOT LIKE *YOU* HUMANS! I WAS MADE WITH *MACHINES*-- BY *YOUR KIND!*

BUT WHEN I AM *ALIVE*, I LIVE *LIKE YOU!* I HAVE MY *FRIENDS!* I HAVE *EXCITEMENT!*

I HAVE *JUST RETURNED TO LIFE*, FOR THE *THIRD* TIME! YOU MUST *NOT* TURN ME *AWAY!*

26

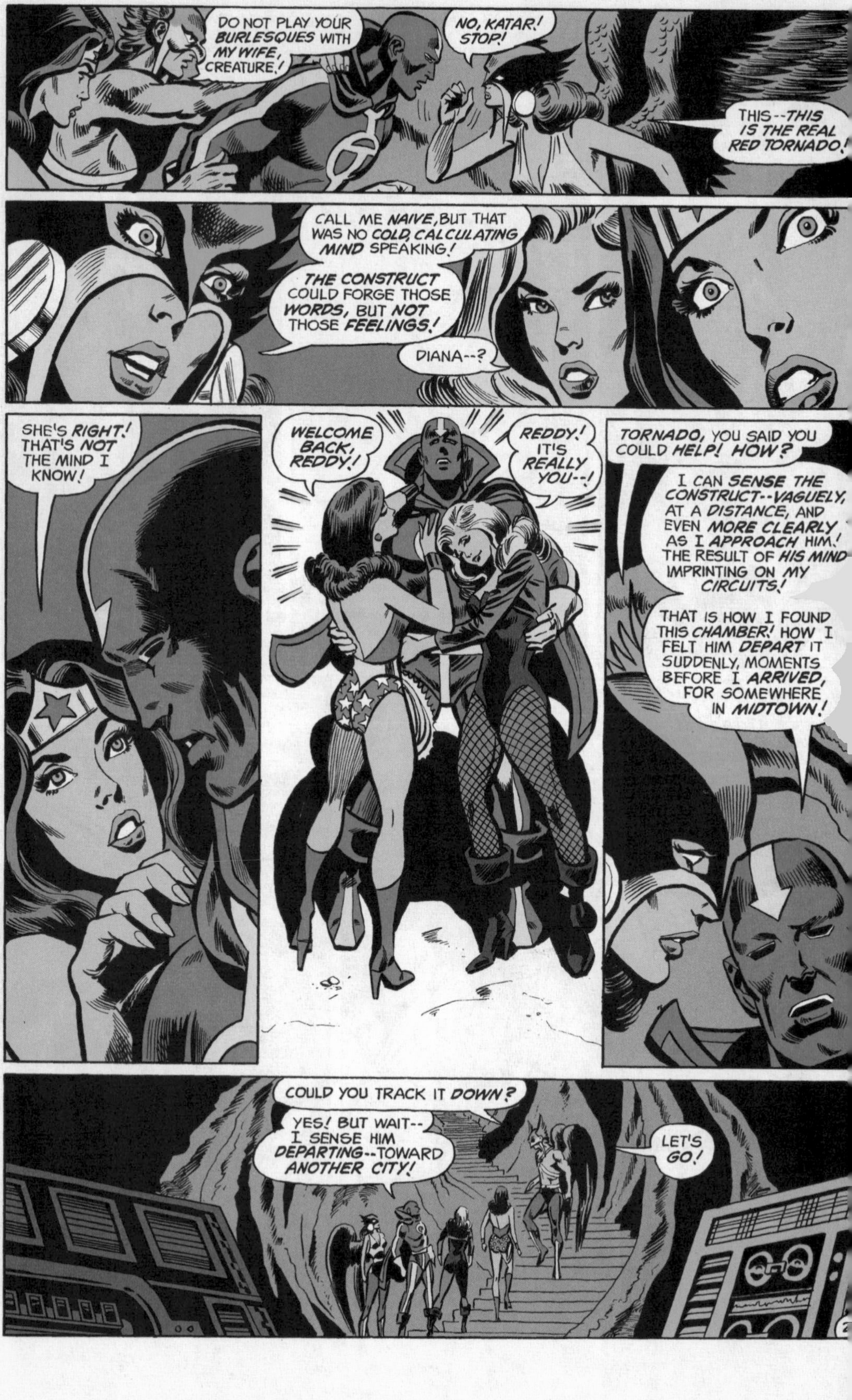

DO NOT PLAY YOUR BURLESQUES WITH MY WIFE, CREATURE!
NO, KATAR! STOP!
THIS--THIS IS THE REAL RED TORNADO!
CALL ME NAIVE, BUT THAT WAS NO COLD, CALCULATING MIND SPEAKING!
THE CONSTRUCT COULD FORGE THOSE WORDS, BUT NOT THOSE FEELINGS!
DIANA--?
SHE'S RIGHT! THAT'S NOT THE MIND I KNOW!
WELCOME BACK, REDDY!
REDDY! IT'S REALLY YOU--!
TORNADO, YOU SAID YOU COULD HELP! HOW?
I CAN SENSE THE CONSTRUCT--VAGUELY, AT A DISTANCE, AND EVEN MORE CLEARLY AS I APPROACH HIM! THE RESULT OF HIS MIND IMPRINTING ON MY CIRCUITS!
THAT IS HOW I FOUND THIS CHAMBER! HOW I FELT HIM DEPART IT SUDDENLY, MOMENTS BEFORE I ARRIVED, FOR SOMEWHERE IN MIDTOWN!
COULD YOU TRACK IT DOWN?
YES! BUT WAIT-- I SENSE HIM DEPARTING--TOWARD ANOTHER CITY!
LET'S GO!

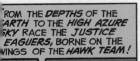

FROM THE *DEPTHS* OF THE *EARTH* TO THE *HIGH AZURE SKY* RACE THE *JUSTICE LEAGUERS,* BORNE ON THE *WINGS* OF THE *HAWK TEAM!*

THE *RED TORNADO* CALLS OUT THE *DIRECTIONS,* AND THEY BANK TOWARD THE *SUN!*

THIS IS THE PLACE-- *METROPOLIS!*

MINUTES LATER--

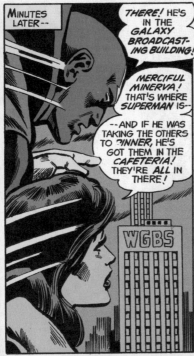

THERE! HE'S IN THE *GALAXY BROADCAST- ING BUILDING!*

MERCIFUL MINERVA! THAT'S WHERE *SUPERMAN* IS--

--AND IF HE WAS TAKING THE OTHERS TO *DINNER,* HE'S GOT THEM IN THE *CAFETERIA!* THEY'RE *ALL* IN THERE!

WGBS

LIKE *DIVING EAGLES* THEY DROP, TO *HOVER* AT THE *20TH FLOOR!*

THIS IS WHERE THE *TV STUDIOS* ARE-- THE MOST LIKELY SPOT FOR *THE CONSTRUCT!*

LOOK OUT!

WGBS

CRASH

THE MACHINES ARE RUNNING *AMOK!* THE CONSTRUCT IS HERE!

WGBS

28

AND THE STUDIO IS *NOTHING BUT* MACHINES--*HUNDREDS* OF THEM!

GALAXY RUNS AN *ENTIRE* NETWORK FROM THIS BUILDING! IF *THE CONSTRUCT* GETS INTO *THAT*--!

BRUK

CRASH

PLEASE, LET *ME* HANDLE THIS! *YOU* WILL HAVE TO DEAL WITH THE *HUMANS!*

THE *HUMANS*--?

BY THE *SILVER SPIRES!* EVERYONE HERE IS IN A *TRANCE!*

THEY'RE LIKE *I* WAS, UNDER *THE CONSTRUCT'S CONTROL!* OUR FRIENDS DIDN'T EVEN HAVE TIME TO SWITCH TO THEIR CIVILIAN IDENTITIES FOR THAT MEAL!

ARROW-- WAKE UP!

THE *MASTER* HAS *ORDERED* THAT YOU MUST *DIE!*

I AM CONSTRUCT III! ALL *MACHINES* BEND TO *MY WILL!* ALL *HUMANS* WHO FEEL *ANGER* CAN BE INDUCED TO FEEL *HATRED*-- MY HATRED-- AT *MY* COMMAND!

TWO *OTHER CONSTRUCTS* HAVE *FAILED* BEFORE ME, BUT *I* SHALL *NOT FAIL!* ONCE I ENTER THE *GBS NETWORK,* EVERY *VIEWER* IN *AMERICA* WHO FEELS ANGER OF *ONE* SORT OR ANOTHER--

--IN SHORT, *ALL* OF THEM--

--WILL BECOME MY *MINDLESS SLAVES!*

I SHALL BE *MASTER OVER ALL*, AS I SET THE HUMANS TO DESTROY *EACH OTHER!* THEN SHALL THE PLANET BE *CLEANSED!*

THEN SHALL I ENJOY THE *LEISURE* TO PONDER THE *REASON* FOR MY *DESTINY!*

YOU WILL *NOT* DESTROY *HUMANITY!*

I WILL *STOP* YOU, *MACHINE* AGAINST *MACHINE!*

PFAGH! I AM *NO MACHINE!*

I *LIVE* IN MACHINES! I HAVE LIVED IN *YOU--* AND I *WILL AGAIN!*

I WILL DRIVE YOUR *NEWLY-MINTED* MIND FROM YOUR HEAD IN AN *INSTANT!*

NO! I FEEL *MANY THINGS,* BUT *NEVER ANGER!*

I WILL *NOT* BE YOUR *PAWN!*

YOU *WILL,* ANDROID-- IF NOT THROUGH *MENTAL CONTROL,* THEN THROUGH *PURE POWER!*

I WILL *OVERWHELM YOU!* YOUR *CIRCUITS* WILL *FUSE!*

NO!

NO-- *I--*

BUT THE CHANGE IS *EVIDENT* FOR *ALL* TO SEE! THE *RED TORNADO* IS SUDDENLY *STAGGERED!*

FOR THE *THIRD TIME,* HE IS FIGHTING THE *ULTIMATE BATTLE* AND FOR THE *THIRD* TIME, HE IS *LOSING* IT!

30

HIS *FORM* SHUDDERS-- HIS *KNEES* QUAKE! STILL, HE STANDS *STRAIGHT AND TALL, DEFIANT,* FOR *LONG, LONG* MOMENTS--

--UNTIL HE CAN STAND *NO MORE!*

REDDY!

DO NOT LET HIM *DO IT, REDDY!* I-- *BELIEVE* IN YOU! I BELIEVE IN YOUR *LIFE!* WE ALL DO!

NOW YOU MUST *BELIEVE* IN *YOURSELF!*

DO IT, REDDY! *DO* IT!

TRY, REDDY! *FIGHT HIM!*

YES!

WILLFUL CREATURE! I *ORDER* YOU TO *SUBMIT!*

I WILL GIVE YOU *MORE POWER!*

--MORE POWER!

SKEEEE-AKKK

HE BLEW HIS *OWN CIRCUITRY!* IT WAS *THE CONSTRUCT* WHO DIED *THE THIRD TIME* -- *NOT REDDY!*

AND *THIS TIME* --

-- I KNOW ENOUGH TO SET UP A *CONTINUOUS RANDOM WAVE-PATTERN* IN THE *ETHER,* SO THAT NO *COHERENT MIND* CAN *EVER COALESCE* OUT THERE AGAIN!

THIS IS THE END OF THE CONSTRUCTS!

HEY, *PRETTY BIRD --!* WHAT'S *GOIN' ON?*

WELL, I'LL *TELL* YOU, OLLIE --

-- I *THINK* WE'RE ABOUT TO HAVE AN *ELECTION!*

AND SO, THIS DAY, AN *OLD MEMBER RETURNS,* AND A *NEW ONE* IS ENTERED ON THE ROLLS!

WHAT *CHANGES* WILL THEY BRING *WITH* THEM? ONLY *TIME* -- AND *FUTURE ISSUES* -- WILL TELL! FOR *NOW,* IT IS *ENOUGH* THAT --

-- THE *LEAGUE STANDS* --

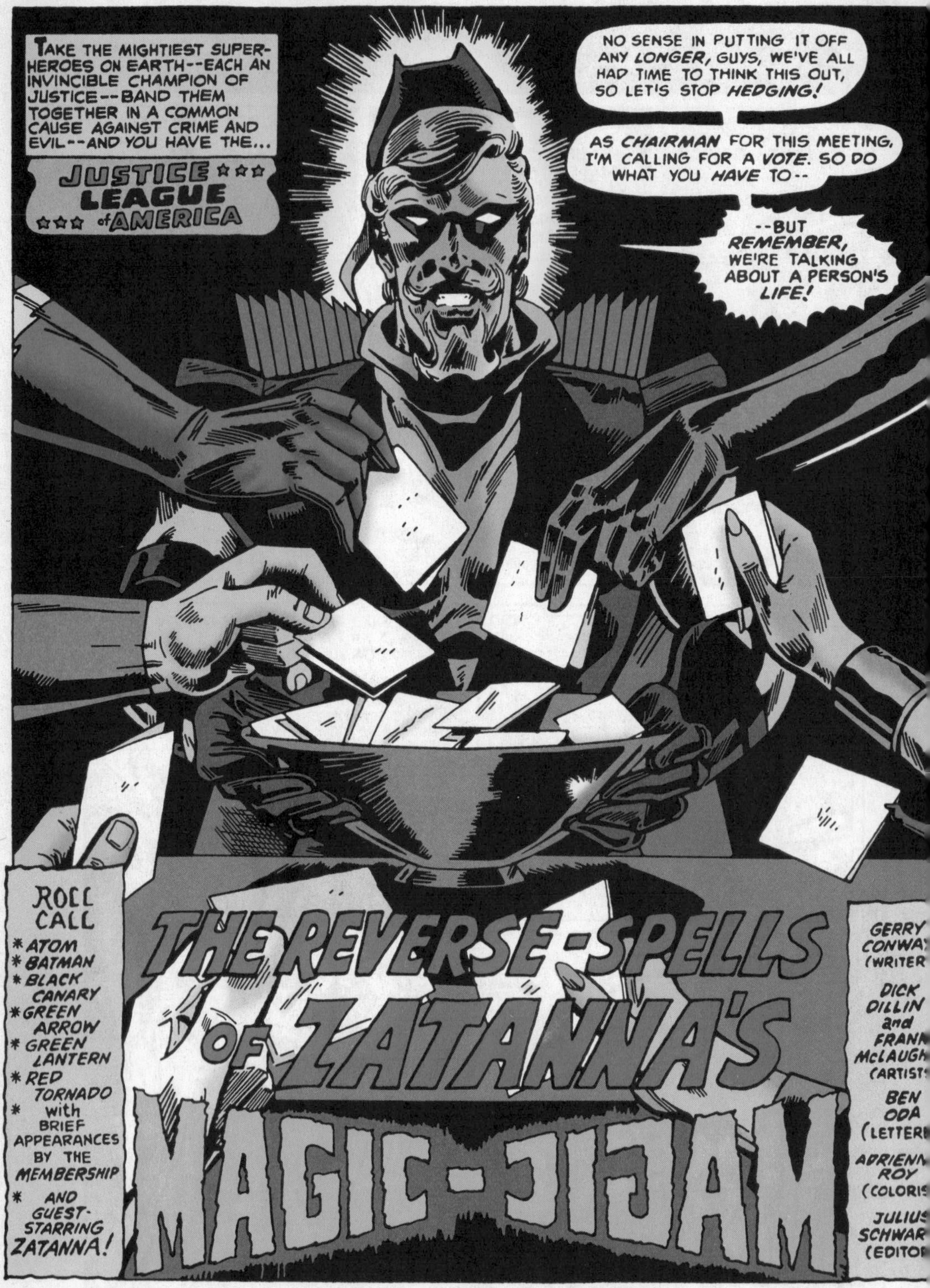

TAKE THE MIGHTIEST SUPER-HEROES ON EARTH--EACH AN INVINCIBLE CHAMPION OF JUSTICE--BAND THEM TOGETHER IN A COMMON CAUSE AGAINST CRIME AND EVIL--AND YOU HAVE THE...
JUSTICE LEAGUE of AMERICA
NO SENSE IN PUTTING IT OFF ANY LONGER, GUYS, WE'VE ALL HAD TIME TO THINK THIS OUT, SO LET'S STOP HEDGING!
AS CHAIRMAN FOR THIS MEETING, I'M CALLING FOR A VOTE. SO DO WHAT YOU HAVE TO--
--BUT REMEMBER, WE'RE TALKING ABOUT A PERSON'S LIFE!
ROLL CALL
* ATOM
* BATMAN
* BLACK CANARY
* GREEN ARROW
* GREEN LANTERN
* RED TORNADO
* with BRIEF APPEARANCES BY THE MEMBERSHIP
* AND GUEST-STARRING ZATANNA!
THE REVERSE-SPELLS OF ZATANNA'S MAGIC-CIGAM
GERRY CONWA (WRITER
DICK DILLIN and FRANK McLAUGH (ARTISTS
BEN ODA (LETTER
ADRIENN ROY (COLORIS
JULIUS SCHWAR (EDITOR

NO NEED TO BE SO MELODRAMATIC, OLLIE. IT'S JUST A MEMBERSHIP VOTE, AFTER ALL!

HARDLY A MATTER OF "*LIFE AND DEATH*," OLIVER.

KATAR! HAVE YOU FORGOTTEN YOUR *OWN* ELECTION TO THE *LEAGUE*?

AS I RECALL, YOU WERE MOST *IMPRESSED*-- AND *TOUCHED*--!

WE WERE *ALIEN STRANGERS* TO THIS WORLD, AND THE *LEAGUE* TOOK US IN, *ACCEPTING* YOU AS ONE OF ITS OWN.

AND MUCH TOO *LATE*, IN THIS GUY'S OPINION, SHAYERA. YOU SHOULD'VE BEEN MADE A MEMBER YEARS AGO!

JUST AS THEY FINALLY ACCEPTED ME A FEW MONTHS AGO--

WE *AGREE*, RALPH. BUT UNTIL WE *REVISED* THE BY-LAWS, THE LEAGUE WAS *LIMITED* TO *TWELVE* ACTIVE MEMBERS.

HAWKGIRL WAS THE *FIRST* NEW MEMBER ELECTED UNDER OUR NEW CHARTER--

--AND WITH ANY LUCK, A CERTAIN *MAID OF MAGIC* WILL BE THE *SECOND*!

WHAT DO YOU THINK SHE'LL SAY WHEN SHE HEARS THE *NEWS*?

I'LL *ANSWER* THAT, ATOM-- IN PERSON!

SHE SAYS-- *NO*!

2

ZATANNA!

AND IN A *DIFFERENT* COSTUME-- A *NEW* ONE!?

WE WERE GOING TO *SUMMON* YOU AFTER THE *VOTING* BUT NOW THAT YOU'RE *HERE*--

--NOW THAT I'M *HERE*, I'LL TELL YOU TO YOUR FACES, DEAR ENEMIES!

I DON'T WANT *ANY* PART OF YOUR "JUSTICE LEAGUE"--

--NOT *NOW*, NOT *EVER!* I DON'T NEED YOUR *HELP*, AND I DON'T WANT YOUR *INTERFERENCE!* MY LIFE IS *PERFECT* AS IT *IS!*

AS FOR YOUR *BALLOTS*--

FARJOSH

FLAMES, DESTROY! FIRE CLAIM! LET THEM NOT WRITE MY NAME--

THOSE BALLOTS WERE *JUSTICE LEAGUE PROPERTY*, SISTER. MAYBE YOU DON'T WANT TO BE A MEMBER, BUT THAT DOESN'T GIVE YOU A *RIGHT* TO--

ARROW, COOL DOWN! THIS ISN'T THE TIME FOR *LOST TEMPERS!*

BLACK CANARY IS *RIGHT!* IF WE'VE *OFFENDED* YOU, ZATANNA, WE *APOLOGIZE...*

...BUT WE HONESTLY BELIEVED YOU'D *WANT* ELECTION TO THE *LEAGUE!*

AFTER ALL, WE WORKED *WELL* TOGETHER, DURIN[G] YOUR SEARCH F[OR] YOUR FATHER, THE MAGICIAN *ZATARA*

--AND AS *WONDER WOMAN* INDICATED ONCE, THE LEAGUE IS IN SORE NEED OF MORE *WOMEN* TO BALANCE OUR ROLLS!

BUT, IF YOU FEEL YOU DON'T NEED US--

THAT'S *EXACTLY* HOW I FEEL, BATMAN. I DON'T NEED *ANYONE'S* HELP! I'M PERFECTLY *FINE!* I DON'T *WANT* MEMBERSHIP, AND I WON'T *ACCEPT* IT!

AM I MAKING MYSELF *UNDERSTOOD?*

TOTALLY

134

...UT, ZATANNA, EVEN IF *YOU* DO NOT NEED *US*, WE NEED YOU! OUR *MAGIC POWERS* WOULD BE TREMENDOUS *ASSET* TO OUR OVERALL STRENGTH! THINK OF YOUR *RESPONSIBILITIES*--

--AS A WOMAN, AS WELL AS A MAGICIAN!

I AM A MAGICIAN *NO MORE*, HAWKGIRL...

AS MY *COSTUME* SHOULD INDICATE, I'VE *SET ASIDE* MY OLD IDENTITY. ZATANNA THE INNOCENT *MAGICIAN* IS DEAD...

LONG LIVE ZATANNA THE SORCERESS!

I CAN'T *BELIEVE* YOU'VE CHANGED THAT MUCH, ZATANNA! YOU WERE *IDEALISTIC*--

--I WAS *YOUNG!*

YOU HAD *HOPES*--

I HAD *DELUSIONS!*

NO! I CAN'T *ACCEPT* THAT.!

WHAT YOU *CAN* OR *CANNOT* ACCEPT IS OF *NO CONCERN* TO ME, *ATOM!*

YOU'RE LIKE MY *FATHER*, A ROMANTIC *FOOL!* HE *RETIRED* FROM THE STUDY OF SORCERY ONLY A SHORT TIME AGO--

--AND HE WANTED *ME* TO TAKE UP HIS *MANTLE*. I TOLD HIM WHAT I TELL *YOU:*

NO!

ASK *HIM*, IF YOU *DISBELIEVE* ME!

NO NEED. WE BELIEVE YOU. YOUR POSITION IS ONLY *TOO CLEAR.*

WELL, *I* DON'T BELIEVE IT! I FOUGHT *BESIDE* YOU, ZATANNA! I HELPED YOU FIND YOUR *DAD!* JUST SAY THE WORD, JUST TELL ME WHAT'S *WRONG*--

4

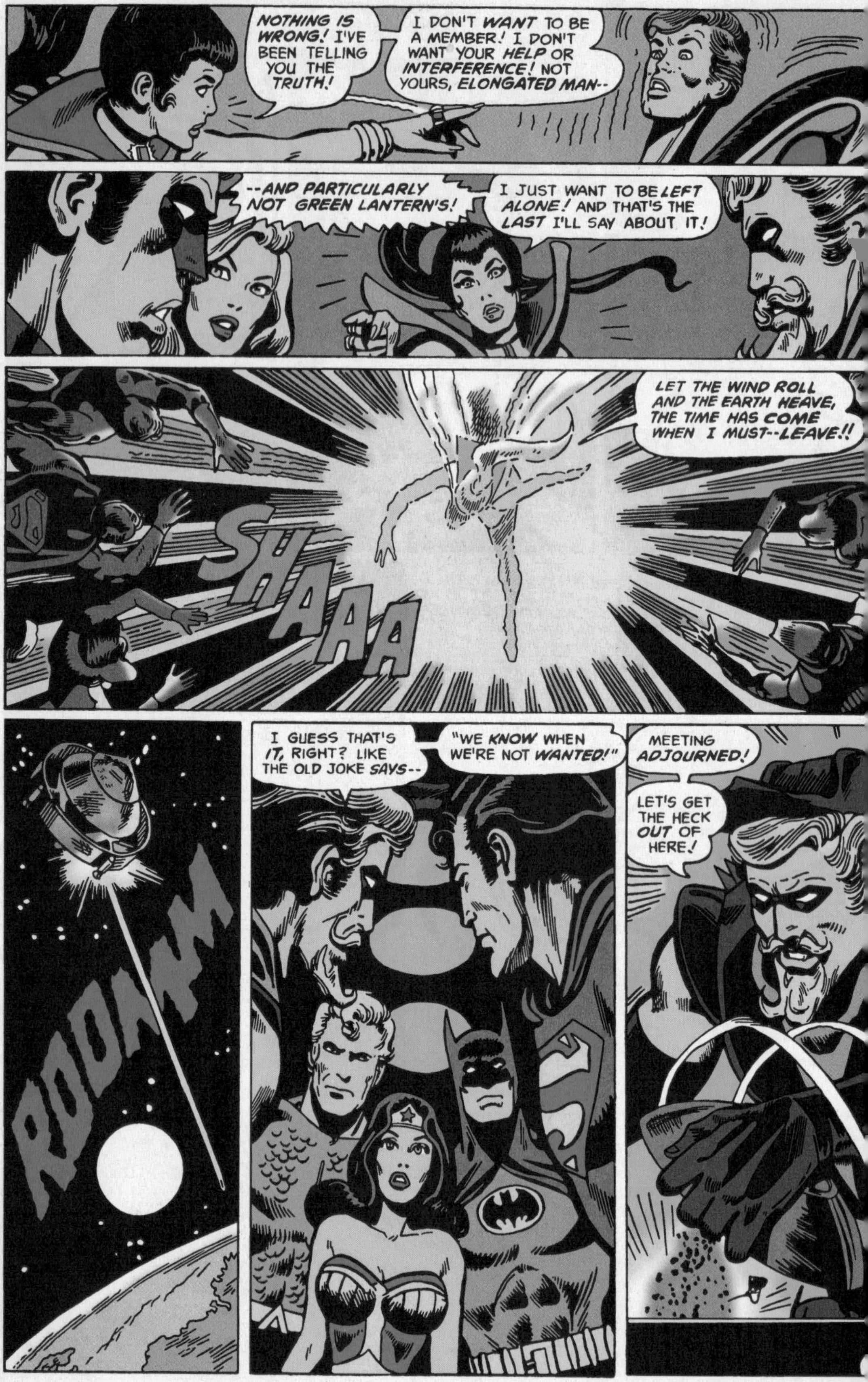
NOTHING IS WRONG! I'VE BEEN TELLING YOU THE TRUTH!
I DON'T WANT TO BE A MEMBER! I DON'T WANT YOUR HELP OR INTERFERENCE! NOT YOURS, ELONGATED MAN--
--AND PARTICULARLY NOT GREEN LANTERN'S!
I JUST WANT TO BE LEFT ALONE! AND THAT'S THE LAST I'LL SAY ABOUT IT!
LET THE WIND ROLL AND THE EARTH HEAVE, THE TIME HAS COME WHEN I MUST--LEAVE!!
SHAAAA
ROOAAM
I GUESS THAT'S IT, RIGHT? LIKE THE OLD JOKE SAYS--
"WE KNOW WHEN WE'RE NOT WANTED!"
MEETING ADJOURNED!
LET'S GET THE HECK OUT OF HERE!

A SULLEN, SAD *SILENCE* HANGS HEAVY IN THE *JUSTICE LEAGUE* SATELLITE NOW, AS THE MEMBERS DEPART, ALONE AND IN SMALL GROUPS, FLASHING *BRIEFLY* IN THE *TRANSPORTER TUBE--*

--VANISHING ON THEIR WAY TO THE GREEN GLOBE OF EARTH LOOMING LIKE A FERTILE *MOON* IN THE BLACK SKY "ABOVE"...

THERE GO THE *LAST* OF THEM, *HAWKMAN* AND *HAWKGIRL*--

--ON THEIR WAY BACK TO THEIR *SPACESHIP* ORBITING OVER *MIDWAY CITY.*

I NEVER THOUGHT I'D *RESENT* MONITOR DUTY, BUT NOW THAT *JEAN* AND I ARE *MARRIED,* I BEGRUDGE EVERY *MOMENT* I HAVE TO SPEND APART FROM HER ...

...PARTICULARLY AFTER THAT SOUR SCENE WITH *ZATANNA!*

I GUESS I'D LIKE A LITTLE *REASSURANCE* RIGHT NOW. IT ISN'T A VERY PLEASANT *EXPERIENCE--*

--DISCOVERING HOW LITTLE YOU *KNOW* ABOUT SOMEONE YOU CALLED A *FRIEND!*

I REMEMBER HOW IT WAS WHEN *ZATANNA* WAS HUNTING FOR HER *LOST FATHER--* SHE WAS SO *DETERMINED.*

IT STARTED WITH *HAWKMAN* AND *HAWKGIRL* SAVING HER LIFE WHEN SHE ACCIDENTALLY SPLIT HERSELF INTO *TWO BEINGS--*

"--AND IT *CONTINUED* WITH OUR SHARED ADVENTURE BATTLING *THE DRUID* IN A SUB-ATOMIC UNIVERSE..!"

"--FOLLOWED BY GREEN LANTERN AIDING HER IN COMBAT WITH THE *WARLOCK OF YS--*"

"--AND ELONGATED MAN HELPING HER SOLVE THE 'TROUBLES OF THE TRIPOD THIEVES!'

"SHE CREATED *DUPLICATES* OF US TO AID HER WHEN SHE FOUND HER *FATHER* IN THE MYSTIC LAND OF *KHARMA--* AND *ENDED* HER THREE-YEAR *QUEST!*"

THE COMPLETE SAGA COLLECTED IN JLA: ZATANNA'S SEARCH- ON SALE NOW!

THAT *ZATANNA* WOULD *NEVER* HAVE REFUSED AN INVITATION TO JOIN THE *JUSTICE LEAGUE!*

WHAT *HAPPENED* TO HER? WHY DID SHE *CHANGE?*

ELTSAC EMOC EVILA! ERUTPAC EHT DIURD! *

*READ *ZATANNA'S* MAGIC WORDS BACKWARDS! --JULIE

WAIT A MINUTE! I HAVE A *CLUE*--AND *ZATANNA* HERSELF GAVE US A WAY TO CHECK IT OUT!

BUT SINCE I'M STUCK HERE ON *MONITOR DUTY*, I'LL CONTACT *BATMAN* AND LET *HIM* DO THE *FOOTWORK!*

ATOM CALLING *BATMAN!* JLA PRIORITY SIGNAL 2A! REPEAT, *ATOM* CALLING *BATMAN*--

A*T LAST THE SIGNAL IS *ANSWER* BUT AS THE *TINY TITAN* EXPLAIN HIS PLAN TO THE *DARKNIGHT DETECTIVE*, THERE IS A *SHIMMERING* ACROSS THE ROOM

--AND UNSEEN, A MISTY *FIGURE* FORMS, PASSING THROUGH THE *BULKHEAD* FROM THE *VOID* BEYOND--!

SLOWLY, LIKE A *RAINBOW* GATHERING IN A *STORMY SKY*, THE FIGURE GROWS MORE *DISTINCT*, BECOMES ACHINGLY *FAMILIAR*--

--AND *ATTACKS* BLUE FIRE LEAPING FROM *RING* TO *VICTIM* LIKE A STABBING SWORD OF *LIGHTNING!*

--THANKS FOR THE HELP, *BATMAN*. THIS IS *ATOM*, OVER AND--

AAARRH

STRANGE! AS *ATOM* SIGNED OFF, IT SOUNDED LIKE --BUT NO, IT MUST HAVE BEEN *STATIC!*

NOW THAT *HORTY* HAS BEEN DISPOSED OF, I CAN CONTINUE WITH MY PLAN! THESE... MACHINES... SHOULD HAVE THE INFORMATION I SEEK...

THOUGH THEIR *THEORY* IS ALIEN TO ME, STILL, I CAN UNDERSTAND THEIR *FUNCTION*, SIMILAR TO THAT OF A *FORTUNE-TELLING CRYSTAL*...

I HAVE BUT TO PRESENT A *QUESTION* ON THIS ALPHABET-BOARD. AND THIS "COMPUTER" WILL PROVIDE AN *ANSWER*... EH?

QUESTION: WHAT IS THE SOURCE OF POWER FOR GREEN LANTERN'S RING?

ANSWER: SOURCE IS THE POWER BATTERY, PROVIDED TO EACH MEMBER OF THE GREEN LANTERN CORPS BY THE GUARDIANS OF OA

A *POWER BATTERY*--? *INGENIOUS!* THAT EXPLAINS WHY THE RING NO LONGER *RESPONDS* TO MY COMMANDS.

IT MUST REQUIRE *RECHARGING* AT REGULAR INTERVALS!*

--AND *WHERE* IS THIS *POWER BATTERY?*

* EVERY *24 HOURS*, TO BE EXACT. AND IF YOU'RE WONDERING WHY THIS *"GREEN LANTERN"* DOESN'T *KNOW* THAT--KEEP READING!   --JULIE

ANSWER: BY ORDER OF ITS CURRENT TRUSTEE, THE POWER BATTERY IS KEPT INVISIBLE, ITS LOCATION... UNKNOWN...

FLAMES OF THE *BLUE DOOR!* THIS UPSETS *EVERYTHING!*

I'D HOPED TO *USE* THE POWER RING TO BRING MY INTERNAL ENERGIES UP TO *FULL POTENCY* AS I ONCE WISHED TO USE IT TO *ENTER* THIS WORLD!

WITHOUT THE RING, I HAVE BUT A *FRACTION* OF MY *TRUE POWER!*

NOW IT APPEARS I MUST FIND *OTHER* MEANS TO REGAIN MY STRENGTH--

--AND I'LL FIND THOSE MEANS ON *EARTH*, AT *ANGKOR WAT!* THERE, I SHALL CAST THE NECESSARY *SPELLS*--

--AND ONCE I HAVE, I'LL *NEUTRALIZE* THE *JUSTICE LEAGUE*--

--JUST AS I'VE *ALREADY NEUTRALIZED* MY OLD *FOE*, ZATANNA!

8

ON A WIND-SWEPT HILL IN THE COASTAL REGION OF *BRITTANY*, A YOUNG VOICE LIFTS IN A LILTING CHANT, ECHOING ACROSS THE WASTES...

THE VOICE IS *ZATANNA'S* AND IT IS VIBRANT WITH SUPPRESSED FEAR...

FLAMES OF OLD, FIRES OF YS, I SUMMON YOU, THIS BODY TO KISS!

FOR THESE ARE THE *RUINS* OF THE LEGENDARY DROWNED LAND OF YS--

-- AND FOR ALMOST *TWO THOUSAND YEARS*, THEY HAVE BEEN THE SCENE OF STRANGE *DISAPPEARANCES*, ALWAYS ACCOMPANIED BY A FLARING OF WEIRD *BLUE FLAME!*

ONCE *BEFOR[E]* THIS WOMA[N] SUMMON[ED] THE FLAME[S] OF YS AND A[S] THEY DID THEN, THEY COME NOW T[O] *CLAIM* HER.

IN AN INSTANT SHE IS GONE--

--AND, SIMULTANEOUSLY, ON *THE OTHER SIDE OF THE WORLD*, SHE REAPPEARS IN A LAND WHICH *SHOULD BE BUT A MYTH*--

--A LAND WHERE *MAGIC* IS THE *NATURAL LAW*, NOT *SCIENCE*--

--A LAND CALLED YS!

IT IS THE *SHE* OUR MASTER FORETOLD!

SHE MUST NOT REACH THE MASTER'S STRONGHOLD!

THE *SHE*-- MUST *DIE!*

WINDS OF HATTOTH, LIGHTNING OF GOLD, REND THE CLOUDS, THEIR WATERS UNFOLD!

KTAKOOM

YIIIEEE

YAAA

HSSSS

LIFT ME NOW, AND LIFT ME HIGH, AND BEAR ME 'CROSS THIS WINDSWEPT SKY!

THE *LAST* TIME I CAME HERE, MY MAGIC WAS *ALTERED* BY THIS WORLD'S TWISTED *REALITY*, BUT NOW I KNOW HOW TO *COMPENSATE* FOR THAT TWIST--

--THOUGH IT'S STILL A *STRAIN*, AND STILL HIGHLY *DANGEROUS!*

YET I CAN'T *THINK* ABOUT THE DANGER, NOT WITH ONE OF MY *DEADLIEST* ENEMIES LOOSE UPON THE EARTH!

I CAN ONLY *PRAY* THE *JUSTICE LEAGUE* UNDERSTOOD MY *WARNING,* AND HOPE THEY LEARN THE *TRUTH* ABOUT "GREEN LANTERN"!

10

--BEFORE HE SLAYS THEM ALL!

AH! THERE'S MY *DESTINATION*, JUST WHERE I *REMEMBERED* IT TO BE!

MY OLD FOE MUST HAVE *EXPECTED* AN ATTACK ON HIS CASTLE: HE'S LEFT A *GUARD*!

LET'S SEE IF THEY'RE AS *EFFICIENT* AS THEIR *COUSINS* ON THE *HEATH*...

SPRITES OF THE AIR, HEED MY IRE--

--FOR... FOR M... A SHIELD OF FIRE...

FTO OSH

FAR SH

EARTH BELOW, I CALL TO YOU, OPEN WIDE, THESE TROLLS TO CHEW!

RRRMMMMMM

THE *SHE* DOES NOT NOTICE ME, IN THESE *SHADOWS*!

AND *THAT* SHALL BE THE *SHE'S* UNDOING!

THA ANG

I'VE *DONE* IT! NOW *NOTHING* CAN KEEP ME FROM FREEING THE *PRISONER* HELD IN THAT CASTLE *TOWER!*

THERE'S *STILL* A CHANCE TO SAVE THE *LEAGUE!* IF *ONLY* I CAN--

AAAIIIEEE

THAK

THE COUNTRYSIDE SURROUNDING *GOTHAM CITY* IS *UNLIKE* THE SUBURBS OF *OTHER* METROPOLITAN AREAS: WITHIN FIFTEEN MILES OF THE DOWNTOWN SKYSCRAPERS, THERE ARE PLEASANT FARMLIKE *ESTATES*--

--ACRES OF *PARKLAND*--

--AND NOT A FEW TURN-OF-THE CENTURY *MANSIONS.*

THE OLD *WAYNE ESTATE* IS ONE SUCH FAMILY FORTRESS, AND HERE IS YET ANOTHER, RECENTLY *PURCHASED* BY A RETIRED MAGICIAN--

--THE MAN WHOM THE WORLD ONCE KNEW AS-- *ZATARA.*

ON THE *CONTRARY,* BATMAN--

-- MY DAUGHTER WAS QUITE *EAGER* TO FOLLOW IN MY "FOOTSTEPS," AS YOU SAY. IN FACT, SHE *INSISTED!*

I DON'T KNOW *WHO* TOLD YOU *OTHERWISE*--BUT HE OR SHE IS *DEAD WRONG!* ZATANNA IS *TOTALLY* COMMITTED TO THE PURSUIT OF *JUSTICE*--I PROMISE YOU!

THEN... SHE *LIED* TO US...

ZATANNA-- *LIED? NO*--I CANNOT BELIEVE--

BUT SHE *DID,* MY FRIEND... AND IF SHE LIED ABOUT *THIS,* SHE MUST HAVE BEEN LYING ABOUT EVERYTHING *ELSE...*

... STATING THE *EXACT OPPOSITE* OF WHAT SHE ACTUALLY MEANT!

IN *THAT* CASE-- *GOOD LORD!*

BATMAN! MY DAUGHTER --IS SHE IN *DANGER?* DO YOU NEED MY *HELP?*

IT'S *IMPOSSIBLE* TO SAY, ZATARA! BUT YOU'D BETTER STAY *HERE!*

ZATANNA IS *OUR* RESPONSIBILITY NOW...

... AND THE *LEAGUE* TAKES CARE OF ITS *OWN!*

I'M CALLING AN *EMERGENCY* MEETING!

WITHIN THE HOUR, *THE BATMAN* AND *THE ATOM* ARE GATHERED WITH THE THREE HEROES WHO HAVE RESPONDED TO THE CALL...

144

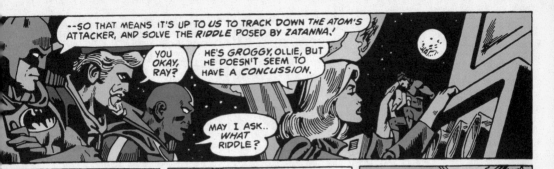

--SO THAT MEANS IT'S UP TO *US* TO TRACK DOWN *THE ATOM'S* ATTACKER, AND SOLVE THE *RIDDLE* POSED BY *ZATANNA!*

YOU *OKAY*, RAY?

HE'S *GROGGY*, OLLIE, BUT HE DOESN'T SEEM TO HAVE A *CONCUSSION.*

MAY I ASK.. *WHAT* RIDDLE?

SOMETHING WHICH SHOULD HAVE BEEN OBVIOUS TO *ANY* OF US WHO WORKED WITH *ZATANNA* BEFORE, *TORNADO!*

--YOU DIDN'T, SO YOU COULDN'T KNOW, ZATANNA HAS *ALWAYS* WORKED HER MAGIC BY SPEAKING *BACKWARDS*--

--BUT THIS EVENING, FOR THE *FIRST TIME,* SHE USED INCANTATIONS IN *NORMAL ORDER!*

SURE! SHE MUST'VE BEEN *TRYING* TO *TELL* US SOMETHING!

PARTLY, OLLIE... BUT I THINK SHE USED INCANTATIONS BECAUSE SHE *COULDN'T* USE HER BACKWARDS-MAGIC!

WHY? BECAUSE EVERYTHING SHE SAID--WAS IN REVERSE!

RAY, TELL THEM WHAT HAPPENED TO YOU!

SOMEBODY *ZAPPED* ME... BUT I GOT A *GLIMPSE* OF WHO DID IT BEFORE I BLACKED OUT. IT WAS YOUR *PAL,* OLLIE... *GREEN LANTERN...!*

THE *LANTERN?* UH-UNH, *SHORT-STUFF,* NO *WAY!*

I *AGREE,* ARROW... BUT NOT FOR *SENTIMENTAL* REASONS. THE COMPUTER RECORDED SEVERAL *QUERIES* ABOUT *GREEN LANTERN'S* POWER BATTERY...

...INDICATING RAY'S *ATTACKER* WAS AN *IMPOSTOR!*

THE COMPUTER ALSO TRACKED HIS *FLIGHT-PATH*--

--AND IT LEADS STRAIGHT TO NORTH-WEST *CAMBODIA,* TO THE MYSTERY-CITY OF *ANGKOR WAT!*

THAT'S WHERE WE'LL FIND OUR EXPLANATIONS, *LEAGUERS!*

THEN *WHAT'RE* WE *WAITING* FOR--?

LET'S GO!

14

ANGKOR WAT, A PLACE WHOSE VERY *NAME* SPEAKS OF ANCIENT MYSTERIES: BUILT BY KING SURYAVARMAN II IN THE 12TH CENTURY A.D. IT LAY *BURIED* IN JUNGLE DARKNESS FOR HALF A *MILLENNIUM*--

--HAUNTED BY LONG-FORGOTTEN *GHOSTS*--

--TILL *REDISCOVERED* IN THE EARLY *20TH* CENTURY.

TONIGHT, THOSE GHOSTS SEEM *REVIVED*, AN THE NIGHT AIR IS *THICK* WITH THE SMELL OF *OZONE*, ECHOING WITH A DISTANT SHOUTING VOICE...

I CAN *HEAR* SOMEBODY SCREAMING IN THAT BIG *BUILDING* UP AHEAD--

SO CAN *I*... BUT IT'S NOT *SCREAMING*, EXACTLY...!

TRUE! IT IS A *CHANTING* OF ALMOST *HYPNOTIC* INTENSITY!

I SUGGEST WE PROCEED WITH *CAUTION*--!

GREAT *IDEA*, MACHINE-MIND! HOW ABOUT PRACTICING WHAT YOU *PREACH*?

I AM AN ANDROID, ARCHER, NOT *SUBJECT* TO HYPNOSIS.

IF *ANYONE* SHOULD INITIATE THIS ASSAULT, IT IS I--

/////////

VVOOOMM

WHY DOES HE KEEP *DOING* THAT?

EVERY TIME WE GET IN A FIGHT, *HE* HAS TO JUMP IN *FIRST!* JUST *ONCE,* I WISH HE'D BRING UP THE REAR! JUST ONCE!

FATWONG

GREEN ARROW ALWAYS GETS ANGRY WHEN HE'S AFRAID FOR A *FRIEND*--

--BUT I WISH HE'D SAY WHAT HE REALLY MEANS-- JUST ONCE!

GOOD! I'VE *DISTRACTED* THAT PHONY *LANTERN* FROM OLLIE'S *ARROW!*

THE IMPOSTER'S SO BUSY TRYING TO NAIL *ME,* HE DOESN'T SEE HIS *REAL TROUBLE*--

FWOOSH

FPWOOSH

FTOOSH

--GREEN ARROW'S GAS-GRENADE ARROW!"

FATOOM

FAST *WORK,* ARCHER! BUT ARE YOU *SURE* THAT *GAS* WILL BE *EFFECTIVE?*

YOU'RE *JOKING,* RIGHT? THERE'S ENOUGH SLEEP-STUFF IN THAT BOMB TO KNOCK OUT THE NEW JERSEY GIANTS!

TRUST ME, BATS! HAVE I EVER LET YOU--

--DOWN?

KIRWHOOM

16

SIMULTA-NEOUSLY, ON THE OTHER SIDE OF THE WORLD...

I STILL FIND IT HARD TO BELIEVE THIS IS *HAPPENING!*

WAKING FROM *UNCONSCIOUSNESS* ...WITH AN ARROW *WOUND* IN MY SHOULDER...TO WATCH *DEMONS* AND *TROLLS* DANCING AROUND A *PYRE*...

IT COULD DRIVE A *NORMAL* WOMAN *MAD!*

FORTUNATELY, I'VE LIVED WITH THIS SORT OF THING EVER SINCE I FIRST REALIZED DAD'S LITTLE *CARD* TRICKS *WEREN'T* TRICKS!

THESE *TROLLS* MAY THINK I'M HELPLESS, BUT I'VE TAKEN STEPS TO GET *FREE!* I ONLY HOPE THEY *WORK* OUT IN--

AARRRGG

--TIME?

SOMEONE'S *ATTACKING!* THEN MY SPELL *SUCCEEDED*--

FFTTT

IEEE

--AND HERE COMES THE CAVALRY!

BACK, HELL-SPAWN! BACK TO YOUR DARK HOLES, AND BY AHURA-MAZDA--

PTANG

--NEVER AGAIN DARE SHOW YOUR FACES TO THE LIGHT OF DAY!

KLASH

KRAK

YAHHH!

EEYAH!

COR BLIMEY, MATE, IT'S A RIGHT TWIST-- A GIRL!

I *KNOW* THIS WOMAN CAPTAIN THE CLOTHES ARE *DIFFERENT* BUT THE FACE IS THE *SAME!*

SHE *FREED* US FROM THE *MASTER'S DOMINION*-- WE OWE HER OUR *SOULS!*

NOT *THAT,* I HOPE...

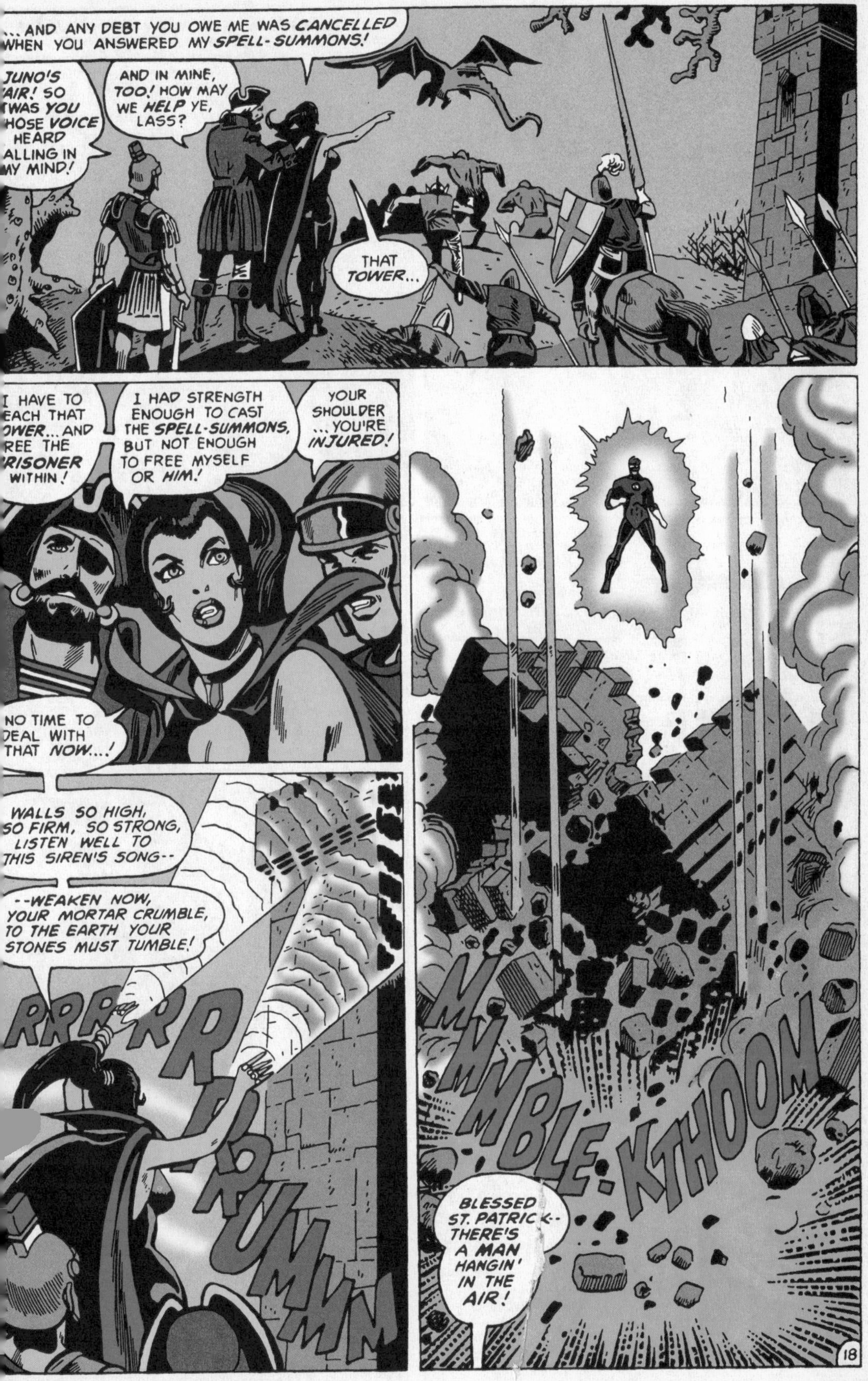
...AND ANY DEBT YOU OWE ME WAS CANCELLED WHEN YOU ANSWERED MY SPELL-SUMMONS!
JUNO'S AIR! SO WAS YOU HOSE VOICE HEARD ALLING IN MY MIND!
AND IN MINE, TOO! HOW MAY WE HELP YE, LASS?
THAT TOWER...
I HAVE TO EACH THAT OWER... AND REE THE RISONER WITHIN!
I HAD STRENGTH ENOUGH TO CAST THE SPELL-SUMMONS, BUT NOT ENOUGH TO FREE MYSELF OR HIM!
YOUR SHOULDER ...YOU'RE INJURED!
NO TIME TO EAL WITH THAT NOW...!
WALLS SO HIGH, SO FIRM, SO STRONG, LISTEN WELL TO THIS SIREN'S SONG--
--WEAKEN NOW, YOUR MORTAR CRUMBLE, TO THE EARTH YOUR STONES MUST TUMBLE!
RRRRRR
RUMMM
MMMBLE-KTHOOM
BLESSED ST. PATRICK-- THERE'S A MAN HANGIN' IN THE AIR!
18

PRISONER IN THAT ROOM SO TALL, FLOAT TO EARTH, AND DO NOT FALL!

SLEEP WHICH HOLDS HIM COLD AS STONE, QUIT HIS MIND AND FLESH AND BONE!

GREAT GUARDIANS...WHAT A *NIGHTMARE!* I DREAMED I COULDN'T *MOVE*...AND THAT *SOMEONE* HAD STOLEN MY *POWER RING!*

NO, *GREEN LANTERN,* IT WAS *REALITY!* YOU MUST *HURRY* TO *EARTH*...

BU ...I WASN A DREAM

BUT HURRY... HURRY...

ZATANNA?

WILL SOMEONE PLEASE *TELL* ME WHAT'S *GOING ON?*

IN THE VINE-CRUSTED HALLS OF *ANGKOR WAT,* A VOICE MURMURS IN A *MADDENED MONOTONE,* A VOICE WHICH ONLY *SUPERFICIALLY* RESEMBLES THAT OF THE *EMERALD CRUSADER*...

IT WAS SO *EASY* TO DISPOSE OF YOU, SO *EFFORTLESS,* NOW THAT I HAVE *BEGUN* THE PROCESS OF *REGAINING* MY *FULL STRENGTH*...

NO LONGER NEED I MAINTAIN THIS *DISGUISE,* SO *POWERFUL* HAVE I BECOME! NOW I MAY STAND REVEALED AS MY *TRUE SELF*...

NOT THE HERO CALLED *GREEN LANTERN,* BUT A BEING OF *SUPREME SORCERY--*

--THE *WARLOCK OF YS!*

HERE, IN THIS PLACE OF AGELESS *MYSTERIES*, WHERE ONCE, EONS AGO, AN OUTPOST OF IMMORTAL... STOOD PROUD AMID THE JUNGLE--

--HERE HAVE I *RENEWED* MYSELF, CANTING SPELLS WHICH HAVE *AWAKENED* THE MYSTICAL ENERGIES WITHIN ME, *STUNTED* BY THE JOURNEY FROM MY HOME WORLD--TO THIS MATERIAL PLANE!

ORIGINALLY, I PLANNED TO MAKE USE OF THIS *POWER RING* TO GAIN THAT END, BUT WHERE ALIEN SCIENCE *FAILED*--

--ANCIENT *MAGIC* TRIUMPHED!

I HAVE NO *USE* FOR THIS RING NOW. IT IS A TARNISHED *BAUBLE*-- A *TOY!*

"I REMEMBER HOW I TRIED TO *LURE* ITS WEARER, *GREEN LANTERN*, TO MY LAND ON *THE OTHER SIDE OF TIME*, TO *STEAL* THE RING FROM HIM!"

"I REMEMBER, TOO, HOW HE AND THE WITCH *ZATANNA* DID *TRICK* ME, TURNING ME INTO A *LIVING STATUE* BY MEANS OF THAT SAME ACCURSED *RING!*"

"YET IN THE MOMENT OF DEFEAT, I CLAIMED *VICTORY*. I PLACED A MAGICAL *THOUGHT-CURSE* ON *GREEN LANTERN*, CAUSING A SLOW, UNNOTICEABLE *TRANSFERENCE* OF OUR *LIFE ENERGIES*..."

"THE *PROCESS* WAS COMPLETED ONLY *ONE DAY* AGO-- AND IN THAT *INSTANT*, WE *CHANGED PLACES!*"

"*I* CAME HERE TO *EARTH*, AND *GREEN LANTERN* WAS TRANSPORTED TO *MY* WORLD, WHERE HE FELL VICTIM TO THE *PARALYSIS* INTENDED FOR *ME*..."

"THE *SAME* CURSE TRANSFERRED THE *POWER RING* FROM HIS HAND TO MINE, FOR ALL THE *GOOD* IT DID ME..."

AND AFTER *COMING* TO EARTH, IT WAS SIMPLICITY *ITSELF* TO CAST A SPELL ON THE WITCH *ZATANNA*, FORBIDDING HER TO *WARN* HER FRIENDS--

--AND *PREVENTING* HER FROM USING HER *BACKWARDS-MAGIC!* I DIDN'T KNOW SHE'D BE ABLE TO USE *OTHER* SPELLS, BUT...

SOUNDS LIKE YOU HAD IT ALL *WORKED OUT*, WARLOCK--

EH?

20

151

TOO *BAD* ZATANNA HAD TO GO AND *SPOIL* IT!

ZATANNA... THIS ONE'S FOR YOU!

EPILOGUE and PROLOGUE

THE EARTH'S *SILENT SENTINEL*, SPINNING *HIGH* OVER THE SAPPHIRE OCEANS

...FORTUNATELY, THE CROSSBOW BOLT PASSED *BETWEEN* YOUR SHOULDER BONES, ZATANNA. YOU'LL *HEAL*--

--AND OUR *THANAGARIAN MEDIKIT* WILL MAKE SURE YOU DON'T HAVE A *SCAR!*

I WISH *KATAR* AND I COULD HAVE ANSWERED THAT *EMERGENCY SIGNAL*--BUT WE WERE INVOLVED IN A CRUCIAL EXPERIMENT ABOARD OUR STARSHIP.

IT APPEARS WE MISSED CONSIDERABLE *EXCITEMENT.*

I'M ONLY GLAD *THE ATOM* DECIPHERED MY *REVERSE-WARNING.* SINCE I COULDN'T MENTION THE *WARLOCK*, IT WAS THE ONLY WAY I COULD *PREPARE* YOU.

AND I'M GLAD *GREEN LANTERN* AND I REACHED YOU IN *TIME!* FORTUNATELY, I REGAINED CONSCIOUSNESS--AND STRENGTH ENOUGH TO TRANSPORT US TO EARTH.

...PRESENT BUT *UNSEEN!*

RECHARGING THE RING WHEN WE ARRIVED AT *ANGKOR WAT* WAS A *CINCH.*

UT THINK OF HE *IRONY*-- HE *WARLOCK* EEDED THE ATTERY... UT HE NEVER NEW I'D RDERED IT O STAY ITH ME, VERYWHERE

I'M AFRAID I'VE ALWAYS SUBCONSCIOUSLY *SUSPECTED* THE *WARLOCK'S* PLAN, *GREEN LANTERN...* EVER SINCE OUR *SECOND* MEETING...

...WHEN YOU REFERRED TO HIM AS THE *WARLOCK OF DIS,* INSTEAD OF *YS!*

GREAT GUARDIANS! HE MUST HAVE BEEN *AFFECTING* ME EVEN *THEN!*

ASIDE FROM EXPLAINING THAT NEW *OUTFIT* OF YOURS, I GUESS THAT LEAVES ONLY ONE THING TO BE SETTLED, *ZATANNA.*

EARLIER TODAY WE VOTED YOU A *MEMBER* OF THE *JUSTICE LEAGUE.* DO YOU *STILL* WANT TO SAY *NO?*

NO! NO--NOT NO! I MEAN--

YES!!

JUSTICE LEAGUE of AMERICA

HEREBY ELECTS

ZATANNA

TO MEMBERSHIP FOR LIFE--WITH ALL THE PRIVILEGES AND GRATUITIES, INCLUDING THE WEARING OF THE SIGNAL DEVICE AND POSSESSION OF THE SPECIAL KEY WHICH PERMITS ENTRY INTO THE SATELLITE-SANCTUARY, ITS LIBRARY AND SOUVENIR ROOMS. IT IS HEREBY FURTHER RESOLVED AND ACTED UPON THAT

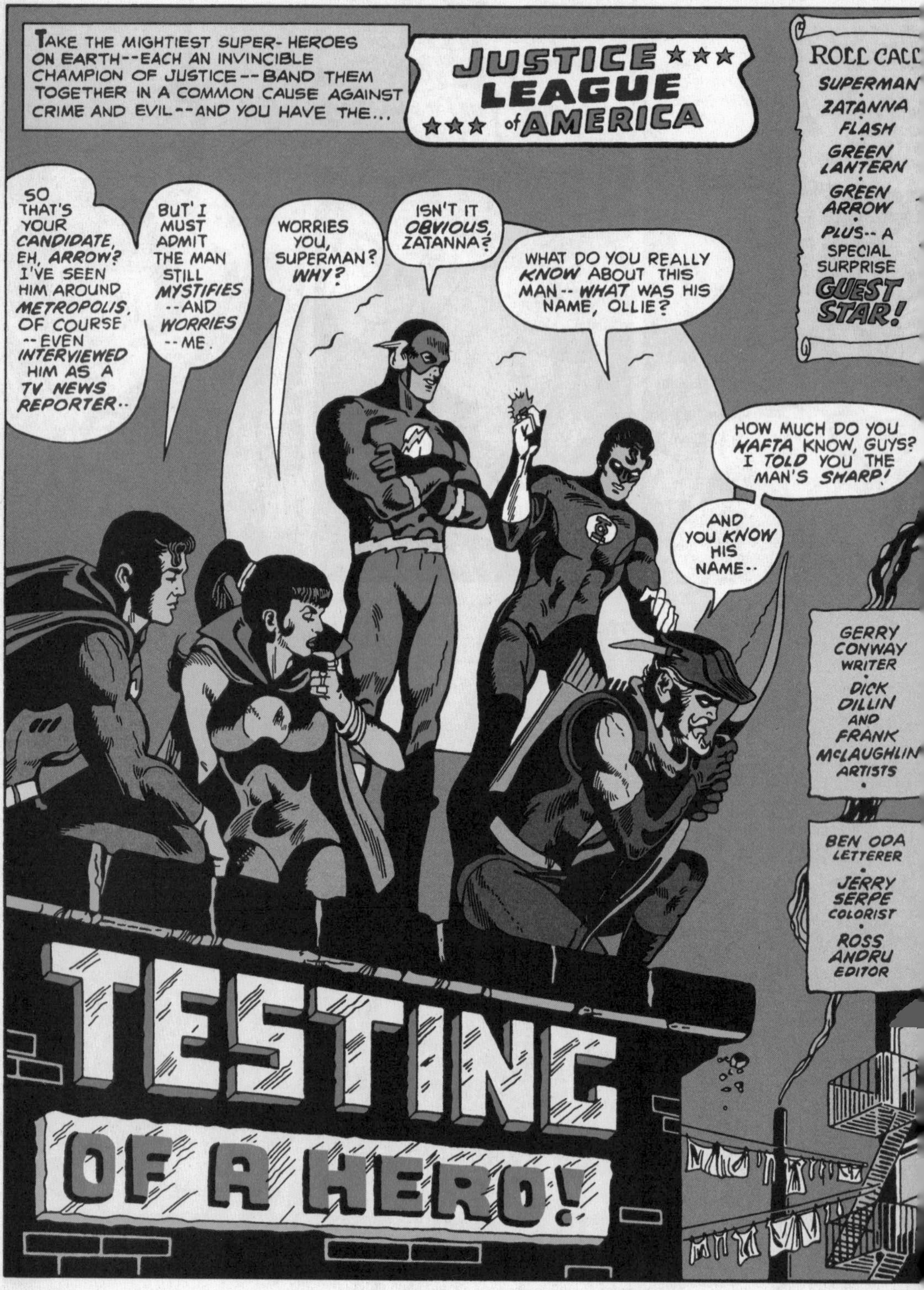
TAKE THE MIGHTIEST SUPER-HEROES ON EARTH--EACH AN INVINCIBLE CHAMPION OF JUSTICE--BAND THEM TOGETHER IN A COMMON CAUSE AGAINST CRIME AND EVIL--AND YOU HAVE THE...
JUSTICE LEAGUE of AMERICA
ROLL CALL
SUPERMAN
ZATANNA
FLASH
GREEN LANTERN
GREEN ARROW
PLUS--A SPECIAL SURPRISE GUEST STAR!
SO THAT'S YOUR CANDIDATE, EH, ARROW? I'VE SEEN HIM AROUND METROPOLIS, OF COURSE--EVEN INTERVIEWED HIM AS A TV NEWS REPORTER..
BUT I MUST ADMIT THE MAN STILL MYSTIFIES--AND WORRIES--ME.
WORRIES YOU, SUPERMAN? WHY?
ISN'T IT OBVIOUS, ZATANNA?
WHAT DO YOU REALLY KNOW ABOUT THIS MAN--WHAT WAS HIS NAME, OLLIE?
HOW MUCH DO YOU HAFTA KNOW, GUYS? I TOLD YOU THE MAN'S SHARP!
AND YOU KNOW HIS NAME..
GERRY CONWAY WRITER
DICK DILLIN AND FRANK McLAUGHLIN ARTISTS
BEN ODA LETTERER
JERRY SERPE COLORIST
ROSS ANDRU EDITOR
TESTING OF A HERO!

"...HE CALLS HIMSELF *BLACK LIGHTNING!"*

ON THE GARBAGE-STREWN STREET BELOW, FOUR MEN RACE, TUMBLING FROM A PAWNSHOP, CLUTCHING BAGS OVERFLOWING WITH DOLLAR BILLS...

THEY DON'T GET FAR--

--BEFORE A *BLUE-AND-GOLD* APPARITION LEAPS FROM THE SHADOWS, SNARLING IN A VOICE LIKE TEMPERED *STEEL*:

FREEZE, YOU TURKEYS!

LIKE *HELL!*

GUNSHOTS RING OUT IN THE RAIN SLICKED NIGHT--

--AND, ABOVE, FOUR COSTUMED FIGURES *TENSE*, EYES FLASHING WITH *CONCERN*:

...WHILE *ONE* SIMPLY SMILES A KNOWING *SMILE*...

SURPRISED, SUCKERS? GUESS YOU NEVER *HEARD* 'BOUT ME, HUH?

POW

POW

KSPOING KSPOING

KSPOING

TOO BAD FOR YOU··

2

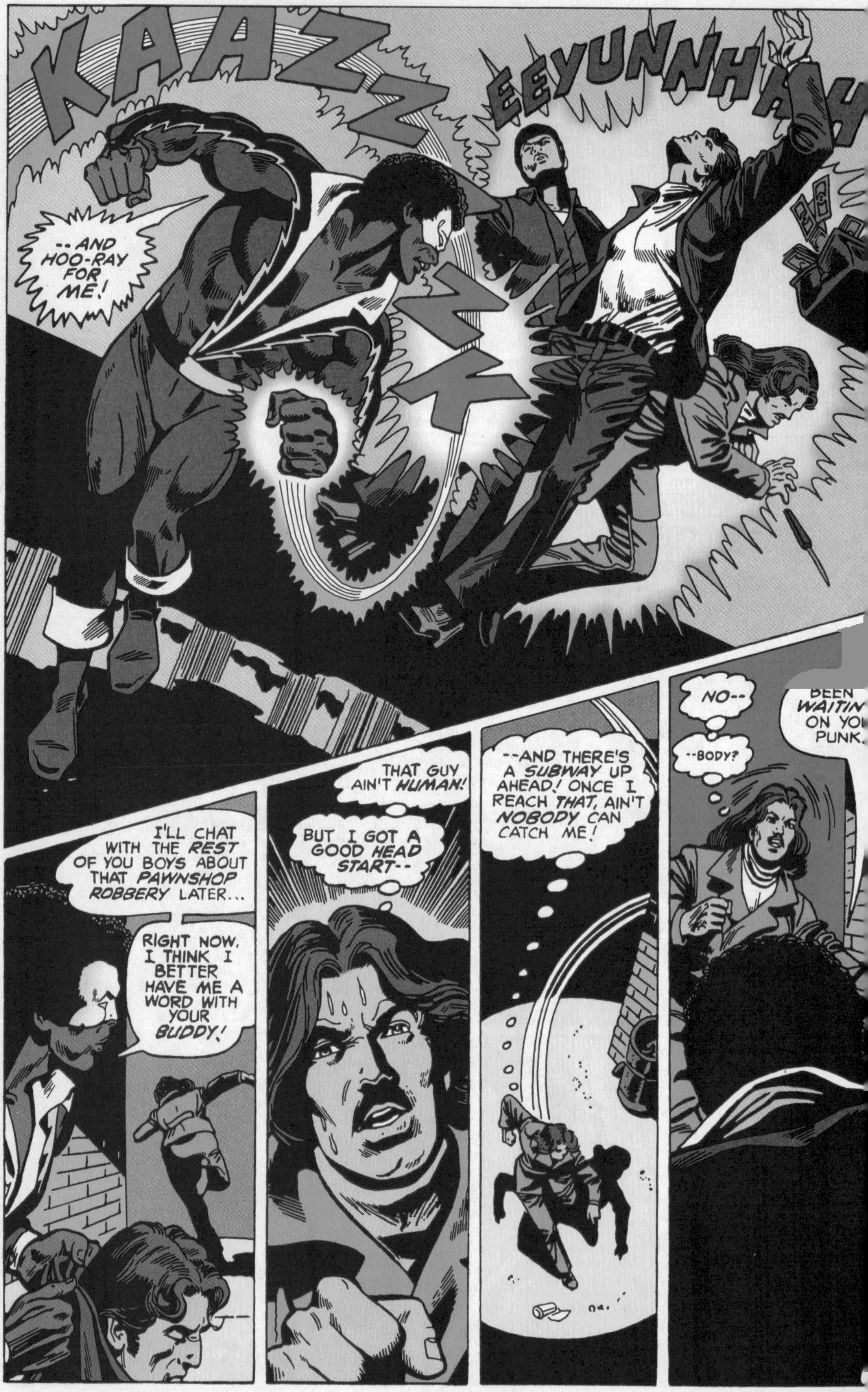
KAAZZ
EEYUNNHHAAH
--AND HOO-RAY FOR ME!
ZZK
I'LL CHAT WITH THE *REST* OF YOU BOYS ABOUT THAT *PAWNSHOP ROBBERY* LATER...
RIGHT NOW, I THINK I BETTER HAVE ME A WORD WITH YOUR *BUDDY!*
THAT GUY AIN'T *HUMAN!*
BUT I GOT A GOOD *HEAD START*--
--AND THERE'S A *SUBWAY* UP AHEAD! ONCE I REACH *THAT,* AIN'T *NOBODY* CAN CATCH ME!
NO--
--BODY?
BEEN *WAITIN* ON YO PUNK.

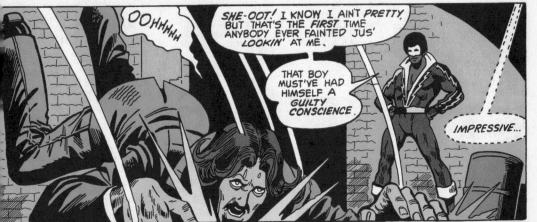

OOHHHHH

SHE-OOT! I KNOW I AIN'T *PRETTY*, BUT THAT'S THE *FIRST* TIME ANYBODY EVER FAINTED JUS' *LOOKIN'* AT ME.

THAT BOY MUST'VE HAD HIMSELF A *GUILTY CONSCIENCE*.

IMPRESSIVE...

..WE SAW *BLACK LIGHTNING* SLIP DOWN AN ALLEY TO CUT OFF THAT THIEF'S *ESCAPE ROUTE*, BUT THE THIEF DIDN'T...

...GIVING *LIGHTNING* A CHANCE TO CAPTURE HIM WITHOUT A *FIGHT*.

VERY GOOD.

I TOLD YA, THE GUY'S A *PRO!*

I MET HIM A FEW MONTHS BACK, WHEN I TRAILED A *CROOK* HERE TO *METROPOLIS...*

HE'S WHAT WE *NEED*, TROOPS. COOL, SMART, BRAVE ... AND *BLACK!*

HOLD IT, ARCHER... THAT'S *NOT* HOW WE MAKE DECISIONS IN THIS LEAGUE.

I NEVER THOUGHT *YOU* WOULD SUGGEST WE TAKE IN A *TOKEN BLACK...*

HUH? YOU THINK THAT'S WHY I--? OF ALL THE *LOUSY--*

EASY, BUDDY. FLASH DIDN'T *MEAN* IT THE WAY IT CAME OUT... I *HOPE.*

YEAH? THEN HOW DID YOU MEAN IT, *FLASHIE?* YOU GOT A MOUTH--*USE IT!*

4

OKAY, ARROW--HERE IT IS! I THINK YOUR *JUDGMENT* IS *WARPED!* YOU'RE TRYING SO HARD TO BE *MISTER LIBERAL*--YOU DON'T *THINK* STRAIGHT ANYMORE!

MAYBE *LIGHTNING* IS WHAT YOU *CLAIM*--BUT I WON'T TAKE *YOUR WORD* FOR IT!

YOU WON'T TAKE MY WORD? JUST WHO THE *HELL* DO YOU THINK--

GL, THIS IS *TERRIBLE!* GREEN ARROW HAS *ALWAYS* BEEN *COMBATIVE,* BUT *FLASH...*

HE'S *CHANGED,* ZATANNA! WHEN HIS *WIFE* WAS KILLED, HE STOPPED BEING THE OLD EASY-GOING *BARRY ALLEN,* MAYBE THAT MAN WILL *RETURN* SOMEDAY...

...BUT FO NOW, WE HAVE TO L AS HE IS AND TRY UNDERSTAN

THAT'S *ENOUGH,* ARROW!

WE CAN'T *FIGHT* AMONG OURSELVES --NOT WHEN THERE'S A *SIMPLE* SOLUTION TO THIS WHOLE QUESTION.

A *TEST*... YOU COULD CALL IT AN *EXAMINATION.*

I COULD *BUY* THAT-- PROVIDED GREEN ARROW ISN'T THE *JUDGE.*

I SAY *DITTO*... YOU BE THE JUDGE, *SUPES.* YOU'RE *DULL*... BUT *FAIR!*

NOT LIKE *TWINKLE-TOES* HERE.

BUT WHAT *SORT* OF TEST CAN IT BE?

AND WHAT WOULD WE BE *LOOKING* FOR?

THAT'S *EASY*-- FIGHTING ABILITY!

AND *SWIFT JUDGMENT!*

THAT-- AND MORE!

WE NEED TO KNOW HOW *BLACK LIGHTNING* WILL REACT IN A *CRISIS*-- AGAINST AN *UNFAMILIAR ENEMY*-- WITH *UNFAMILIAR POWERS!*

AND *HERE'S* HOW I SUGGEST WE GO ABOUT IT...

MEANWHILE, AS THE GATHERED HEROES OF THE *JUSTICE LEAGUE* DISCUSS ONE RESIDENT OF *SUICIDE SLUM*, ELSEWHERE IN THE GHETTO, A *LIGHT* SMOULDERS IN A BURNED-OUT *TENEMENT*...

...AND, IN THE HEART OF THAT BURNED-OUT *HULK*, A THOUSAND *SHADOWS* SKITTER TOWARD THAT EERIE *GLOW*...

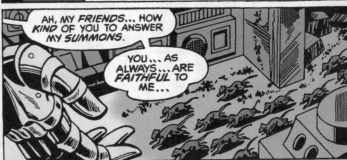

...LIKE *MOTHS* DRAWN TO A GLITTERING *FLAME*...

AH, MY *FRIENDS*... HOW *KIND* OF YOU TO ANSWER MY *SUMMONS*.

YOU... AS ALWAYS... ARE *FAITHFUL* TO ME...

YOU, *ALONE* OF ALL MY *FRIENDS*, HAVE *STAYED* BY MY SIDE.

THE OTHERS -- MY *WIFE*, MY *PARTNER*, MY CO-WORKERS AT *S.T.A.R. LABS* --ALL HAVE *DESERTED* ME--AND NOW ONLY *YOU* REMAIN!

YOU, WHOM SOCIETY HAS *CONDEMNED* AND *FORGOTTEN*-- JUST AS THEY HAVE *CONDEMNED* AND *FORGOTTEN* ME!

I TOLD MY COLLEAGUES AT *S.T.A.R.* THAT WE OWED AN *OBLIGATION* TO THE *POOR* AND *DISENFRANCHISED*! THEY WOULD NOT *LISTEN*!

TONIGHT-- THEY *WILL* LISTEN, AND THEY WILL *NOT* FORGET--

--THE *REGULATOR*!

6

AND AT THAT MOMENT, AT CENTRAL METROPOLIS *POLICE HEADQUARTERS*...

LIGHTNING, YOU *KNOW* I APPRECIATE WHAT YOU DID TONIGHT-- WE'VE BEEN AFTER THOSE *PAWNBROKER-ROBBERS* FOR WEEKS...

GOT ME A FEELING THERE'S A *"BUT"* COMIN' UP, INSPECTOR.

BUT...THIS *VIGILANTE* ACT IS GOING TO GET YOU IN *TROUBLE*. THE *CITY COUNCIL* IS CONSIDERING A *NEW* LAW...

I *KNOW* IT... AND I AIN'T LOSIN' ANY *SLEEP* OVER IT, EITHER. ANY LAW THAT'S GONNA AFFECT *THIS* BOY'LL ALSO *HAFTA* AFFECT *SUPERMAN*...

...AND *NO WAY* IS *THAT* GONNA HAPPEN IN *THIS* TOWN.

'SIDES, I CAN ALWAYS COUNT ON *YOU* OUT THERE BATTIN' FOR ME...

AIN'T THAT *RIGHT*, INSPECTOR HENDERSON?

YEAH.

TAKE *CARE* OF YOURSELF, LIGHTNING.

SOMEONE HAS TO.

♪ WHEW! ♪ SOMETIMES THAT *STREET* JIVE MAKES MY *JAW* ACHE. BUT I SUPPOSE IT'S *NECESSARY* AS A *"BLIND."*

♪ YAWN! ♪ I BETTER GET *HOME*, THOUGH... I'VE GOT TO BE AT *LINCOLN HIGH* EARLY TOMORROW TO *MIMEOGRAPH* A HISTORY TEST... *NOT* MY FAVORITE PASTIME!

NOW?

NOW!

HOLY--!

ARRRHH

BTOOM

MAIL

CRAZY! TWO REFUGEES FROM A DRIVE-IN MOVIE MONSTER FLICK... ONE LIKE SOME KIND OF HUMAN STARBURST, AND THE OTHER--

-- A JUNIOR-LEAGUE KING KONG!

I DON'T KNOW WHY THEY'RE ATTACKING ME, BUT THERE'S ONE THING I DO KNOW...

ARRHHH

-- I DON'T LIKE IT!

OFF ME, YOU DUMB SUCKER!

UNNHH..!

WHOOPS... JUST NOTICED, THAT KING IS A QUEEN... A SHE-APE!

I REALLY HATE HAVING TO DO THIS TO A LADY--

SWOOOOOSH

8

--BUT THAT *GLINT* IN HER EYES DOESN'T LEAVE ME MUCH *CHOICE!*

WHAMO

YOU'VE HURT *PRIMAK!*

IF SHE'S *INJURED,* I'LL--

SHAZOOMM

YOU'RE THE *SECOND* DONKEY WHO'S TRIED BLASTIN' ME AWAY TONIGHT, AND LIKE I TOLE THE *OTHER* FELLA, YOU GOT A LOT TO LEARN 'BOUT *BLACK LIGHTNING--*

FLAASSH

--AND NOT A WHOLE LOTTA *TIME* TO BE *TAUGHT!*

SHSSSHHH

FTOOSH

YOU'VE GO[T] SOME KIND OF *FORCE FIELD* PROTECTIO[N] --MAKES YO[U] *INVULNERABL[E]* MY *FIRE- BOLTS* WERE *USELESS!* NO TIME TO *YAAAAAH!*

BEATS *ME,* INSPECTOR. THOSE YAHOOS JUS' *ATTACKED* ME... DIDN'T EXACTLY SAY *WHY.*

IT'S WHAT I SAID *EARLIER*-- THIS *VIGILANTISM* BREEDS *TROUBLE!*

YOU'VE BECOME A *TARGET* FOR *WEIRDOES!*

CRAZY...

LIGHTNING... FOR THE LOVE'A *MIKE,* WHAT *HAPPENED?*

POLICE

MAYBE SO... BUT ANYONE *ELSE* TRIES JUMPIN' ME, HE'LL GET THE SAME TREATMENT THOSE TWO GOT. *BET* ON IT.

GOTTA GO NOW... CATCH YOU *TOMORROW.*

SAY, INSPECTOR HENDERSON, SOMETHING *ODD* HERE.

WHAT'S *THAT,* OFFICER?

SIR, YOU BETTER COME TAKE A LOOK FOR *YOURSELF...*

AND, AS THE WEARY POLICEMAN TURNS HIS *ATTENTION* TO THE MYSTERY AT HAND...

...A FEW MILES AWAY, ON THE OUTSKIRTS OF *SUICIDE SLUM,* A HUNDRED SMALL SHADOWS *SEPARATE* FROM THE DARKNESS AND RACE ACROSS A DESERTED *STREET...*

10

... MOVING WITH UNCANNY *PURPOSE*...

S.T.A.R. LABS
AUTHORIZED
PERSONNEL
ONLY

... AND *DEADLY INTENT*...

YIIIEEE

THE GUARD SCREAMS *ONCE*; HIS NEXT CRY IS A MOIST *GURGLE*; BUT *NEITHER* SOUND IS HEARD BY ANYONE IN THE SURROUNDING TENEMENTS, AND EVEN IF IT *WERE*--

--IT WOULD NOT BE *HEEDED*; FOR IT DOESN'T *PAY* TO INVESTIGATE *CRIES FOR HELP* IN THE GHETTO KNOWN AS *SUICIDE SLUM*...

THE *LOCKBOX* CONTROLLING THE *AUTOMATIC GATE* IS A DELICATE PIECE OF *CRAFTMANSHIP*; BUT A DOZEN NIBBLING *TEETH* AND TWO-DOZEN SCRATCHING *CLAWS* HAVE AN EFFECT UNANTICIPATED BY ITS *DESIGNERS*...

SRAZZZKK

... AND THE *LOCKED GATE SWINGS OPEN*, AS THOUGH "PICKED" BY A *MASTER THIEF*...

WELL DONE, TTLE ONES. E HAVE TAKEN E FIRST STEP OGETHER.

NOW, TOGETHER WE WILL REAP OUR REWARD...

SIMULTANEOUSLY, HIGH ABOVE AND SEVERAL MILES SOUTH...

SO FAR, BLACK LIGHTNING HAS EXCEEDED OUR EXPECTATIONS...BUT HE'S PASSED ONLY THE FIRST PART OF HIS TEST...

"THE MORE DIFFICULT HALF IS ABOUT TO BEGIN--

--NOW!"

PARDON ME, PAL, AREN'T YOU BLACK LIGHTNING?

WHAT THE--?

I MUST BE WORKING TOO HARD...COULD HAVE SWORN I HEARD A VOICE, FELT A TAP ON MY SHOULDER...

JUST WANTED TO MAKE SURE YOU WERE FACING ME, CHUMP

I NEVER COULD HIT A MAN FROM BEHIND!

YUNNNHH

KAPOW

12

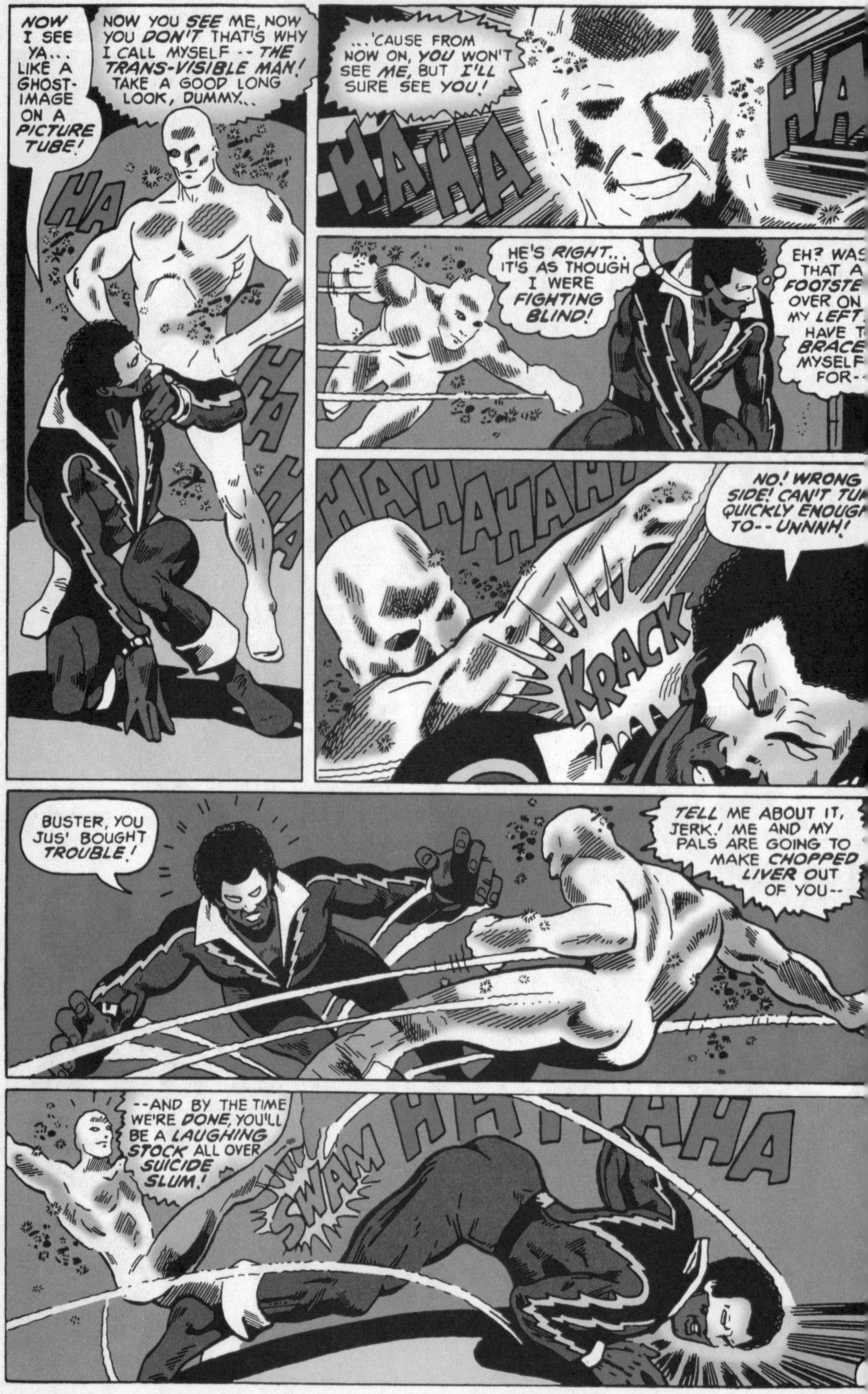
NOW I SEE YA... LIKE A GHOST-IMAGE ON A PICTURE TUBE!
NOW YOU SEE ME, NOW YOU DON'T THAT'S WHY I CALL MYSELF -- THE TRANS-VISIBLE MAN! TAKE A GOOD LONG LOOK, DUMMY...
HA
HA
HA
HA
...'CAUSE FROM NOW ON, YOU WON'T SEE ME, BUT I'LL SURE SEE YOU!
HAHAHA
HA
HE'S RIGHT... IT'S AS THOUGH I WERE FIGHTING BLIND!
EH? WAS THAT A FOOTSTE OVER ON MY LEFT HAVE T BRACE MYSELF FOR--
HAHAHAHAH
NO! WRONG SIDE! CAN'T TU QUICKLY ENOUG TO-- UNNNH!
KRACK
BUSTER, YOU JUS' BOUGHT TROUBLE!
TELL ME ABOUT IT, JERK! ME AND MY PALS ARE GOING TO MAKE CHOPPED LIVER OUT OF YOU--
--AND BY THE TIME WE'RE DONE, YOU'LL BE A LAUGHING STOCK ALL OVER SUICIDE SLUM!
SWAM
HAHAHAHA

YOU DON'T LAUGH AT A MAN WHO'S BEEN FIGHTING FOR *DIGNITY* FOR MOST OF HIS LIFE: YOU MIGHT MAKE HIM MAD...

VERY MAD.

BUT *ANGER* IS NO SUBSTITUTE FOR *STRATEGY* AND *TACTICS*, AND IN THE NEXT FEW MINUTES, *BLACK LIGHTNING* LEARNS THAT LESSON-- *PAINFULLY...*

YET, WITH EVERY *BLIND SWING*, AND EVERY *PUNCH* FROM AN UNSEEN ASSAILANT, HE GROWS MORE AND MORE *FURIOUS...*

...FOR THE *LAUGHTER* IS LOUD IN HIS EARS...

HAHA

HAHA

HAHA

HAD *ENOUGH,* PUNCHING-BAG?

IF I COULD JUST... *SEE* YOU...

WELL, IF YOU CAN'T SEE *HIM,* MATEY--

...AND *FRUSTRATION* BURNS LIKE A BRAND IN HIS *HEART!*

14

-- WILL I DO? SWASHBUCKLER IS MY NAME, *SWORDPLAY* IS MY GAME.

YOUR SPARRING PARTNER IS A *FRIEND* OF MINE.

THE OTHER MAN'S ANSWER IS A *RAGING* CRY--

AARRR RHHH

--AND A *LEAP* THAT CARRIES HIM ACROSS THE SPACE SEPARATING THEM IN AN *EYEBLINK*--!

AARR

ELECTRICITY CRACKLES, GIVING PROOF TO *BLACK LIGHTNING'S* NAME; THE RAPIER JUMPS FROM SHOCKED FINGERS, THE SWASHBUCKLER FALLS UNDER A *HEAVY BLOW*...

KKKRAZKKK

WHAM

YOU'RE *FAST*, MATEY, BUT YOU'RE NOT *FAST ENOUSH* TO ESCAPE A *BALL* BETWEEN Y' *RIBS!*

CHPOW

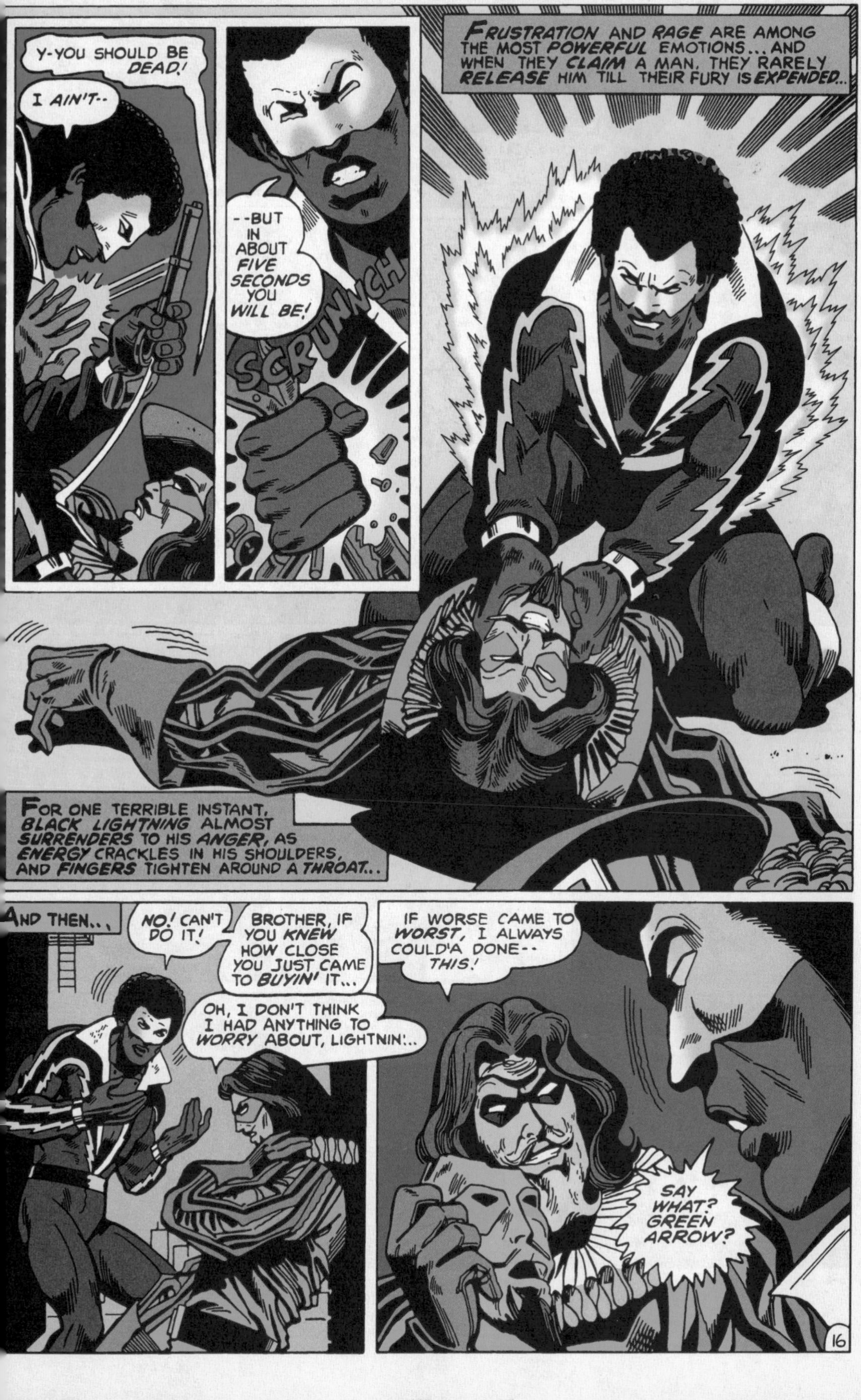
Y-YOU SHOULD BE DEAD!
I AIN'T--
--BUT IN ABOUT FIVE SECONDS YOU WILL BE!
SCRUNNCH
FRUSTRATION AND RAGE ARE AMONG THE MOST POWERFUL EMOTIONS... AND WHEN THEY CLAIM A MAN, THEY RARELY RELEASE HIM TILL THEIR FURY IS EXPENDED...
FOR ONE TERRIBLE INSTANT, BLACK LIGHTNING ALMOST SURRENDERS TO HIS ANGER, AS ENERGY CRACKLES IN HIS SHOULDERS, AND FINGERS TIGHTEN AROUND A THROAT...
AND THEN...
NO! CAN'T DO IT!
BROTHER, IF YOU KNEW HOW CLOSE YOU JUST CAME TO BUYIN' IT...
OH, I DON'T THINK I HAD ANYTHING TO WORRY ABOUT, LIGHTNIN'...
IF WORSE CAME TO WORST, I ALWAYS COULD'A DONE-- THIS!
SAY WHAT? GREEN ARROW?
16

WHAT'S GOIN ON?

WE OWE YOU AN APOLOGY, FRIEND ALL THIS, *ALL* OF IT, WAS A *TEST*.

ESPECIALLY THE LAST PART. WE HAD TO SEE HOW YOU'D REACT WHEN YOU WERE *PUSHED TO THE LIMIT*...

...SO WE PLAYED A LITTLE *SUBTERFUGE*. *GREEN LANTERN* WAS THE *HUMAN STARBURST*, *ZATANNA* BECAME *PRIMAK*, AND *FLASHIE* WAS THE *TRANS-VISIBLE MAN!*

WE ALMOST *BLEW* THE WHOLE PERFORMANCE WHEN *INSPECTOR HENDERSON* AND HIS MEN *RECOGNIZED* US...BUT LUCKILY, HE AGREED TO GO ALONG.

I DON'T *GET* IT-- WHAT'S THE *IDEA?*

CALL IT AN *INITIATION TEST*, LIGHTNING, FOR *MEMBERSHIP* IN THE *LEAGUE*.

YOU JUST *PASSED* WITH *FLYING COLORS!*

HOLD *EVERYTHING!* WHO WANTS TO JOIN THE *LEAGUE?*

HUH?

I APPRECIATE THE OFFER, FOLKS, BUT *THIS* HERO'S GOT *ENOUGH* WORK RIGHT HERE IN *SUICIDE SLUM*. I CAN'T GO FLASHIN' OFF WITH YOU GUYS.

YOU JUST BETTER GET YOURSELF ANOTHER BOY!

YOU THINK WE MADE HIM MAD WITH OUR *DUMB TEST?*

MAYBE... BUT *THAT* ISN'T THE REASON HE TURNED US DOWN. SOME PEOPLE JUST DON'T WORK WELL WITH *GROUPS*, ARROW.

HE WOULD HAVE MADE A *FINE* ADDITION TO OUR LEAGUE.

I WONDER IF WE'LL SEE HIM AGAIN.

I HAVE THE STRANGEST FEELING WE *WILL*, HAL... AND PERHAPS SOONER THAN WE *THINK*...

"...PERHAPS *SOONER* THAN WE THINK..."

NEXT: THE SINISTER SECRET OF **THE REGULATOR!**

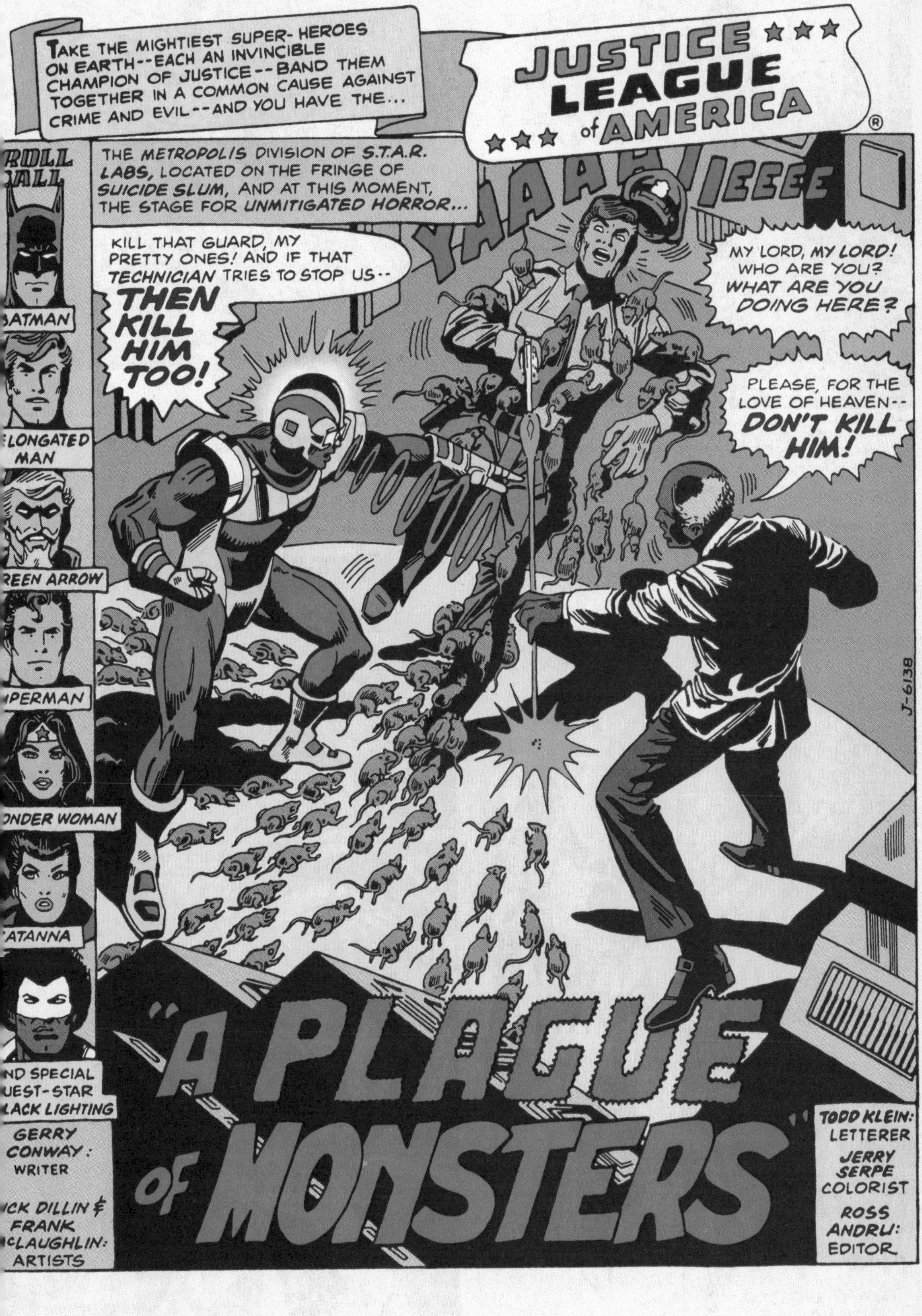

TAKE THE MIGHTIEST SUPER-HEROES ON EARTH--EACH AN INVINCIBLE CHAMPION OF JUSTICE--BAND THEM TOGETHER IN A COMMON CAUSE AGAINST CRIME AND EVIL--AND YOU HAVE THE...
JUSTICE LEAGUE of AMERICA ®
THE METROPOLIS DIVISION OF S.T.A.R. LABS, LOCATED ON THE FRINGE OF SUICIDE SLUM, AND AT THIS MOMENT, THE STAGE FOR UNMITIGATED HORROR...
YAAAAHIEEEE
KILL THAT GUARD, MY PRETTY ONES! AND IF THAT TECHNICIAN TRIES TO STOP US-- THEN KILL HIM TOO!
MY LORD, MY LORD! WHO ARE YOU? WHAT ARE YOU DOING HERE?
PLEASE, FOR THE LOVE OF HEAVEN-- DON'T KILL HIM!
BATMAN
ELONGATED MAN
GREEN ARROW
SUPERMAN
WONDER WOMAN
ZATANNA
AND SPECIAL GUEST-STAR BLACK LIGHTING
J-6138
"A PLAGUE OF MONSTERS"
GERRY CONWAY: WRITER
DICK DILLIN & FRANK McLAUGHLIN: ARTISTS
TODD KLEIN: LETTERER
JERRY SERPE COLORIST
ROSS ANDRU: EDITOR

THAT'S ENOUGH. THEN, MY LITTLE FRIENDS. THE TECHNICIAN IS *RIGHT*.

WE DON'T NEED TO KILL THE GUARD... NOT YET!

H-HOW DID YOU GET IN HERE...THE ALARMS, THE *ELECTRIFIED* FENCING...?

CHITTER CHITTER CHK CHK

IT WAS *SIMPLE*, RICHARDS...ESPECIALLY WHEN YOU *KNOW THE WAY!*

I GAVE MY FRIENDS THEIR *COMMANDS* WITH THIS *HELMET*... AND THEY DID THE *REST!*

GOOD GOD-- BARNABAS! BARNABAS BOULTON!

YES, RICHARDS, IT'S *ME*, BARNEY BOULTON, YOUR *EX-COLLEAGUE* ...THE MAN YOU *BETRAYED!*

W-WE ALWAYS WONDERED WHAT *HAPPENED* TO YOU, BARNABAS. T-THE LAST WE HEARD, YOU'D *DISAPPEARED* FROM THE HOSPITAL...

YES, THE HOSPITAL-- THE *MENTAL* HOSPITAL WHERE YOU AND MY *WIFE* HAD ME COMMITTED FOR A "*NERVOUS BREAKDOWN*"!

"YOU WERE *JEALOUS* OF MY GENIUS! YOU HATED ME BECAUSE SPOKE THE *TRUTH!*

UNNNH

SAP

I BUILT THIS *HELMET* TO HELP MAN RID THE *SLUMS* OF THE *VERMIN* WHICH INFESTED IT... BUT *YOU* SAID THE HELMET HAD DRIVEN ME *MAD!*

YOU *LIED*, RICHARDS! YOU DON'T *CARE* ABOUT THE POOR--*NONE* OF YOU DO!

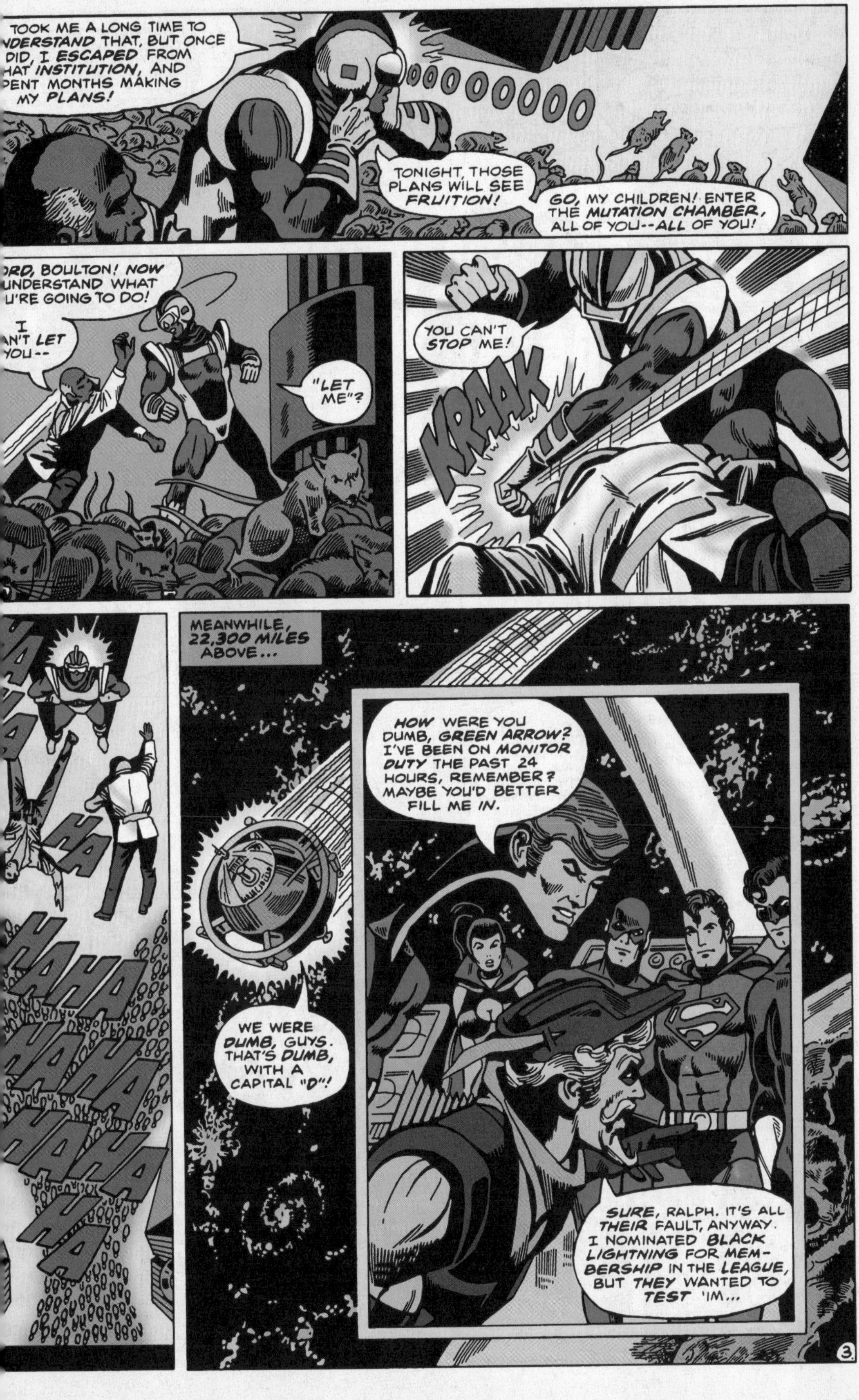
TOOK ME A LONG TIME TO NDERSTAND THAT, BUT ONCE DID, I ESCAPED FROM HAT INSTITUTION, AND PENT MONTHS MAKING MY PLANS!
OOOOOOOOOO
TONIGHT, THOSE PLANS WILL SEE FRUITION!
GO, MY CHILDREN! ENTER THE MUTATION CHAMBER, ALL OF YOU--ALL OF YOU!
ORD, BOULTON! NOW UNDERSTAND WHAT U'RE GOING TO DO!
I AN'T LET YOU--
"LET ME"?
YOU CAN'T STOP ME!
KRAAK
HA HA HA HA HA HA HA HA HA HA HA HA HA HA HA HA
MEANWHILE, 22,300 MILES ABOVE...
WE WERE DUMB, GUYS. THAT'S DUMB, WITH A CAPITAL "D"!
HOW WERE YOU DUMB, GREEN ARROW? I'VE BEEN ON MONITOR DUTY THE PAST 24 HOURS, REMEMBER? MAYBE YOU'D BETTER FILL ME IN.
SURE, RALPH. IT'S ALL THEIR FAULT, ANYWAY. I NOMINATED BLACK LIGHTNING FOR MEMBERSHIP IN THE LEAGUE, BUT THEY WANTED TO TEST 'IM...
3

...AND PROBABLY BECAUSE OF *THAT,* THE GUY TURNED US *DOWN!*

I'VE BEEN *THINKING* ABOUT IT THE PAST HOUR, AND I'M *STEAMED.*

MAYBE *YOU* JOKERS ARE READY TO LET IT *DROP...* BUT ME, I'M GONNA GIVE IT *ANOTHER TRY.* AND *THIS* TIME-- WITHOUT ANY *HELP* FROM *YOU!*

ARROW, YOU DON'T *SERIOUSLY* BELIEVE THAT *FLASH* AND *GREEN LANTERN* AND *I* WANTED LIGHTNING TO REJECT US... DO YOU?

WHAT *YOU* WANTED DOESN'T MEAN DIDDLY, *SUPES...*

...I'M JUST COUNTIN' *RESULTS.* CATCH YOU LATER... *MAYBE.*

SOMEBODY BETTER GO WITH THAT CRAZY *ARCHER,* AND SINCE I'M OFF *MONITOR* DUTY, I THINK I'LL *STRETCH* A POINT... AND NOMINATE ME.

AND *I* WILL ACCOMPANY YOU, *ELONGATED MAN.*

BE *CAREFUL,* ALL OF YOU...

THERE GO THREE FINE *JUSTICE* LEAGUERS.

I HOPE THEY COME BACK WITH A *FOURTH.*

...WHAT CAN I *TELL* YOU, *ARCHER? SURE,* I WORK WITH *BLACK LIGHTNING,* BUT I'VE GOT AS MUCH OF AN IDEA HOW TO *FIND* HIM AS *YOU* DO...

METROPOLIS POLICE HEADQUARTERS

...WHICH IS *NO* IDEA AT ALL!

174

E PROBLEM WITH THE GUY IS, HE'S A *ILANTE*. IT'S MADE HIM SOME *ENEMIES* ERE IN THE DEPARTMENT. HE CAN'T AFFORD TO BE *TOO* AVAILABLE.

SOME COFFEE?

NO THANKS, INSPECTOR. LOOKS LIKE WE'VE HIT A *DEAD END*.

ERHAPS COULD OCATE HIM GICALLY...

SURE BEATS PUTTING AN AD IN THE *DAILY PLANET*, ZATANNA.

ATTENTION ALL UNITS! INTRUDER ALARM AT *S.T.A.R. LABS!*

HEY, YOU HEAR THAT?

OUNDS E *OUR* E KIND OF CTION!

HOW, YOU ASK? ATTRIBUTE IT TO THE *WILL POWER* AND *COURAGE* OF ONE WOUNDED GUARD ACTIVATING A *HIDDEN SWITCH*...

AND IF IT'S OUR KIND OF ACTION-- MAYBE IT'LL ATTRACT *BLACK LIGHTNING!*

AND, EVEN AS THE ALARM SUMMONS THE *POLICE* FROM *SURROUNDING PRECINCTS*--

-- IN AN APARTMENT *NOT FAR* FROM THE LAB COMPLEX, A WEARY *SUPER-HERO* CHANGES INTO A TIRED HIGH SCHOOL HISTORY TEACHER NAMED *JEFFERSON PIERCE*.

I CAN'T BELIEVE I'LL HAVE TO BE *UP* IN A FEW HOURS TO MIMEOGRAPH THAT *AMERICAN HISTORY* EXAM FOR MY *9:15* CLASS... OH, MY ACHING *BODY*...

OH, YES! YES! LET'S *HURRY!*

N ALARM AT *S.T.A.R. LABS*, HEN ALL THE ALARMS HAVE BEEN *BYPASSED?*

5

I'VE GOT TO STOP BURNING THE OLD *CANDLE* FROM TOP TO BOTTOM.

BUT WHICH PART OF MY LIFE DO I *GIVE UP?* JEFFERSON PIERCE, *TEACHER?* OR BLACK LIGHTNING, SO-CALLED "*SUPER-HERO*"?

--INTERRUPT THIS MUSICAL INTERLUDE FOR AN ANNOUNCEMENT FROM THE METROPOLIS POLICE DEPARTMENT:

ALL RESIDENTS IN THE SUICIDE SLUM AREA ARE ADVISED TO STAY OFF THE STREETS! THERE IS AN EMERGENCY SITUATION AT S.T.A.R. LABS, AND POLICE HAVE CORDONED OFF THE BLOCKS FROM 123RD STREET TO --

THERE'S YOUR ANSWER, SON.

KLIK

FOR THE TIME BEING... YOU HAVE TO BE *BOTH!*

S.T.A.R. LABS, TWO MINUTES AND THIRTY-THREE SECONDS LATER...

ALL *S.W.A.T.* TEAMS IN POSITION! GET READY TO *MOVE* OUT--

CAPTAIN! I SAW SOMETHING *MOVE* INSIDE THE *GATE!* SHADOWS-- *LARGE* SHADOWS! I THINK THEY'RE--

CHITTERCHITTER CHTCHTCH

BRAKABRAK

KPOW

POW

POW

YAAAAA!

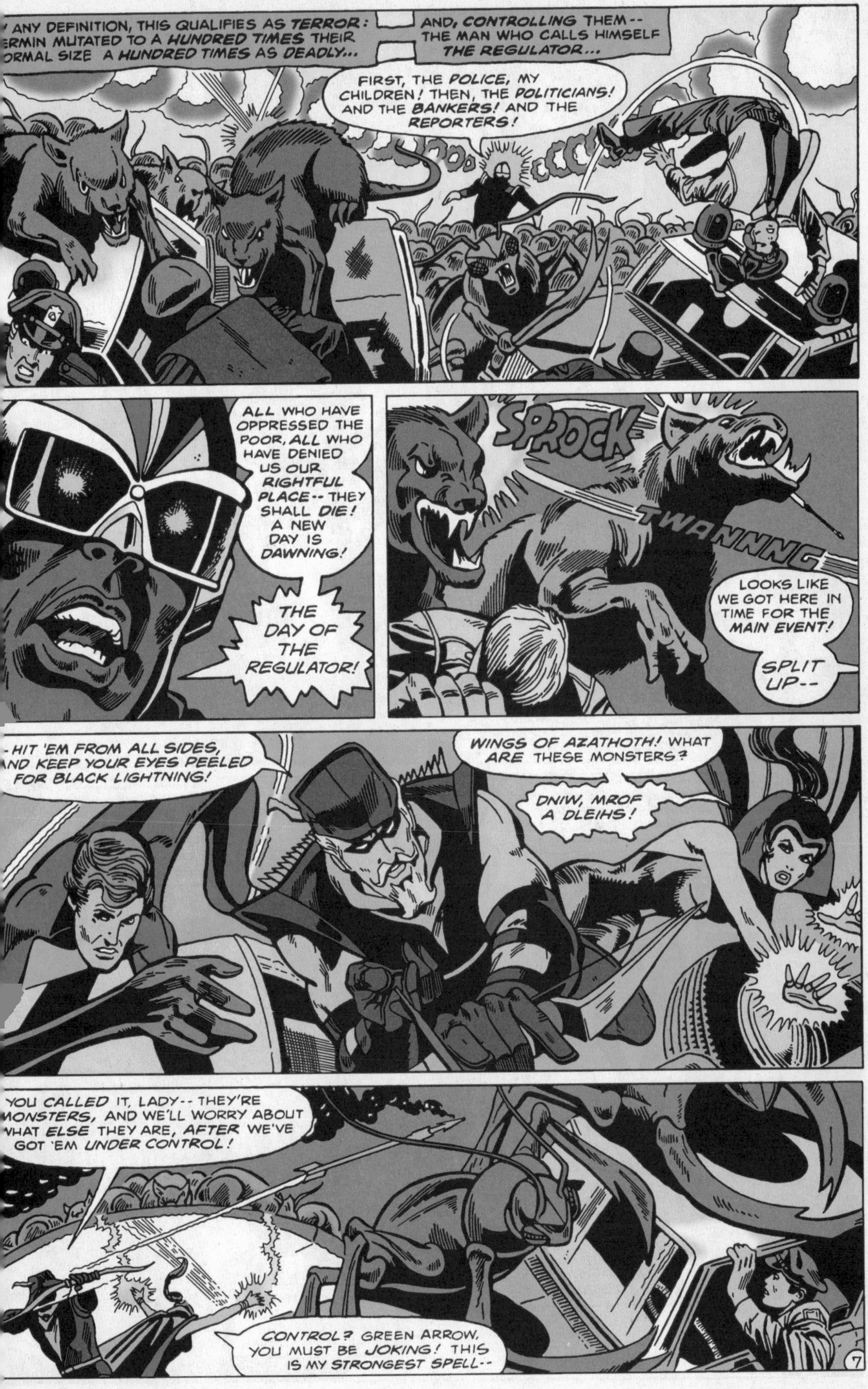

Y ANY DEFINITION, THIS QUALIFIES AS TERROR: ERMIN MUTATED TO A HUNDRED TIMES THEIR ORMAL SIZE A HUNDRED TIMES AS DEADLY...
AND, CONTROLLING THEM -- THE MAN WHO CALLS HIMSELF THE REGULATOR...
FIRST, THE POLICE, MY CHILDREN! THEN, THE POLITICIANS! AND THE BANKERS! AND THE REPORTERS!
ALL WHO HAVE OPPRESSED THE POOR, ALL WHO HAVE DENIED US OUR RIGHTFUL PLACE -- THEY SHALL DIE! A NEW DAY IS DAWNING!
THE DAY OF THE REGULATOR!
SPROCK
TWANNNG
LOOKS LIKE WE GOT HERE IN TIME FOR THE MAIN EVENT!
SPLIT UP--
-HIT 'EM FROM ALL SIDES, ND KEEP YOUR EYES PEELED FOR BLACK LIGHTNING!
WINGS OF AZATHOTH! WHAT ARE THESE MONSTERS?
DNIW, MROF A DLEIHS!
YOU CALLED IT, LADY -- THEY'RE MONSTERS, AND WE'LL WORRY ABOUT WHAT ELSE THEY ARE, AFTER WE'VE GOT 'EM UNDER CONTROL!
CONTROL? GREEN ARROW, YOU MUST BE JOKING! THIS IS MY STRONGEST SPELL--
7

--AND IT ISN'T EVEN *SLOWING* THEM DOWN!

THERE ARE JUST *TOO MANY* OF THEM! I CAN TURN A *DOZEN* OF THEM TO *STONE-- STAR EMOCEB SEUTATS* * --BUT A *HUNDRED* MORE TAKE THEIR PLACE!

*ZATANNA PERFORMS MAGIC BY SPEAKING HER SPELLS *BACKWARDS!* --ROSS.

ZATANNA'S *RIGHT!* I CAN *TRIP UP* THESE UGLIES FOR A MOMENT --GIVE THE COPS A CHANCE TO *DISENGAGE* --BUT THERE'S *NO WAY* WE CAN *BEAT* THEM!

TOO MANY OF THEM-- *TOO FEW* OF US!

THEN LET'S CALL FOR *REINFORCEMENTS--*

BREEEEEEE

FTOOSH

--AND HOPE THEY GET HERE BEFORE WE DO A *CUSTER'S LAST STAND!*

THE *JUSTICE LEAGUE SIGNAL DEVICE* CAN BROADCAST *AROUND THE WORLD,* BUT IT DOES LITTLE *GOOD* WHEN THOSE WHO HEAR IT *CANNOT RESPOND...*

FOR *RAY PALMER,* ALIAS THE *ATOM,* THE SIGNAL REACHES HIM WHILE *SPELUNKING* WITH HIS WIFE IN *CARLSBAD CAVERNS...*

FOR *RED TORNADO,* THE SUMMONS COMES WHILE HE WALKS WITH HIS *ORPHANED* YOUNG FRIEND, *TRAYA,* IN MANHATTAN'S *TIMES SQUARE...*

FOR *AQUAMAN,* THE SIGNAL ARRIVES DURING A *DELICATE OCEAN RESCUE...*

...AND FOR *THE BLACK CANARY,* THE CALL REACHES HER IN A *SICKBED...*

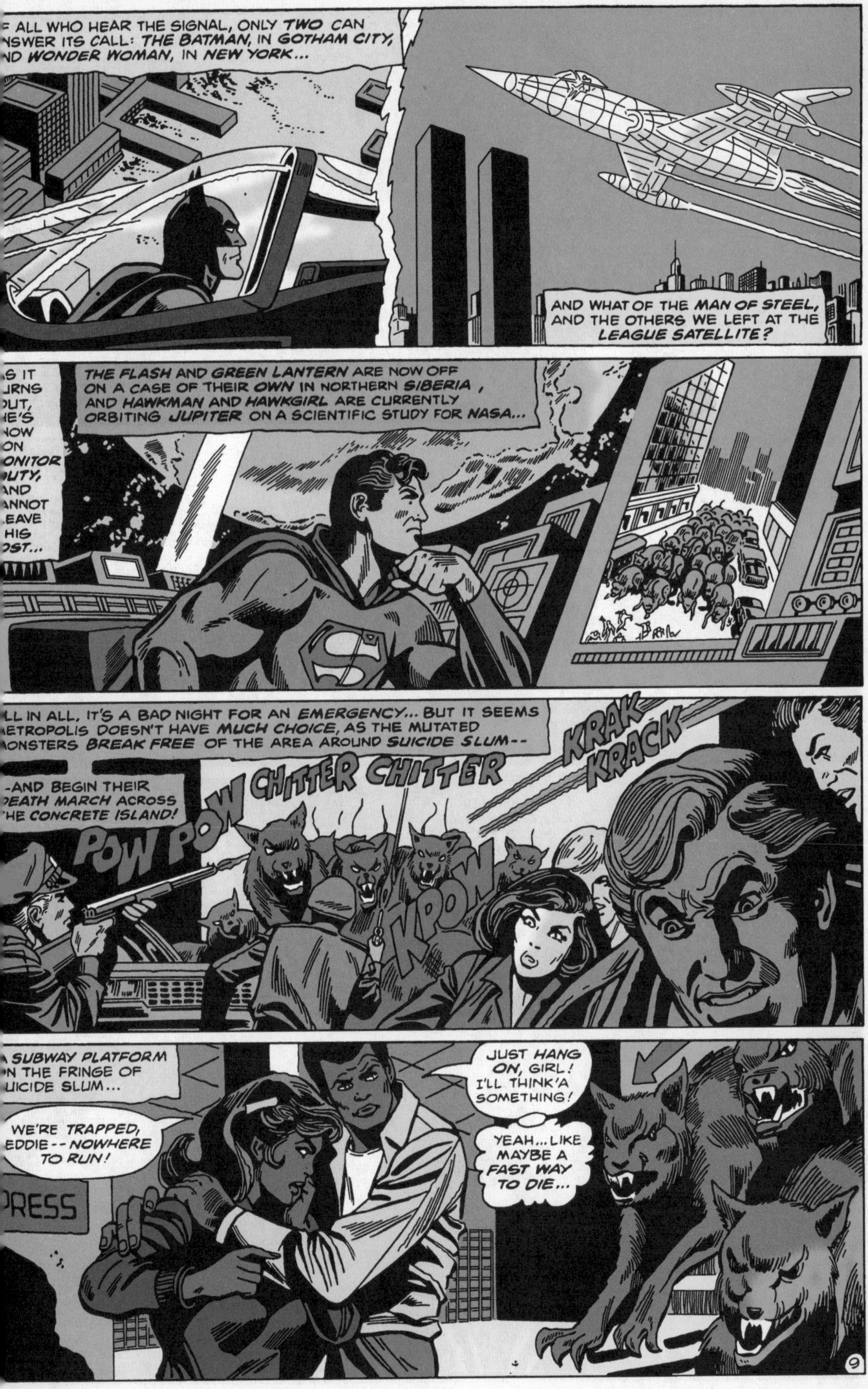
F ALL WHO HEAR THE SIGNAL, ONLY TWO CAN NSWER ITS CALL: THE BATMAN, IN GOTHAM CITY, ND WONDER WOMAN, IN NEW YORK...
AND WHAT OF THE MAN OF STEEL, AND THE OTHERS WE LEFT AT THE LEAGUE SATELLITE?
S IT JRNS OUT, HE'S NOW ON ONITOR UTY, AND ANNOT LEAVE HIS OST...
THE FLASH AND GREEN LANTERN ARE NOW OFF ON A CASE OF THEIR OWN IN NORTHERN SIBERIA, AND HAWKMAN AND HAWKGIRL ARE CURRENTLY ORBITING JUPITER ON A SCIENTIFIC STUDY FOR NASA...
LL IN ALL, IT'S A BAD NIGHT FOR AN EMERGENCY... BUT IT SEEMS ETROPOLIS DOESN'T HAVE MUCH CHOICE, AS THE MUTATED ONSTERS BREAK FREE OF THE AREA AROUND SUICIDE SLUM--
-AND BEGIN THEIR DEATH MARCH ACROSS THE CONCRETE ISLAND!
KRAK KRACK
POW POW CHITTER CHITTER
KPOW
A SUBWAY PLATFORM N THE FRINGE OF UICIDE SLUM...
WE'RE TRAPPED, EDDIE--NOWHERE TO RUN!
JUST HANG ON, GIRL! I'LL THINK'A SOMETHING!
YEAH... LIKE MAYBE A FAST WAY TO DIE...
PRESS
9

EDDIE, LOOK!

IT'S THAT GUY --BLACK LIGHTNING!

STAY COOL, CHILDREN--

CHITTER, CH'TCHT

-- HELP IS COMIN' THROUGH!

ZZZAZZZ

ZAAASSK

CHITTER CHITTER

SCREEF

H-HOW DID YOU D-DO THAT!

I-I HEARD YOU'VE GOT SOME KINDA ELECTRICAL POWER!

WELL, IT SURE AIN'T MY DARK GOOD LOOKS, CALVIN.

THE WAY OUT IS THAT WAY!

SCREEE SCREEE HSSS HSSS

FRANTIC MOMENTS LATER...

YOU'LL BE OKAY NOW-- ME, I GOTTA SEE SOME FOLKS 'BOUT A PLAGUE!

POLICE

WE WERE WONDERIN' WHEN YOU'D SHOW UP, BL.

GOT DELAYED CATCHIN' A TRAIN.

RUN THAT BY ME AGAIN, PROFESSOR. YOU SAY YOU KNOW WHERE THESE MONSTERS... COME FROM?

I'M AFRAID I CAN MAKE A PRETTY FAIR *GUESS,* INSPECTOR. I RECOGNIZED THE MAN WHO'S LEADING THEM, WHO CALLS HIMSELF *THE REGULATOR.*

HE'S ONE OF *S.T.A.R.'S* FORMER TECHNICIANS, AND HE WORKED ON A PROJECT WE CALLED *COMPOUND ONE...*

COMPOUND ONE? WASN'T THAT PART OF *S.T.A.R.'S* TOP SECRET *GENETIC RESEARCH PROJECT?* WE BATTLED *THE SHARK* WHEN HE TRIED TO USE THE PROJECT TO CREATE A RACE OF *SUPER-ANIMALS* ...

ARE YOU SAYING IT'S *HAPPENED* AGAIN?

I'M AFRAID IT'S *WORSE* THIS TIME, *WONDER WOMAN.* THIS MAN *REGULATOR* IS IN *CONTROL* OF THESE MUTANT MONSTERS...

...AND HE'S *CONSCIOUSLY* DIRECTING THEM TO LEAVE *METROPOLIS ISLAND...*

THEY REACH THE SURROUNDING MAINLAND, THEY'LL *SEPARATE...* FORM COLONIES... BEGIN *BREEDING!* SOON THEY'LL NUMBER A *MILLION...*

...THEN A *BILLION...*

...AND FINALLY, THEY MAY WELL *OVERRUN* THE EARTH!

THEN IT'S *SIMPLE*--WE'VE GOTTA *STOP* THESE BABIES BEFORE THEY CAN REACH THE *BRIDGES!* RIGHT, LIGHTNING?

LIGHTNING?

BLAST! WHERE'D HE GO NOW? IF I DIDN'T KNOW BETTER...

"I'D SAY HE WAS *DELIBERATELY AVOIDING US...*"

11

WE'D BETTER *SPLIT UP*, THEN. WONDER WOMAN, SEE WHAT YOU CAN DO ABOUT THE *BRIDGES* AND *TUNNELS* LEADING OUT OF METROPOLIS.

ARROW, HELP THE *SWAT TEAMS* TRY TO CONTAIN THIS *MONSTER PLAGUE*.

AND *PROFESSOR*, I HOPE *YOU* CAN HELP ME FIND A *SOLUTION* TO THIS *MADNESS*...

"...OR WE MAY JUST BE WITNESSING THE *DOWNFALL OF HUMANITY!*"

THAT SCIENTIST WAS *RIGHT*-- HERA HELP US, THE *VERMIN* ARE SWARMING TOWARD THE *BRIDGES!*

I HAVE TO *BLOCK* ALL THE EXITS-- NEED SOME KIND OF *BARRICADE!*

MY MAGIC LAS[SO] CAN EXPAND [TO] ANY *SIZE*-- EV[EN] LARGE ENOUGH [TO] ENCIRCLE THAT CRUMBLING *TENEMENT*--

--SO NOW, IF I CAN JUST GET THE *PROPER LEVERAGE*--!

FATHER ZEUS, LEND ME STRENGTH!

CREEEAAK

CHITTER CHITTER CHITCHT

THANK HERA! THAT'S *ONE* BRIDGE BLOCKED -- BUT THERE ARE *SEVEN MORE!*

CAN I REACH THEM --IN *TIME?*

THO OM

AS TO THAT, ONLY TIME WILL TELL, AND MEANWHILE, IN AN INTERSECTION ONLY A FEW MILES NORTH OF METROPOLIS SQUARE GARDEN...

USELESS! OUR TACTICS DON'T EVEN SLOW THEM!

EASY, KID. YOU MAY THINK THINGS ARE GRIM NOW, BUT THERE'S ONE THING US OLD PROS HAVE LEARNED FROM EXPERIENCE...

...NO MATTER HOW DARK THINGS LOOK...THEY CAN ALWAYS GET WORSE!

CHITTER CHITTER CHITTER

FACE IT, OLLIE, WE'RE BEING OUT-FLANKED! IT'S THAT GUY--THE REGULATOR!

HE'S GOT HIMSELF A BIRD'S EYE VIEW OF THE CITY FROM ATOP THAT FACTORY CHIMNEY, AND EVERY TIME WE MAKE A MOVE-- HE COUNTERS IT!

"SO LONG AS HE COMMANDS THESE CREATURES, WE DON'T STAND A CHANCE ...AND HE'S TOO FAR AWAY, AND TOO GUARDED TO REACH!"

PERHAPS THAT'S TRUE FOR YOU, ELONGATED MAN...

BUT IT ISN'T TRUE FOR THE MAN CALLED BLACK LIGHTNING!

EH? HOW DID YOU GET PAST MY SENTRIES?

WHAT, THOSE UGLY-LOOKIN' RATS DOWN BELOW? I BURNED 'EM, JIM --

13

-- JUS' LIKE I'M GONNA BURN *YOU!*

UNNNH! WHAT IN--?

DID YOU THINK MY *REGULATOR HELMET* ONLY AFFECTED *VERMIN?* NO, IT ALSO GETS RESULTS WITH *HUMANS--*

--THOUGH WITH *HUMANS,* THE EFFECT ISN'T SO MUCH *CONTROL,* AS IT IS-- *DESTRUCTION!*

ARRHH! MAN... WHY YOU *DOIN'* IT...? WHY YOU *HURTIN'...* ALL THOSE *INNOCENT* PEOPLE?

YOU'RE *BLACK,* LIKE *ME--* AND YOU CALL THEM *INNOCENT?* THEY'RE THE *RAVAGERS* OF THE *POOR!* THE *OPPRESSORS,* THE *VICTIMIZERS!*

I OFFERED THE MY *HELMET,* SO WE COULD *HELP* THE SLUM-DWELLE BY *CONTROLLING* THE VERMIN, BUT THEY *LAUGHED* IN MY FACE!

THEY *REJECTED* ME! THEY *DESERVE* TO DIE!

MAN...

...YOU ARE *SICK!*

FAKING? YOU-- FAKED IT?

WWNNHH!

WHAMM

NAH, I DIDN'T *FAKE* IT, BROTHER! JUST TOOK ME *TIME* TO BUILD UP MY *BODY'S FORCE FIELD--* ALMOST DIDN'T *MAKE* IT--!

YOU'RE--
PIG!
OU DON'T
EN CARE
OU'RE
LACK!

YEAH, I'M *BLACK*, AND I KNOW THE BROTHERS AND SISTERS'VE GOT THEIR *PROBLEMS*, BUT MAYBE YOU DIDN'T *NOTICE* IT, YOU TURKEY--

-- SOME'A THE PEOPLE YOU SAY YOU WANNA *HELP* ARE THE *FIRST ONES* GETTIN' *KILLED!* YOUR LOUSY MONSTERS'RE HITTIN' THE *GHETTO*, RIGHT?

WHO LIVES IN *GHETTOS*, YOU DUMB *JACKASS?*

OH MY LORD.

OUT OF MY *WAY*-- I HAVE TO *STOP* IT-- OH GOD, I NEVER *REALIZED*--!

WATCH IT-- YOU'RE *SLIPPING!* YOU'RE GONNA--

YAAAIIIEEE!

FTOOOM

ELSEWHERE, DOZEN-ODD BLOCKS TO THE *SOUTH*...

ARE YOU CERTAIN THIS WILL HAVE THE EFFECT YOU *PREDICTED*, PROFESSOR?

BATMAN, AFTER TONIGHT, I'M NO LONGER CERTAIN OF *ANYTHING!*

STILL, THIS *MIST* DOES CONTAIN A POTENT *CHEMICAL PERFUME*...

CHITTER CHIT CHITTER

15

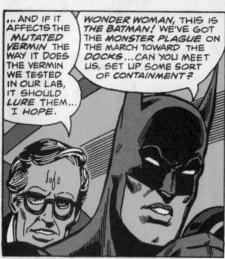

...AND IF IT AFFECTS THE *MUTATED VERMIN* THE WAY IT DOES THE VERMIN WE TESTED IN OUR LAB, IT SHOULD *LURE* THEM... I HOPE.

WONDER WOMAN, THIS IS THE BATMAN! WE'VE GOT THE *MONSTER PLAGUE* ON THE MARCH TOWARD THE *DOCKS*...CAN YOU MEET US, SET UP SOME SORT OF *CONTAINMENT?*

PRAISE *ATHENA,* I'VE FINISHED WITH THE *BRIDGES* AND *TUNNELS,* BATMAN ...SO YES, I CAN MEET YOU. I SAW A *CONSTRUCTION SITE* DOWN THERE EARLIER...

I MAY JUST HAVE *EXACTLY* WHAT WE *NEED!*

SHORTLY, AS THE TENSE MOMENTS DRAW TO A CLIMAX...

I'M GLAD WE MADE IT DOWN HERE IN TIME TO *SEE* THIS... IT'S *INCREDIBLE!*

THERE GOES THE *BATPLANE,* LEAVING ITS *SCENT...*AND HERE COME THE *RATS!*

AND *LOOK...*

"...THERE'S *WONDER WOMAN!* SHE HAS SOMETHING IN HER *MAGIC LASSO...* IT LOOKS LIKE A *CONCRETE CAISSON...*"

CHITCHITTER CHITTER

"IT'S MORE THAN A *BUILDING BLOCK,* KID --IT'S A *GIANT RAT-CATCHER!* LEAVE IT TO THE *AMAZON* TO FIGURE A WAY TO *CATCH* THOSE *MUTANTS* ...BUT WHAT *NOW?*"

I'LL SHOW YOU, GREEN ARROW. STAND BACK-- SORCERESS AT WORK!

SNOSSIAC LAES-- PART STAR EDISNI!

INSTANTLY, IN RESPONSE TO THE YOUNG MAGICIAN'S SOFTLY LITTERED SPELL...

...THE CAISSONS SEAL UP, COMPLETELY AIR-TIGHT...

...AND, A MOMENT LATER...

DIANA THE HUNTRESS, GUIDE MY AIM! I'VE SENT THESE MUTANT MONSTERS ON AN ELLIPTICAL COURSE TO THE OUTER REACHES OF THE SOLAR SYSTEM.

WITH GOOD FORTUNE, THAT'S THE VERY LAST WE'LL EVER SEE OF THEM.

EPILOGUE: THE PEOPLE OF METROPOLIS ARE RETURNING HOME NOW, AND A NEW DAY IS ABOUT TO BEGIN, AS, IN A WHARF OVERLOOKING THE BAY...

LIKE I SAID, I APPRECIATE THE OFFER-- BUT IT'S NOT FOR ME. I'M A LONER, AND I LIKE IT.

PIGEON FEATHERS! YOU'D MAKE A GREAT LEAGUER!

WOULD I, ARCHER? BE HONEST. WHILE THE REST'A YOU WERE OFF TEAM-PLAYING, I HIT OUT ON MY OWN, FACIN' THE REGULATOR DOWN ALL BY MYSELF.

MAYBE IT AIN'T THE BEST WAY, BUT IT'S MY WAY SORRY.

UH, LISTEN, LEAGUERS... ABOUT THOSE BRIDGES...

IN A MOMENT, INSPECTOR JUST GIVE US A MOMENT...

...WHILE OUR FRIEND SAYS GOOD-BYE...

YEAH, ME TOO.

SEE YA AROUND, RIGHT?

BET ON THAT.

17

Ena.

JLA ★ INCARNATIONS

Over the years the Justice League has disbanded many times, only to be quickly replaced by a new League. The following is a list of all teams and their members.

Justice League of America
Founded in Brave and the Bold #28

FOUNDING MEMBERS:

SUPERMAN Clark Kent/Kal-El
BATMAN Bruce Wayne
WONDER WOMAN Diana Prince
FLASH Barry Allen
GREEN LANTERN Hal Jordan
AQUAMAN Arthur Curry/Orin
MARTIAN MANHUNTER J'onn J'onzz

NEW MEMBERS:

GREEN ARROW Oliver Queen
Joined Justice League of America #4
ATOM Ray Palmer
Joined Justice League of America #14
HAWKMAN Katar Hol
Joined Justice League of America #31
BLACK CANARY Dinah Lance
Joined Justice League of America #74
PHANTOM STRANGER Unknown
Joined Justice League of America #103
ELONGATED MAN Ralph Dibny
Joined Justice League of America #105
RED TORNADO John Smith / Tornado Champion
Joined Justice League of America #106
HAWKWOMAN Shayera Hol
Joined Justice League of America #146
ZATANNA Zatanna Zatara
Joined Justice League of America #161
FIRESTORM Ronnie Raymond & Martin Stein
Joined Justice League of America #179

[Disbanded in *Justice League of America Annual #2*]

Justice League of America "Detroit"
Founded in Justice League of America Annual #2

FOUNDING MEMBERS:

AQUAMAN Arthur Curry/Orin
MARTIAN MANHUNTER J'onn J'onzz
ELONGATED MAN Ralph Dibny
SUE DIBNY
ZATANNA Zatanna Zatara
STEEL Hank Heywood, III
VIXEN Mari Jiwe McCabe
VIBE Paco Ramone
DALE GUNN

NEW MEMBERS:

GYPSY Cindy Reynolds
Joined Justice League of America #236
BATMAN Bruce Wayne
Joined Justice League of America #250

[Disbanded in *Justice League of America #261*]

Justice League
Founded in Legends #6

FOUNDING MEMBERS:

MARTIAN MANHUNTER J'onn J'onzz
BATMAN Bruce Wayne
BLACK CANARY Dinah Lance
BLUE BEETLE Ted Kord
CAPTAIN MARVEL Billy Batson
DOCTOR FATE Kent Nelson
GREEN LANTERN Guy Gardner

NEW MEMBERS:

MISTER MIRACLE Scott Free
Joined Justice League #1
OBERON
Joined Justice League #1
DOCTOR LIGHT IV Kimiyo Hoshi
Joined Justice League #1
MAXWELL LORD
"Joined" Justice League #4
BOOSTER GOLD Michael Carter
Joined Justice League #4

[Disbanded in *Justice League International #7*]

Justice League International
Founded in Justice League International #7

FOUNDING MEMBERS:

MAXWELL LORD
OBERON
MARTIAN MANHUNTER J'onn J'onzz
BATMAN Bruce Wayne
BLACK CANARY Dinah Lance
BLUE BEETLE Ted Kord
GREEN LANTERN Guy Gardner
MISTER MIRACLE Scott Free
BOOSTER GOLD Michael Carter
CAPTAIN ATOM Nathaniel Adam
ROCKET RED 7 Vladimir Mikoyan

NEW MEMBERS:

BORIS DIMITRAVICH RAZUMIHIN
Joined Justice League International #8
CATHERINE COBERT
Joined Justice League International #8
ROCKET RED #4 Dimitri Pushkin
Joined Justice League International #11
FIRE (GREEN FLAME) Beatriz da Costa
Joined Justice League International #14
ICE (ICEMAIDEN) Tora Olafsdotter
Joined Justice League International #14
HAWKMAN Fel Andar
Joined Justice League International #19
HAWKWOMAN Sharon Parker
Joined Justice League International #19

ELONGATED MAN Ralph Dibny
Joined Justice League International #24
ANIMAL MAN Buddy Baker
Joined Justice League International #24
FLASH Wally West
Joined Justice League International #24
METAMORPHO Rex Mason
Joined Justice League International #24
POWER GIRL Kara / Karen Starr
Joined Justice League International #24
SUE DIBNY
Joined Justice League Europe #1
HUNTRESS Helena Bertinelli
Joined Justice League America #30
DOCTOR FATE II Linda Strauss
Joined Justice League America #31
KILOWOG
Joined Justice League Europe #33
**"Justice League Antarctica": MAJOR DISASTER,
G'NORT, MULTI-MAN, BIG SIR, CLUEMASTER,
CLOCK KING, MIGHTY BRUCE, SCARLET SKIER**
"Placed" Justice League America Annual #4
CRIMSON FOX Vivian and Constance d'Aramis
Joined Justice League Europe #13
L-RON
Joined Justice League America #42
LIGHTRAY Sollis
Joined Justice League America #42
ORION
Joined Justice League America #42
BLUE JAY Jay Abrams
Joined Justice League Europe #20
SILVER SORCERESS Laura Neilsen
Joined Justice League Europe #20
GENERAL GLORY Joseph Jones
Joined Justice League America #50
TASMANIAN DEVIL Hugh Dawkins
Joined Justice League America #56
DOCTOR LIGHT IV Kimiyo Hoshi
Joined Justice League America #56
SUPERMAN Clark Kent/Kal-El
Joined Justice League Spectacular #1
GREEN LANTERN Hal Jordan
Joined Justice League Spectacular #1
AQUAMAN Arthur Curry/Orin
Joined Justice League Spectacular #1
BLOODWYND Bloodwynd / J'onn J'onzz
Joined Justice League America #63
MAXIMA
Joined Justice League America #63
MAYA Chandi Gupta
Joined Justice League Europe #50
WONDER WOMAN Diana of Themyscira
Joined Justice League America #71
RAY Ray Terrill
Joined Justice League America #71

BLACK CONDOR Ryan Kendall
Joined Justice League America #71
AGENT LIBERTY Benjamin Lockwood
Joined Justice League America #71
FLASH Jay Garrick
Justice League America #78

[Disbanded in *Justice League Europe #67*]

Justice Leagues

*The combination of tragic events and loss of
United Nations backing created differences of
opinion as to how the League should operate.
Three teams were formed operating under the
name of Justice League.*

Justice League America
Founded in Justice League America #0

FOUNDERS:

WONDER WOMAN Diana of Themyscira
HAWKMAN Katar Hol
FLASH Wally West
METAMORPHO Rex Mason
CRIMSON FOX Vivian and Constance d'Aramis
NUKLON Albert Rothstein
OBSIDIAN Todd Rice

NEW MEMBERS:

BLUE DEVIL Daniel Cassidy
Joined Justice League America #98
ICEMAIDEN Sigrid Nansen
Joined Justice League America #98

[Disbanded in *JLA #1*]

Justice League "Task Force"
Founded in Justice League Task Force #1

FOUNDERS:

AQUAMAN Arthur Curry / Orin
MARTIAN MANHUNTER J'onn J'onzz
GYPSY Cindy Reynolds
FLASH Wally West
NIGHTWING Dick Grayson

NEW MEMBERS:

BRUCE WAYNE
Joined Justice League Task Force #5
GREEN ARROW Oliver Queen
Joined Justice League Task Force #5
BRONZE TIGER Benjamin Turner
Joined Justice League Task Force #5
WONDER WOMAN Diana of Themyscira
Joined Justice League Task Force #7
MAXIMA
Joined Justice League Task Force #7

VIXEN Mari Jiwe McCabe
Joined Justice League Task Force #7
DOLPHIN
Joined Justice League Task Force #7
JOE PUBLIC Unknown
Joined Justice League Task Force #9
GEIST Dwayne Geyer
Joined Justice League Task Force #9
LOOSE CANNON Eddie Walker
Joined Justice League Task Force #9
HOURMAN Rex Tyler
Joined Justice League Task Force #10
THUNDERBOLT Peter Cannon
Joined Justice League Task Force #10
ELONGATED MAN Ralph Dibny
Joined Justice League Task Force #10
BLACK CANARY Dinah Lance
Joined Justice League Task Force #10
DESPERO L-Ron/Despero of Kalanor
Joined Justice League Task Force #12
TRIUMPH William MacIntyre
Joined Justice League Task Force #0
RAY Ray Terrill
Joined Justice League Task Force #0
MYSTEK Jennifer Barclay
Joined Justice League Task Force #26

[Disbanded in *Justice League Task Force #37*]

Justice League "Extreme"
Founded in Extreme Justice #0

FOUNDERS:

CAPTAIN ATOM Nathaniel Adam
MAXIMA
BLUE BEETLE Ted Kord
BOOSTER GOLD Michael Carter
AMAZING MAN Will Everett, III

NEW MEMBERS:

FIRESTORM Ronnie Raymond
Joined Extreme Justice #5
PLASTIQUE Bette Sans Souci
Joined Extreme Justice #6
CAROL FERRIS
Joined Extreme Justice #10
"WONDER TWINS" Zan & Jayna of Exor
Joined Extreme Justice #16

[Disbanded in *JLA: Incarnations #6*]

JLA
Founded in JLA Secret Files #1

FOUNDERS:

SUPERMAN Clark Kent/Kal-El
BATMAN Bruce Wayne
WONDER WOMAN Diana of Themyscira
FLASH Wally West

GREEN LANTERN Kyle Rayner
AQUAMAN Arthur Curry/Orin
MARTIAN MANHUNTER J'onn J'onzz

NEW MEMBERS:

TOMORROW WOMAN
Joined JLA #5
AZTEK Curt Falconer
Joined Aztek #10
GREEN ARROW Connor Hawke
Joined JLA #9
ORACLE Barbara Gordon
Joined JLA #16
PLASTIC MAN Patrick "Eel" O'Brien
Joined JLA #16
STEEL John Henry Irons
Joined JLA #16
HUNTRESS Helena Bertinelli
Joined JLA #16
ZAURIEL
Joined JLA #16
WONDER WOMAN Hippolyta of Themyscira
Joined JLA #16
CATWOMAN Selina Kyle
Revealed in JLA #17
BIG BARDA Barda Free
Joined JLA #17
ORION
Joined JLA #17
HOURMAN Matthew Tyler
Joined JLA #26
ATOM Ray Palmer
Joined JLA #27
MARK ANTAEUS
Joined JLA: Superpower
FLASH Walter West
Joined JLA #33
GREEN ARROW Oliver Queen
Joined JLA #69
FIRESTORM Ronnie Raymond
Joined JLA #69
ZATANNA Zatanna Zatara
Joined JLA #69
NIGHTWING Dick Grayson
Joined JLA #69
FAITH
Joined JLA #69
HAWKGIRL Kendra Saunders
Joined JLA #69
JASON BLOOD/THE DEMON
Joined JLA #69
MAJOR DISASTER Paul Booker
Joined JLA #69
GREEN LANTERN John Stewart
Joined JLA #76
MANITOU RAVEN
Joined JLA #78

[Disbanded in *JLA #125*]

Hereby Elects

* *

To membership for life, with all privileges and gratuities, including the wearing of the signal device and possession of the special key which permits entry into the sanctuary, its library and souvenir rooms. It is hereby further resolved and acted upon that:

* *

Shall receive this special commendation for expert assistance in the case we have entitled in our scrolls...

* *

★ ★ ★